Covenant and Republic investigates the cultural politics of historical memory in the early American republic, specifically the historical literature of Puritanism. By situating historical writing about Puritanism in the context of the cultural forces of republicanism and liberalism, this study reconsiders the emergence of the historical romance in the 1820s, before the work of Nathaniel Hawthorne. *Covenant and Republic* not only aids the Americanist recovery of this literary period but also brings together literary studies of historical fiction and historical scholarship of early republican political culture; in doing so, it offers a persuasive new account of just what is at stake when one reads literature of and about the past.

CAMBRIDGE STUDIES IN AMERICAN LITERATURE
AND CULTURE

Covenant and Republic

Books in the series

(continued after page 273)

COVENANT AND REPUBLIC

Historical Romance and the Politics of Puritanism

PHILIP GOULD

Brown University

CAMBRIDGE
UNIVERSITY PRESS

Published by the Press Syndicate of the University of Cambridge
The Pitt Building, Trumpington Street, Cambridge CB2 1RP
40 West 20th Street, New York, NY 10011-4211, USA
10 Stamford Road, Oakleigh, Melbourne 3166, Australia

First published 1996

Printed in the United States of America

Library of Congress Cataloging-in-Publication Data
Gould, Philip (Philip B.)
Covenant and republic : historical romance and the politics of
Puritanism / Philip Gould.
p.   cm. – (Cambridge studies in American literature and
culture : 103)
Includes bibliographical references.
ISBN 0-521-55499-3
1. Historical fiction, American – History and criticism.
2. Politics and literature – United States – History – 19th century.
3. Literature and history – United States – History – 19th century.
4. American fiction – 19th century – History and criticism.
5. Cooper, James Fenimore, 1789-1851.   Wept of Wish-ton-wish.
6. Sedgwick, Catharine Maria, 1789-1867,   Hope Leslie.   7. Child.
Lydia Maria Francis, 1802-1880,   Hobomok.   8. Puritans – United
States – Historiography   9. Puritan movements in literature.
10. Puritans in literature.   I. Title.   II. Series.
PS374.H5G68   1996
813'.08109 – dc20   96-6233
                                                              CIP

A catalog record for this book is available from the British Library.

ISBN 0-521-55499-3 Hardback

For *Athena and the Nickel-Man*

"I am a fool
To weep at what I am glad of"

—*The Tempest* III, i

CONTENTS

vii

ACKNOWLEDGMENTS

I was fortunate to do my graduate training at the University of Wisconsin-Madison, an intellectually rich environment for anyone involved in American literary and historical studies. Courses with Bill Andrews, Al Feltskog, Tom Schaub, and Jeffrey Steele modeled distinctive brands of superlative scholarship that in the long run helped me cultivate my own practice. Chuck Cohen's seminar in the American Revolution provided invaluable intellectual-historical foundations to the following study, and to him I wish to express my (truly republican) gratitude. I owe special thanks to Gordon Hutner for his consummate abilities as a student of American literary studies as well as his challenging questions about the critical stakes of the arguments I was developing. Dale Bauer read every chapter of this work, and I can tell you that there is no more thorough, incisive reader than she. She has been both critic and friend.

Numerous people were willing to read various chapters of my work-in-progress and offer constructive advice about how and where to improve it: Jane Donahue Eberwein, Larry Gragg, Philip Gura, David Levin, Carla Mulford, John McWilliams, and Linda Smith Rhoads. Charles Harmon has been a true friend and kindred spirit. At Cambridge University Press I owe thanks to Eric Sundquist, the anonymous reader of the manuscript (whoever she or he may be!), and, most of all, to Susie Chang, whose eminent professionalism is matched only by her warm sense of humor. I wish her good luck at Oxford University Press.

While I was researching this project, I was awarded a dissertation fellowship by the Wisconsin Alumni Research Foundation. It allowed me significant time to focus on my work with minimal distractions. The respective staffs at Memorial Library of the University of Wisconsin, the State Historical Society of Wisconsin, and the Newberry Library all have been very helpful. Various portions of this work have appeared previously as articles: "Catharine Sedgwick's 'Recital' of the Pequot War," *American Literature* 66 (December 1994): 641–62; "Virtue, Ideology and the American Revolution: The Legacy of the Republican Synthesis," *American Literary History*, 5 (Fall 1993); 564–77; "Representative Men: Jeremy Belknap's *American Biography* and the Political Culture of the Early Republic," *Auto/Biography Studies* 9 (Spring 1994): 83–97; and "New England Witch-Hunting and the Politics of Reason in the Early Republic," *New England Quarterly* 68 (March 1995): 58–82. I take this opportunity to thank each of their editors for allowing me to reprint previously published materials.

Most of all, I want to thank Sargent Bush, Jr., who has served as an exemplary scholar and mentor to me for years now. Amid what William Bradford has called "the uncertain things of this world," Sarge is a constant source of stability and direction. His scholarly acumen, integrity, and commitment to the profession make him truly "representative" in the Emersonian sense of the word.

All criticism is autobiographical. Reared by kind, loving parents one of Puritan and one of Judaic descent, I have ventured – rather unsurprisingly – into the subjects of virtue and community. In doing so, I have collaborated not only with the people listed above but also with many good friends too numerous to name here. Throughout the cycles of presumption and humility during this project, I have been lucky to enjoy the love and fellowship of my wife, Dr. Athena Poppas, and our son, Nicholas Gould (who knows "Daddy works in the basement"). To them I dedicate this work. Bless you both.

INTRODUCTION

THE HISTORICITY OF HISTORICAL FICTION

One of the early American republic's most hostile critics of the Salem witchcraft trials, Charles Wentworth Upham, concluded his *Lectures on Witchcraft* (1831) with some rather pointed remarks about his own era. Upham, a Unitarian minister, argued that the episode held particular meaning for contemporary New Englanders. As if his immediate audience might be too obtuse to interpret the lesson of Salem correctly, Upham instructed them in no uncertain terms to read the hysteria of 1692 as a political trope for an immediate problem. "[W]henever a community," he warned, "gives way to its passions . . . and casts off the restraints of reason, there is a delusion that can hardly be described in any other phrase. We cannot glance our eye over the face of our country, without beholding such scenes. . . . It would be wiser to direct our ridicule and reproaches to the delusions of our own times, rather than to those of a previous age, and it becomes us to treat with charity and mercy the failings of our predecessors, at least until we have ceased to imitate and repeat them."[1] One is struck immediately by the sense of urgency with which Upham displaces colonial history with a contemporary crisis, one where the people's civic behavior is contingent upon the faculty of reason. (In fact, in Chapter 5 I take up the politics of faculty psychology surrounding the period's historical literature about the Salem witchcraft trials.) Chastising his readers to get out of the seventeenth century, Upham rather abruptly reorients them to nineteenth-century politics, as though their obsession with their ancestors' foibles has dulled their capacity for self-examination.

Upham's exhortation, I believe, actually raises crucial theoretical and methodological issues for reading historical literature about Puritan New England. Indeed, critics of this genre might

1

do well to heed his call. Such a reorientation significantly affects our understanding of both the historicity and the canonicity of historical fiction. Instead, modern criticism generally has assumed that the textual signs of historical literature fundamentally represent a colonial past, even though it acknowledges that the genre may have contemporary relevance. In this study of the emergence of historical romance about Puritanism during the 1820s, I have challenged this assumption. Here's why.

One reason involves the stature of Nathaniel Hawthorne. The long, imposing shadow that Hawthorne casts on the entire genre of the historical romance of New England dates back quite some time, and has distorted both the texts and the contexts that precede his work. Whether motivated by high regard, or even by skeptical revision, critics of the genre consistently situate Hawthorne at the hermeneutic center of things. For both traditionalists and revisionists, admirers and detractors, he has managed to serve as an interpretive touchstone, an apparently fixed standard by which we measure either the aesthetic deficiencies or (more recently) the relatively progressive politics of both his immediate predecessors and his contemporaries.[2] As Jane Tompkins has shown, the political contexts for Hawthorne's critical reputation extend back into antebellum America and "to the social and institutional structures that shaped literary opinion."[3] Such a claim, of course, is part of a larger project in American literary studies examining the politics of canon formation, which involve in this case the cultural and ideological contexts contributing to both Hawthorne's reputation and that of an elite coterie of literary kingpins around whom F. O. Mathiessen defined "the American Renaissance."[4]

The modern roots of Hawthorne's reputation lay largely in the skeptical intellectual currents of postwar liberalism. As both Thomas Hill Schaub and Russell Reising have noted, Hawthorne became something of a trope for the "new" liberalism that arose during the late 1930s and 1940s out of the wreckage of Leftist politics in America.[5] Disenchantment with the Soviet Union, particularly in the wake of Stalin's purge trials and his nonaggression agreement with Nazi Germany in 1939, propelled a self-consciously centrist and "anti-ideological" movement in American liberalism. Revisionist liberals scorned the naively optimistic progressivism of older liberals; they associated pure reason and ideology with the fallacies of Marxist dogma; viewed mass culture with a new horror that resonated with the specter of Russian and German totalitarianism; and generally embraced a "realistic" political vision derived from a Christian postlapsarian view of human nature that displaced an older idealism with a hard-eyed recognition of irony and tragedy, and a class-conflict model of history with a consensual one. Hence the invention of an "American" mind. Liberals, moreover, co-opted an older Hegelian and Marxist discourse of the "dialectic" of history and psychologized it to signify the contradictions of the mind, a maneuver that in effect minimized the importance of social realism in life and in literature. This new suspicion of ideology, historical determinism, and moral crusading was expressed in various forms: Arthur Schlesinger, Jr.'s notion of "the vital center" to American politics; the historian Louis Hartz's belief that American history was essentially free of the class conflict describing Europe; or even the distinction Lionel Trilling drew between a static "ideal" and a the complex, irresolvable tensions of a literary "idea."[6] The polarities of the new liberalism, as Schaub notes, contrasted "totalitarianism and democracy, utopianism and politics, certitude and ambiguity" and maintained that reality itself is essentially "an experience of complexity that has its generative roots in the ineradicable conflicts of the private self."[7]

Influential works on Hawthorne during the 1950s and 1960s inscribe the predispositions of liberal politics. The very premise of Richard Fogle's *Hawthorne's Fiction: The Light and the Dark* (1952) is to defend his subject from being "naive and old-fashioned." As Fogle praises Hawthorne's "pervasive irony" he proudly upholds a writer wielding moral allegory for psychological ends, one whose work is "enriched with ambiguity" and "so entirely unsentimental."[8] Such praise for Hawthorne is premised on the same ideology that led Arthur Schlesinger, Jr., to deride "the sentimental abstractions of Doughface [i.e., progressive] fantasy."[9] As Harry Levin's *The Power of Blackness: Hawthorne, Poe, Melville* (1958) attests, Hawthorne's sense of innate depravity ("the dark wisdom of deeper minds" characterizing Poe and Melville as well) made him attractive to postwar liberals, who themselves were engaged in an ideological project of rejecting the principles of reason, progress, and perfection.[10] When Frederick Crews published his Freudian study of Hawthorne, *The Sins of the Fathers* (1966), he decidedly intended to rescue his subject from a host of critics who had tried to turn him into a genteel, optimistic, politically involved man of the world. The contrast Crews drew between the false view of Hawthorne as a "dogmatic moralist," a "plodding democrat and religious tutor," and the more profound one of a "self-divided, self-tormented man" actually encodes a much larger political and cultural debate over human nature and artistic consciousness that was taking place between traditional and revisionist American liberals.[11]

The legacy of postwar liberalism has shaped as well more recent evaluations of Hawthorne and the antebellum practice of historical romance. In the name of "complexity," "ambiguity," and "irony," influential critics have placed Hawthorne at the center of a nineteenth-century literary genre, revealing as much about their own political inheritance as they do about Hawthorne's historical craft. For example, at the end of the Introduction of the influential *Hawthorne and the Historical Romance of New England* (1971), Michael Davitt Bell argues that the "problem for patriotic historical romancers was immense. They were torn between the patriotic impulse to idolize the [Puritan] founders as heroes and the romantic impulse to criticize them as enemies to independence and individual liberty."[12] As Bell examines these writers' various attempts to resolve this tension, a host of presumably lesser practitioners are cast as confused progressives – not unlike those troubled idealists of the postwar era whom Schlesinger calls "Doughface" idealists – who cannot shed the premises of progressive history. As opposed to these "confused" writers, who were unable to reconcile contradictions about Puritanism, Hawthorne exploited such ambiguities for "artistic" purposes. Hence what distinguishes Hawthorne from his peers in effect is his ability to grasp a new liberal understanding of the inherent irony of historical process. The value of historical irony is not lost on George Dekker, whose monumental, erudite *The American Historical Romance* (1987) lauds Hawthorne's sense of how "historical circumstances create situations ironic, comic, and tragic by curtailing or liberating the human actors' potential for understanding or action."[13] For Michael J. Colacurcio, in *The Province of Piety: Moral History in Hawthorne's Early Tales* (1984), Hawthorne's "historical prescience" makes him an apt parallel to Perry Miller himself, one who sees, for example, the malaise of the New England Way among third-generation Puritans in "Young Goodman Brown;" Hawthorne also shows "ambivalence about 'the meaning of America' " and "hatred of every sort of historical absolutism" in "Endicott and the Red Cross."[14] Moreover, the ideological medium of revisionist liberalism has sustained Hawthorne's reputation as a historical romancer specifically against literary rivals such as Lydia Maria Child, Catharine Maria Sedgwick, and John Neal whose works are filled, as one critic claims, with "anachronisms" and "improbabilities."[15]

One might see the recent dissent from this tradition as an

attack on the "sins of the fathers." The critical recuperation of writers like Lydia Maria Child, Catharine Maria Sedgwick, and others owes much of its success to Rutgers University Press's American Women Writers Series, which during the 1980s began to reprint important editions of works by nineteenth-century American women writers. The critical editions of *Hobomok* and *Hope Leslie* are filled with important scholarly notes and accompanied by introductory essays that provide important biographical and critical material, all of which makes a case for rethinking Child's and Sedgwick's place in the American canon. These writers certainly *did* know something about colonial history. According to the editor of *Hobomok*, Carolyn L. Karcher, Child "went about writing an alternative history of the Puritan experiment – one that highlighted its underside and shifted the focus from the saints to the sinners, from the orthodox to the heterodox, from the white settlers to the Indians, from the venerated patriarchs to their unsung wives."[16] Likewise, Mary Kelley maintains that in writing *Hope Leslie*, Sedgwick successfully interrogated Puritan historians – William Bradford, John Winthrop, William Hubbard – whose work she knew well.[17]

Just as significant as the obvious revisionism here is a less immediately apparent line of continuity between these two schools of critics of historical romance. Whereas liberal critics once praised Hawthorne for rewriting the historical record of seventeenth-century New England, revisionist critics praise Hawthorne's female predecessors during the 1820s for virtually the same thing. The essential difference here is the substitution of antipatriarchalism for irony as the elixir of legitimacy. Such a reevaluation of women's historical fiction quite rightly disrupts the traditionally exclusive nature of the nineteenth-century American canon. But the interpretive continuities here, I would argue, tend to reshuffle canon hierarchies rather than reexamine their premises. By locating the genre's "historicity" in the seventeenth century, critics of this historical literature of New England consistently have assumed a stable relationship between text and context, a fact that ultimately obscures the many ways in which these novels do not merely make analogies between past and present but actually inscribe *contemporary* history.

Before proceeding, I should acknowledge that virtually all critics of the genre do argue that historical fiction had some sort of contemporary relevance in the early republic. Colacurcio, for example, argues rigorously for Hawthorne's ironic treatment of the standard democratic pieties of his day, perhaps best exemplified by George Bancroft's historical theories of the evolutionary progress of liberty in America, even though Hawthorne was publishing much of his work in James P. O'Sullivan's *United States History and Democratic Review*.[18] Likewise, for Kelley, Sedgwick's historicism carries out an "investigation into the roots of American moral character"; for Karcher, Child uses history to provide early national Americans with an "alternative vision of race and gender relations."[19] Most recently, Nina Baym has put women's historical romances into the broader context of all of women's history-writing, maintaining that a novel like *Hope Leslie* attacks Puritanism because colonial/patriarchal origins were incompatible with the cultural refinement of America.[20] Even Baym's cogent assessment, however, overlooks significant cultural tensions between premodern and modern ideologies in the post-Revolutionary era (a subject which I take up in Chapter 3). For all of these critics, historical fiction revises the past as a way of sending political messages germane to the early republic. Yet they all assume that the literary materials of historical romance – its language and love plots, its stern patriarchs and rebellious women, the conventions of marriage and miscegenation – fundamentally represent the colonial past.[21]

Even cultural critics of historical fiction make similar assumptions. Both Lawrence Buell and David Reynolds have articulated how the rivalries between Unitarians and Orthodox Calvinists during the early nineteenth century made the historical romance of New England a major site of sectarian warfare.[22] As Buell has shown, the Unitarian embrace of belles lettres as a surrogate source of biblical authority quickly made historical romance a Unitarian possession. Yet even his notion of "the historicity of historical literature" concerns the issue of whether or not the genre "captures the past." Under the influence of Sir Walter Scott, the argument goes, American historical novelists pursued a "mixed mode" of documentary mimesis and imaginative liberation that inevitably led to problems fulfilling antebellum critics' demand that fiction show a fidelity to historical fact.[23] As opposed to critics emphasizing the religious culture of nineteenth-century New England, Lucy Maddox recently has argued that contemporary cultural assumptions about race and Indian removal inform a wide variety of antebellum literature. Maddox contextualizes the treatment of race in historical fictions such as *Hobomok, Hope Leslie,* and *The Scarlet Letter* (as well as in other genres), showing how in varying ways male and female writers negotiated race within the prevailing cultural ideologies of the day. Despite her sense of these novels' significance to early republican politics, however, Maddox fundamentally sees *Hobomok* and *Hope Leslie* as representations of colonial history that imply comparisons and analogies to the nineteenth century: "Working backward from their own circumstances in the early years of the nineteenth century, when women . . . are sufficiently liberated to debate ideas with men and publish novels that revise male-transmitted history, they can argue the changed status of women is the result of a process of reform begun nearly two-hundred years before by the small rebellions of a few spirited and intelligent women against the Puritan patriarchy."[24] So for all of these readers of historical romance – liberals, cultural critics, feminists, and revisionists – the cultural logic of this literary genre works according to the principle of historical analogy.

This brief survey of the field cannot help but simplify the complexities of these valuable critical studies. But it does begin to show a line of critical continuity regarding the historicity of historical literature that helps to clarify my own approach to the genre. This book is indebted to the above critics, but its methods and motives involve two crucial, related strategies of displacement. One of them concerns the issue of the American canon. In what follows I displace the issue of canon hierarchies with a cultural dialogue that was taking place in "history-writing"[25] during the early republic. This period I am defining as the time between the end of the American Revolution and the 1830s, a period that, of course, witnessed the emergence of historical fiction in general and the historical romance of New England in particular. This cultural dialogue concerned the nature of citizenship in the early republic, and the subject of Puritan history provided an important (though not exclusive) discursive site for it. The second strategy involves the recovery of fiction's cultural signification by displacing Puritan history with early republican history. I read historical texts as culturally specific expressions of the post-Revolutionary era.

   To do this, I incorporate both older and newer modes of historical criticism. At the time of this writing, it has been roughly fifteen years since the publication of Stephen Greenblatt's *Renaissance Self-Fashioning: From More to Shakespeare* (1980) and the beginnings of what became the "new historicism." As one will see, my methods have been influenced by the new historicism, particularly the ambivalent signification of the "subject" of history, which positions writers as both agents of textual authority and vessels of cultural ideologies, as well as the theoretical equivalence this methodology draws between the "historicity of texts" and the "textuality of history."[26] Fifteen years after the fact, however, there should be no theoretical qualms about employing both newer and more traditional historicist methods. I take seriously those primary sources which early nationals consulted in reconstructing Puritan history: who read what, who borrowed what from whom, and so on. But I articulate the historical transmission of Puritan sources in the context of early national culture and politics, in order to show how such borrowing (or outright stealing) was mediated by immediately resonant ideologies. Instead of analyzing, as others have done, Puritan history as an analogue for the early republic, I divest these narratives of their colonial garb altogether. Anyone who carefully reads historical fiction of the 1820s soon sees that these texts speak a language of anachronism, one fraught with immediate social, political, and ethical concerns. Puritanism is much less a stable analogue than a protean metaphor for the early republic.

The metaphoric significance of Puritanism registers the central civic and political issues of the day that revolved around the subject of republican "virtue." In *Patricide in the House Divided: A Psychological Interpretation of Lincoln and His Age* (1979), George Forgie has argued: "It was taken for granted from the start that the survival of the Republic for any length of time would depend heavily on the virtue of its citizens. Character was perceived to be the point of contact between individual lives and national fate."[27] Early nationals continually groped for new definitions of republican citizenship, and, in doing so, refashioned the meaning of "virtue" in new, complex, and often inconsistent ways. The meaning of this key word was devilishly elusive during this era, and a host of troubling questions lay behind its signification. What kinds of personal and civic qualities were necessary to republican life? What were the terms of political association? How could women be expected to fulfill a political role in the republic without really being citizens at all? Hence this discourse of virtue (which included a related lexicon of "industry," "vigor," and "valor," as well as "benevolence," "affection," and "refinement") signified in highly contextual ways that were contingent upon gender, class, race, purpose, audience, and personal sensibility. Sometimes these rhetorical and ideological factors collided. Forgie's study of a "post-heroic" generation following the American Revolution psychologizes the domestication of political discourse and the transferal of authority from real fathers to Revolutionary fathers as a way of securing the future of the republic. I extend this concept from the Revolutionary to the Puritan fathers themselves, and yet rediscover the cultural role of patriarchal/historical authority in political rather than psychological terms. Puritanism afforded an arena in which early nationals negotiated the contemporary meanings of republican "virtue." The period's cultural politics of Puritanism, in other words, can be understood as a function of its complex political culture.

If we are to articulate the cultural politics of a literary genre, we should read it in the same context that early nationals did – that is, in this case, alongside the other kinds of historical writing, such as the election-day sermons, commemorative orations, biographies, as well as state, regional, and national histories. All of these saturated early republican letters. History and historical fiction were intimately related genres during this era. As I show throughout, they at once complemented and competed with one another over the ideological stakes of republican "virtue." There is, of course, a purely theoretical rationale for reading these genres together. The study of historiography as a fictional mode of discourse, in which historical "reality" is as much created as recorded, has held significant critical attention for more than twenty years.[28] The chief spokesman for "metahistory," Hayden White, has argued that historical writing can be nothing more or less than a discursive act. As much as poets do, historians impose what White has called "poetic figurations" (e.g., metaphor, metonymy, synechdoche, irony) on historical "facts" that themselves have no meaning without a "tropological" system of relations with which they can be conjoined – or "emplotted" – into narrative form. The facts of any historical narrative, in other words, cannot exist without an overarching "story" (e.g., romance, comedy, tragedy, or satire). Historical narratives are "verbal fictions, the contents of which are as much invented as found and the forms of which have more in common with their counterparts in literature than they have in the sciences."[29]

Such a dismantling of generic borders, however, only affirms ex post facto the entanglement between fiction and history during the post-Revolutionary era. Historical fiction emerged during the 1820s in context of an already established, thriving literary industry of historiography. As others have noted, history-writing of all sorts held a significant place in early national letters.[30] After all, over 85% of the nation's best sellers during the 1820s were books of history, a trend that paralleled the rise of state historical societies.[31] Not only adults but schoolchildren were readers of these new texts. One crucial factor behind the proliferation of written histories was the rise of public education in early-nineteenth-century America. Between the time that religious disestablishment (under Thomas Jefferson's leadership) began in Virginia in 1786, to its final eradication in Massachusetts in 1833, public schools were increasingly institutionalized in America.[32] The study of history in these new public schools became a formal and separate discipline. During the 1820s, moreover, a number of states required by law that history be taught in state-supported schools.[33] In 1827, for example, six years before the formal disestablishment of religion in Massachusetts, the state legislature passed a law requiring that history be part of the public school curriculum.[34] Moreover, this new industry of history textbooks led to the creation of journals, such as the *United States Literary Gazette* and the *American Journal of Education,* to review and often promote them.[35] History-writing was becoming the New Word of the republic.

This New Word was sanctioned by its capacity to inculcate virtue in republican citizens. A quick glance at the period's primary sources reveals a peculiar brand of didacticism shaped by the experience of the American Revolution. An essayist for the *North American Review,* for example, declared that the chief value of history-writing was to make "us better and more valuable members of society." Unless we diligently study the "truths" that history afforded, the writer asked, "how shall we ever improve ourselves, and thus act beneficially upon society; or develope [sic] those germs of virtue and knowledge which exist within us?"[36] Popular history-writers like Emma Willard, founder of the Troy Female Seminary, framed their productions in similar ways: "And may not these generous feelings of virtue arise, respecting nations as well as individuals; and may not the resolution which the youth makes, with regard to himself individually, be made with regard to his country, as far as his future may extend?"[37] Even *The Christian Spectator,* a forum for stodgy Orthodox Calvinists, who viewed novel reading suspiciously, allowed that historical fiction in the tradition of Scott offered characters whose "virtue" consisted of "those principles which hold society together, and keep the world from falling into chaos."[38] Such patriotic didacticism modulated discussions of historical fiction as well. Like nationalist history, historical fiction theoretically instructed readers in republican behavior. The Massachusetts jurist Rufus Choate even claimed that historical fiction did a better job than history did of entertaining readers. Its didactic mission, however, of "hold[ing] up to our emulation and love great models of patriotism and virtue" was essentially the same as history's.[39]

The ideological intimacy between historiography and histori-

cal fiction actually blurred their generic distinction, a fact that
buttresses my intertextual reading of these two modes of historical literature. Those, like Rufus Choate, who called for an original, American historical romance, only ended up muddling the
distinction between history and fiction. In 1823, for example, the
author of "American Genius" tried to argue for the superiority of
historical fiction because of its ability to maintain readerly interest. But his claim that "the novelist's chance for immortality is . . .
at least equal to that of the historian's,"[40] reveals how virtually all
of these kinds of rallying cries for a great American historical
novel actually were premised on generic equivalence. If historical
fiction might better enhance the nation's literary reputation at
home and abroad, both genres similarly fulfilled the cultivation
of republican citizenship.

Such a conflation of historical genres was mystified by the
insistence of historical romancers that their productions did not
qualify as "history." The first words that Catharine Sedgwick utters
in the Preface to *Hope Leslie* protests that her work is not "an
historical narrative, or a relation of real events." But of course it
was. The novel's fourth chapter, as I show in Chapter 2, offers a
revisionist history of the Pequot War meant to compete with
early national accounts of the conflict. Sedgwick goes on to state
ambiguously that historical reality is merely "alluded to" and that
her aim is "to illustrate not the history, but the character of the
times."[41] But if historical romance was not, as Sedgwick phrases
it, a "substitute for genuine history," what was it? A twin? A cousin?
A younger (more sprightly) sibling who possessed captivating
charms? If novels, as Cathy N. Davidson has suggested, provided
an alternative, radical form of education to schoolbook texts in
early republican America,[42] we might consider historical novels
as somewhere between these extremes. Historical novels certainly
offered no dalliance for early national readers; rather, they offered a compromise to the dangers of idleness and moral dissipation associated with novel reading. This mediating role of the
historical romance further contributed to generic instability, for
its cultural position at once called attention to and denied its
status as a "novel." Hence writers like Sedgwick tripped over
themselves trying to sort out and stabilize the generic status of
their work. The safe distance and yet inevitable intimacy between
the two genres is apparent as well in Choate's claim that the critic
"would wish at length to hear such a genius *mingling the tones* of a
ravishing national minstrelsy with the grave narrative, instructive
reflections, and chastened feelings of Marshall, Pitkin, Holmes

and Ramsay."[43] Historical fiction, it would appear, actually should *absorb* elements of historiography within itself. It was supposed to be what Choate called a "supplement," rather than a substitute, for the more mundane narrative of nationalist history. So the genre whose renaissance Choate calls for in 1833 approximates what we call "intertextuality" today. He wants historical fiction paradoxically to emobody and transcend the conservative didacticism of its chief colleague and competitor.

These similar premises created a host of ambiguities. Early national critics simultaneously panned historians for not being sufficiently "literary" and historical fictionists for not being sufficiently "historical." The histories written by Massachusetts minister Charles Goodrich and the South Carolinian physician David Ramsay both suffered criticisms of style and presentation. In the case of Ramsay, the *North American Review*'s suggestion of plagiarism faulted him not for having borrowed other history-writers' interpretations, but for his failure in having "taken his materials and wrought them up with his own skillful hand"; the crime involved narrative originality rather than research, differentiating artistic "genius" from "mere copyists."[44] On the other hand, historical fiction writers were often were subjected to historians' standards of objectivity. Charges of plagiarism stuck just as noxiously to historical fiction as to histories. Jared Sparks, for example, simply railed at the anonymous author of the historical novel *The Witch of New England* (1824) for having plagiarized Nathaniel Ward's *The Simple Cobbler of Aggawam* (1647), Jeremy Belknap's *American Biography* (1794–8), and other well-known histories of the day. The author, Sparks complained, "interweav[es] with his narrative a number of facts, which he has collected and used without ceremony. . . . We could easily trace his progress through several of these [histories], and were amazed, that, after having read them, he should still remain so ignorant of the early history of the country."[45] In context of this critique of Ramsay, a certain irony emerges: Plagiarism for a "historian" involved an unoriginal style; for a "novelist," a feeble effort in research.

The intimacy between history and historical fiction sometimes collapsed altogether.[46] If material from histories – through carelessness, design, plagiarism, or similar narrative qualities – sometimes made their way into historical fiction, the opposite held true as well. Lydia Child's rendition of James Otis's speech in *The Rebels* (1825), a romance of the American Revolution, later appeared in school readers. James Fenimore Cooper's account of

Lexington and Concord in *Lionel Lincoln* (1825) was similarly appropriated by Caleb Snow in *A History of Boston* (1825).[47] Historians and novelists, moreover, seem to have been acutely aware of each other. Emma Willard lamented that school histories sadly lacked historical fiction's more interesting focus on "a few individuals, of whose geographical course we are never allowed to lose sight."[48] Fiction writers showed the same self-consciousness. In their historical novels about Puritanism, James Fenimore Cooper and James McHenry each critiqued Benjamin Trumbull's *A Complete History of Connecticut* (1797) in order to distinguish their own *historical* interpretations, Cooper calling attention to how "graver improbabilities creep into the doubtful pages of history," and McHenry taking Trumbull to task specifically for erasing the historical record of Connecticut's involvement in witch-hunting.[49] All such instances of generic entanglement, outright literary theft, or historical commentary suggest the ways in which these dual modes of historical writing complemented and competed with one another.

In light of these generic ambiguities, I treat historical fiction as an identifiable, though not autonomous, mode of history-writing in the early republic. The kind of revisionist history with which we are familiar today did not really exist in early republican America. Dissenting and conflicting interpretations of key events certainly did appear in nationalist history-writing between the 1780s and 1830s, but the genre's emphasis on personal and public virtue, as well as national destiny, made it generally conservative. In the absence of a school of revisionist historiography, historical romance provided one outlet for cultural dissent. Without overestimating the radical politics of historical romance, one should recognize that the genre engaged, subverted – sometimes participated in – the dominant ideologies of status quo historiography. Indeed, the cultural role of historical fiction as a mediator between novels and histories marks its liminal political position. As a medium for dissent, however, historical romance provided greater flexibility than historiography did, especially for women writers who manipulated literary conventions to critique the contemporary republic.

The flexibility that historical fiction provided, however, should not obscure its nationalistic tenor. As Benedict Anderson has argued, if nationalism itself is a cultural construct, early-nineteenth-century creations of the "imagined nation" reinvented historical continuity between heroic origins and the present generation:

Hence, for the members of what we might call "second-generation" nationalist movements, those which developed in Europe between about 1815 to 1850, and also for the independent national states of the Americas, it was no longer possible to "recapture/The first fine careless rapture" of their revolutionary predecessors. For different reasons and with different consequences, the two groups thus began the process of reading nationalism *genealogically* – as the expression of an historical tradition of serial continuity.[50]

Anderson raises an important issue for early republican culture and the period's historical literature. The comparison between Puritan New England and the early republic spawned commentaries that cast the present generation alternately as enlightened beings or as enfeebled backsliders. All forms of history-writing in early national New England, including, of course, historical romance, negotiated with difficulty the "serial continuity" between contemporary and colonial history. To fulfill the directives of cultural nationalism, the "nation" was engineered by bourgeois and aristocratic New Englanders through the agency of historical memory. But what sort of continuities existed – or were even desirable? Or were thought to be hopelessly impossible? Historical literature about Puritanism describes a selective process of culling and pruning ancestral qualities that simultaneously compressed and distended the historical distance between Puritan and early republican cultures.

The very definition of early republican culture, however, is itself problematic. One of the more cogent critiques of new historical methods is that they can totalize culture into a giant, meaningless monolith. Instead of proceeding by a strategy of chiasmus, as Brook Thomas has argued, where literary discourse is situated as only one cultural practice among many other cultural practices, new historicist studies sometimes tend to slip into synecdoche, where one form of discourse is mistakenly taken for "culture" in general.[51] This issue affects my admittedly rigorous – though not exclusive – focus on New England, particularly on writers who come from its bourgeois and aristocratic ranks.[52] At the risk of totalizing early national culture as New England writ large, I should note that my regional focus results largely from the fact that during this era both histories and historical fictions about Puritanism were produced by New Englanders. Moreover, as scholars of nineteenth-century historiography have noted, the very subject of New England dominated the discipline.[53] These

conservative, genteel amateurs (and often ministers), who fashioned themselves as moral stewards of the republic, exerted a
disproportionate influence on historical writing about Puritanism. Popular histories by such New Englanders as Charles
Goodrich and Salma Hale reached well beyond regional borders:
Hale's work, after all, won an award from the New York Academy
of Language and Belles Lettres, and Goodrich's went through
more than a hundred editions during the nineteenth century.
Hence the regional and cultural mythologies perpetuated by privileged New Englanders emigrated more widely than one might
initially expect.

The context of civic and political culture allows for clarity in
demystifying the politics of historical literature. Too often critics
carelessly bandy about epithets like "radical" and "conservative,"
as though they were universal terms transcending time and place.
Although I recognize Foucauldian objections to pure subjectivity,
and admit the epistemic impossibility of writing from a zone of
ideological neutrality, I have tried to locate in historical literature
culturally specific debates over the nature of that elusive term
"republicanism." Context, moreover, provides an ideological map
with which to reread literary convention. Whereas formalist critics
once emphasized the presumably clichéd nature of women's historical romance[54] – rebellious daughters, tyrannical fathers, progressive marriages – feminist critics like Kelley and Karcher cogently have reinterpreted them to argue for their political
significance. Building on this reappraisal, I pursue the early national debates encoded within literary convention and thus not
only emphasize the historical distance between gender politics of
the 1820s and that of the 1990s, but also reconceive the very
nature of literary "convention" itself. These formal features are
signposts with which early national readers were meant to interpret their own lives and determine their own valuations of "republican" citizenship. Many such formal conventions derive, of
course, from the model of Sir Walter Scott. But rather than plot
out the literary-historical coordinates between Scott and American romancers, I investigate the emergence of a literary genre in
context of political–cultural issues about republicanism.

The anxieties surrounding these issues derived largely from
the great, and sometimes unsettling, changes taking place in
America between the 1790s and 1830s. It is always easy to overstate these movements, or to lose a sense of historical continuity
by isolating this period. But the social, political, and economic
transformations during this era did create internal convulsions

among many Americans, including elite New Englanders, whom I consider in Chapter 1, over the future of the republic. One major change involved the nature of property itself. Charles Sellers has characterized the early antebellum period as a process of transformation from "land" to "market," that is, from premodern farming to modern agricultural capitalism.[55] Older household economies, which were based on task labor and produced primarily for local markets, began to give way to agricultural production for expanding domestic and international markets. This change in turn spurred the development of more sophisticated transportational networks: new roads, canals, and eventually railroads by the 1820s and 1830s. As fertile agricultural lands along the eastern seaboard, and especially in New England, began to become scarce during the early nineteenth century (through overuse or limited quantities), American society underwent explosive demographic movements, especially toward the West. Moreover, the growth of commercial capitalism, and the inchoate beginnings of industrialization, changed the definition of "property" in both the legal and legislative systems. Common-law courts, which traditionally had upheld an agrarian or "natural" conception of property, increasingly adjudicated property rights according to productivity.[56] Whereas state legislatures formerly had granted corporate status exclusively to public institutions, such status now became available to private businesses that benefited the "public welfare" and also themselves. This era also saw the rise of American political parties that openly avowed self-interests, thus violating older, eighteenth-century understandings of republican politics. All these changes characterized an emergently liberal republic whose ethos of self-interest challenged many traditional beliefs. Historical romance emerged, then, during an era in which traditional meanings of "republicanism" became increasingly fractured and in which Americans were compelled to adapt traditional ideologies to new realities.

The decade of the 1820s was particularly acute in this regard. Indeed, nowhere is an historical epithet more misleading than "the era of good feelings" for the extended period after the War of 1812. The 1820s began with the immediate aftermath of the Panic of 1819, and witnessed rising sectional tensions over the Missouri Compromise of 1824. From James Monroe's presidency through Andrew Jackson's second term, the subject of Indian removal was especially resonant and at times volatile. Political issues concerning tariffs, internal improvements, and the federal government's role in the promotion of capitalist enterprises began to splinter the Republican Party – the old, sacred party of Jefferson – which had been in power since 1800. If these contemporary controversies created uncertainties about the state of the Union, they did so amid constant reminders of the heroic purity of the Revolutionary generation. As scholars of the early republic have shown, a central tension during this era describes the emergence of liberal America out of a culture of commemorative nostalgia about republican origins.[57] Historical literature about Puritanism emerged at such a moment. The tour of the Marquis de Lafayette in the 1820s only highlighted the historical distance between that decade and the Revolution. The fifty-year anniversaries of Lexington and Concord and the Declaration of Independence fell in 1825 and 1826. Jefferson and John Adams, the last of the Framers, died in 1826 – both on the night of July Fourth. Most importantly, the 1820s were bracketed by the bicentennial commemorations of the founding of Plymouth and the Massachusetts Bay colony. The decade witnessed the reprinting of numerous original Puritan texts: Cotton Mather's *Magnalia Christi Americana* in 1820, John Winthrop's *History of New England* in 1825, Nathaniel Morton's *New England's Memorial* in 1826, as well as many others. Historical romance appeared amid a larger, cultural recirculation of Puritan discourse at a time fraught paradoxically with both anxieties and exuberance about the modern republic.

Chapter 1 examines the representation of Puritanism in early national historiography within the context of these cultural changes. What I call "metaphorical Puritanism" locates colonial New England as a complex trope for republican virtue that at once recovered the ideologies of classical republicanism and translated them into modern liberalism via an elastic, protean language. These ideologies lent a rhetorical multivalence to historical discourse about Puritanism, a phenomenon that instances the Bakhtinian concept of heteroglossia – the dialogue among various interanimating social discourses. The confrontation of republican and liberal discourses dialogize one another, and create new meanings through the medium of historical discourse.

Chapters 2 and 3 pursue the gendered ramifications of Puritanism as a cultural trope for masculine republicanism. Women writers took up the subject of Puritan history as a way of renegotiating the values codified by the Puritan/republican ideal. Their revisions of Puritan history served the ends of redefining the republic itself. As I show, the gradual feminization of virtue during the late eighteenth and early nineteenth centuries helped facilitate this project. In Chapter 2, I demonstrate how Catharine

Sedgwick's "recital," or performance, of the Pequot War in *Hope Leslie* was engaged primarily with histories of her own day that used the war to recover an already outmoded form of republican manhood. This analysis of a small, though crucial, section of *Hope Leslie* segues to a larger consideration of the contemporary struggle over the terms of civic ethics that both *Hope Leslie* and Lydia Child's *Hobomok* undertake. Chapter 3 explores the civic and political meanings of female virtue during this transitional era where the meaning of republicanism was itself unstable and thus eminently contestable. In writing about colonial history, women writers selectively critiqued, appropriated, and refashioned Revolutionary republicanism. Hence their historical novels, not unlike Noah Webster's dictionaries, recodify republican language. With this context in mind, we may reread the literary conventions of women's historical romance as the site of contemporary political critiques of female ontology, civic authority, and republican marriage.

Chapter 4 reconsiders Cooper's well-known disdain for the Puritans. I challenge the view held among numerous Cooperians that *The Wept of Wish-ton-Wish* is a psychological commentary on Puritan history by recontextualizing the novel within a larger field of contemporary narratives about King Philip's War. Cooper's sometimes satiric treatment of frontier Puritans actually challenges those accounts by New England historians in his own day who used the war to legitimate the acquisitive logic of liberalism. *The Wept*, in other words, contests the naive optimism and self-congratulatory euphoria of an emergently liberal republic by exposing the unmitigated greed contemporary New England historians rationalized in order to defend their Puritan ancestors. Cooper also engages the gender and racial politics of women's historical writing during the 1820s by revising the formulas for androgynous manhood that writers like Child and Sedgwick earlier had promoted. His novel marks a dialogue in historical romance of the 1820s about the ethical contours of republican manhood.

Chapter 5 examines the subject of Puritan witch-hunting as a political metaphor for the modernization and democratization of American politics between the 1790s and the 1830s. In the wake of the development of popular political parties, the Salem witchcraft trials of 1692 became a trope for a contemporary breakdown of social and political order, a phenomenon exacerbated by the example of the French Revolution. Historical writing about witch-hunting inscribes the legacy of classical republican theory.

Words such as "delusion" and "superstition" signify an ideology of reason and moderation upon which traditional deferential politics rested. The early national narrative of Salem mediates a contemporary dilemma for early nationals of the meaning of Revolutionary republicanism in a post-Revolutionary political world. By examining a variety of literary texts, however, including John Greenleaf Whittier's *Legends of New England* (1831), John Neal's *Rachel Dyer* (1828), and James Nelson Barker's drama *Superstition* (1824), we can see that romantic ideas complicated the subject of reason in literary texts.

An argument this book decidedly does *not* attempt to make is that these historical novels and plays of the 1820s and 1830s should be considered part of an "American Renaissance." This category still occupies the hermeneutic center of American literary studies, and it reflects what one critic has aptly called the "neoromantic organicist models of American literary history."[58] Whether it be F. O. Mathiessen's "American Renaissance" in 1941, or such later reformulations as "The Other American Renaissance," or "The American Renaissance Reconsidered,"[59] both exclusionists and revisionists perpetuate a model of nineteenth-century literature in which midcentury works take a dominant place. This not only marginalizes earlier writing but also tends to misplace historical contexts germane to the 1850s onto earlier texts of the 1820s. As it is so often told, the "story" of nineteenth-century American literature rides a kind of metonymic train to the destination of the American Renaissance (wherever that may be these days) and then begins anew. For this reason, I intentionally reorient these literary works from the Renaissance to the Revolution. In this way, early historical romances do not become cheapened adumbrations of Hawthorne and other romantic writers. Historical romance of the 1820s is the site of various intersections between literary and political cultures, a place where literary didacticism, historical memory, and post-Revolutionary politics converge.

1

THE NEW EBENEZER:

REPUBLICAN VIRTUE, THE PURITAN FATHERS, AND EARLY NATIONAL HISTORY-WRITING

It must not be imagined that the piety of the Puritans was merely speculative, taking no notice of the course of worldly affairs. Puritanism . . . was almost as much a political theory as a religious doctrine.

– Alexis de Tocqueville, *Democracy in America*

But the dead have no rights.

– Thomas Jefferson, "Letter to Samuel Kercheval," July 12, 1816

Several years before he was elected to the state senate of New Hampshire in 1824, Salma Hale, the son of a Revolutionary war hero, published his *History of the United States*. It was a big success, winning the highly coveted prize awarded by the New York Academy of Language and Belles Lettres for the best history textbook for schools. This is no surprise, since Hale had been writing for years, publishing his first book – a grammar of English – as a teenager. Before the publication of his *History*, Hale also had been elected to Congress as a Republican in 1816; later in life he served in the New Hampshire House of Representatives. What is significant about his ongoing dual careers in politics and letters is that they mark his prize-winning *History* as the product of an avocation; it is a text, in other words, whose well-advertised utility to American citizens closely paralleled Hale's activities in politics and government. Like virtually all history-writers during the early republic, Hale understood the duality of his life as something perfectly reconcilable. His literary efforts, like his public service in government, fulfilled an ethos of citizenship. Readers of his writings, young and old alike, would be socialized as good "republicans."

Hale's narrative of Puritan New England is particularly striking in this context. Even more apparent than the disproportionate weight he gives to the Puritans – they cover about 40% of the entire history of colonial America – is the obvious instruction in civic and political ethics that early New England afforded contemporary readers. Puritanism offered a particular lesson in community.

To show this, Hale turns to the authoritative word of the Fathers themselves. Citing a letter included in William Bradford's *Of Plymouth Plantation,* in which the Pilgrim leaders in 1618 are trying to sell themselves to the Virginia Company as a reliable investment, Hale claims that the Plymouth immigrants " 'were knit together by a strict and sacred bond, by virtue of which they held themselves bound to take care of the good of each other and of the whole.' "[1] Such a communitarian spirit also informs Hale's treatment of the Mayflower Compact, the agreement whereby the Pilgrim newcomers, having arrived north of Virginia, and now faced with possible dissension from their nonbelieving colleagues, desperately formed a government. Here Hale again excises key phrases from Bradford's history and pastes them together in new and condensed form to show that the Compact created "a body politic, for the purpose of making equal laws for the general good."[2] This thematic design, moreover, shapes the entire narrative of colonial New England. During the 1660s, for example, when the colonies were "threatened with punishment" by the English government against abetting the fugitive regicides of Charles I, both Massachusetts Bay and New Haven "evinced the republican spirit"[3] by hiding two of the fugitives. And despite the irony that Hale finds in Puritan persecution of Quakers during the 1650s, he still admires New England's "adventurous and hardy labourers."[4] It is no surprise, then, according to Hale, that Massachusetts Bay was treated more favorably than Virginia by Cromwell during the Interregnum because the Puritans "were republicans in politics, and Puritans in religion."[5]

What did it mean during the 1820s to call the Puritans "republicans," to separate, in this case, theology from politics? This chapter examines the politics of early national historical writing *about* Puritanism in just this context. The ideology of civic-mindedness surrounding Hale's Puritans, however, is not as simple as it initially appears. One should not overlook the fact that, even as Hale wrote didactically, his *History* won him four hundred dollars – and a gold medal worth fifty dollars.[6] This monetary reward is perhaps indicative of the increasingly commercialized literary marketplace beginning to evolve in early-nineteenth-century America. Moreover, such remuneration suggests financial considerations commensurate with the emergence of a liberal republic, ones that do not invalidate but that certainly complicate the presumably pristine didacticism of post-Revolutionary history-writing. Hale's "virtue" lay in both his capitalist and his civic energies. The capacity of his *History* to teach "virtue," in other words, was complicated during this transitional era by the kinetic instability of the word itself. Cultural change in early national America tellingly leaves its mark on the narrative of Puritan New England. Consider, for example, Hale's praise for his industrious forebears, for it shows an irrepressible fascination with a freely competitive arena describing his *own* era:

> Such . . . were the character and virtues of the [Puritan] emigrants; such the power over difficulties which their reso-lute minds, and bodies hardened by labour, had imparted to them, that they continued to increase with astonishing ra-pidity in wealth and numbers. And a vote of the house of commons, stating "that the plantations in New England had had good and prosperous success, without any public charge to the state," is quoted by an historian of those times as an honourable testimony of the high merit of the colonists.[7]

Republican language here is imbedded with newer, liberal mean-ings. One sees that the exemplary status of Puritan "labour" implies both prosperity and expansion – the "astonishing rapidity in wealth and numbers." However, in the context of New En-gland's presumably communal values, there would seem to be something troublingly incongruous about the mere suggestion of, much less effusive praise for, competition and acquisitiveness. Yet language itself somehow sanctifies such a narrative of Puri-tanism: "The habits of industry and economy, which had been formed in less happy times, continued to prevail, and gave a competency to those who had nothing, and wealth to those who had a competency."[8] This is the myth of America, as we know it today; this is the free-wheeling and unfettered promised land that has produced the representative likes of Benjamin Franklin, Horatio Alger, and H. Ross Perot – and, in the 1820s, Salma Hale's Puritans.

Like any right-minded Puritan minister, I suppose, I take Hale's *History* as my "text": It is representative of history-writing about Puritanism during the early republic. It crucially registers the protean meanings of citizenship amid dynamic changes in American society. There are *two* discourses of Puritanism here, simultaneously inhabiting the same set of "republican" signifiers. These distinct yet reciprocal and mutually animating discourses of "virtue" simultaneously reveal a fascination with and repugnance for modernity. The language surrounding Hale's treatment of Puritan prosperity – their vigorous character, their "bodies hardened by labour," their indomitable will in the face of adversity – invokes the sturdy yeoman freeholder that the American Revolution had popularized. In this resonant context, the ideological and rhetorical power of language defuses the dangers to republican morality lurking within prosperity itself. Uncannily, then – through language if not by logic – Puritan New England can be construed both to promote and to contain cultural change. In order to articulate how this was possible in the early republic, one needs to understand it within the context of changes in American civic and political culture between the 1780s and 1830s. This involves the problem of "republicanism."

Virtue, Ideology, and the American Revolution

What did "virtue" mean during the Revolutionary era? Ever since the excavation of republican ideology by historians nearly thirty years ago, this issue has consumed the study of eighteenth- and early-nineteenth-century America. Over the years, historians gradually have moved away from using the strident dichotomy of "republicanism" and "liberalism," and take a more nuanced, contextual approach to the intellectual and cultural life of early America. After the Second World War, liberal "consensus" historians, such as Arthur Schlesinger, Jr., Louis Hartz, and Richard Hofstadter, dominated the study of Revolutionary America.[9] Driven by the desire to extricate American history from Leftist politics, liberal historians argued that the Revolution lacked any discernible "ideology" – a code word, as I have tried to emphasize in the Introduction, for Marxist totalitarianism – besides a loosely consensual faith in individual property rights derived largely from John Locke's *Two Treatises of Government* (1690). Revision of the liberal consensus in Revolutionary studies began during the 1960s, as "republican" historians, such as Bernard Bailyn, Gordon S. Wood, and J. G. A. Pocock, unabashedly restored ideology to the causes of the Revolution and to the intellectual and cultural life of the nation.[10] Like their liberal forebears, they rejected earlier "progressive" historians' neo-Marxist belief that class interests had shaped the political history of the Revolution (captured in Carl Becker's famous phrase that the Revolution was about "home rule and who shall rule at home"),[11] but they significantly displaced the intellectual inheritance of Locke with that of Polybius, Renaissance civic humanism, the seventeenth-century English Commonwealthmen, and Montesquieu.

The common ground of such a diverse intellectual inheritance lay in the very conception of a "republic" itself, which was understood in simultaneously ethical and institutional terms. Classical republicanism, which made its way into American political thought, as Pocock has shown, via Machiavelli and English Whiggery, theorized that political life depended largely upon a citizenry's capacity for "virtue." The importance of this term in American Revolutionary culture is apparent in the myriad pamphlets, broadsides, invectives, treatises, satires, and editorials during the rising tensions the 1760s and 1770s. American Whigs opposing British imperial policy were themselves influenced by Opposition writers in England who earlier had excoriated the regime of Sir Robert Walpole during the 1720s and 1730s. Whig historicism, as Bailyn has shown, was essentially a hermeneutics of conspiracy. It envisioned "Power" and "Liberty" in an ongoing archetypal struggle that was then being staged in the New World. Because Power was predatory and masculine, and Liberty feminized and passive, only masculine virtue theoretically could protect the people's freedom. Such an exclusively masculine understanding of virtue derived from the classical concept of *virtu* (the lexical root of "virility"), which denoted the martial courage and disinterested devotion to the state expressed by all male citizens: rulers, in political service, and the masses, in a call to arms. At its core, then, republicanism embraced a view of society and politics that was corporate, consensual, and hierarchical.

The dual foci of republicanism were property and liberty. As I show in this chapter, elite conservatives believed that social and political order was requisite to preserving both of them, and this shaped the post-Revolutionary era's discourse of Puritanism. As a distinctly premodern ideology of society and politics, republicanism traditionally resisted modern, commercial capitalism, with its supposedly corrupt mechanisms of banks, paper credit, and financial interests that were sure to compromise the *res publica*. In a traditionally republican context, property constituted the bare, necessary means to independence. One worked industriously to maintain one's land and hence one's free will; one's property, in other words, prevented one from becoming dependent – or "enslaved." To republican theorists, however, from Polybius through Machiavelli to John Adams, the experience of history sadly demonstrated that all republics inevitably declined because citizens eventually succumbed to "corruption" and "effeminacy," the passionate desires of greed and ambition that sacrificed the public good on the altar of self-interest. As Pocock has shown, the anticapitalistic strain within republicanism was amplified in early-eighteenth-century England during a period of increasing commercial capitalism. Many Opposition writers lamented these changes – not really trade, per se, but the insidious networks of stockjobbers and speculators associated with venture capitalism – which helped to create a corrupt den of placemen in Parliament who were beholden to special interests and looked to fatten themselves at the expense of the people. Indeed, the luxuries associated with modern capitalism enervated citizens' capacity for disinterestedness, making them "slaves" as much to their own greedy appetites as to the larger designs of conniving, ambitious capitalists and politicians.

What one historian more than twenty years ago tellingly called the "republican synthesis"[12] restored ideology to the American Revolution in ways that reflected the work of cultural anthropologists such as Clifford Geertz. From the outset, republican historiography articulated how political discourse operates as a cultural system. Hence it synthesizes; it serves as an ideological force shaping all forms of behavior in a specific cultural context. It is important to note, however, that republican historians isolated a political-cultural inheritance as it existed *in language* alone. The fact that these historians largely ignored the relationship between language and the complex social and economic conditions in Revolutionary America began to elicit revisionist interpretations by such historians as Joyce Appleby, who as early as the mid-1970s addressed the troubling idea of a causative theory of the Revolution that was divorced from social and economic realities. "If a classical republicanism imbued with traditional notions of political authority dominated colonial thinking," Appleby asked, "where are the roots of that liberalism which flowered so quickly after independence?"[13] No less ideological than republicanism, the liberalism that Appleby and others began to promote as part of Revolutionary American culture posits that the natural laws of the unregulated marketplace ultimately benefit society. In this context, "virtue" becomes the salutary pursuit of private self-interest that brings forth national prosperity (as in Hale's frontier Puritans); thus luxury, in turn, is conceived of as the sign of civilization rather than of corruption and decay. Commerce promotes not only the exchange of goods but also the exchange of ideas, continually civilizing and uplifting society to greater heights of taste, sensibility, and refinement. Liberal ideas about the market, society, competition, and individualism, as Appleby's

158,164

rhetorical question suggests, quickly gained currency in nineteenth-century America. And they had to come from somewhere.[14]

So historians over the past two decades have debated the relative importance of republicanism and liberalism in early America. One should recognize the political sensitivity of historiographic debates that implicitly raise issues about the presumed nature of the "American character" or "the American mind" (even though this trope has itself been questioned in an era increasingly more aware of cultural diversity). Was the nation, in other words, founded on an anticapitalist ideology or on a materialist one?

The issue of "virtue" in early America is complicated even further by the word's gradual feminization, its increasing association with Christian benevolence and genteel sociability. The severe austerity of classical *virtu* became increasingly obsolete during the late eighteenth century for an American elite that self-consciously fashioned itself according to principles of sociability and refinement deriving from Scottish Common Sense philosophers such as Francis Hutcheson, Lord Kames, Archibald Alison, Thomas Reid, and others.[15] American aristocrats, as Gordon Wood recently has argued, embraced the polished company of modern society wherein one was judged by standards of taste, gentility, and moral feeling: "They were men of leisure, graceful without foppishness, polite without arrogance, tasteful without pretension, virtuous without affectation, . . . natural without vulgarity."[16] So a convoluted, interanimating complex of intellectual traditions – classical republicanism, liberalism, Scottish affectionalism – rendered the meaning of "virtue" a sometimes tortured multivalence during this era. In light of these traditions, historians increasingly take more innovative approaches to the very idea of ideological inheritance. As one has put it, "republican society and liberal society did not stand diametrically opposed in America . . . . [for] republican traditions served as a seedbed for the growth of liberal commitments."[17] What once critically was cast as polarity now tends toward synthesis, pluralism, and even multivalence.[18] Most are now willing to acknowledge that, as another historian has put it, "there was *no single republican ideology*. Republicanism was not an immutable set of commandments, but a malleable series of ideas and beliefs."[19] As many have recently argued – including Wood himself – classical and liberal discourses were not mutually exclusive: "Just as monarchy was transformed rather than supplanted by republicanism, so too was republicanism transformed rather than supplanted by liberalism."[20] Scholars thus see classical and liberal ideologies in a syncretic relationship that eventuated in an " 'Americanization' of discursive traditions [which] represented a distinctive blend of many voices."[21]

This eighteenth-century trinity, so to speak, bestowed a complex ideological legacy upon early republican America, an inheritance which early nationals negotiated in synthetic and sometimes inconsistent ways. Example: It was possible to trade vigorously in increasingly sophisticated capitalist markets and simultaneously to declaim the dangers of luxury and "effeminacy" on the republic. But the danger of luxury was itself problematic because modern virtue in early America recast it as something positive. Another tension: The republican sin of "effeminacy" was complicated by self-consciously modern tenets of virtue that demanded a quasi-feminized ethos of feeling and benevolence. One might even say that the legacies of republican vigor and Common Sense affection implicitly made androgyny – in certain contexts – the unspoken logic of early republican manhood. As one historian has shown, the rural elite of Massachusetts deliberately cultivated their identities according to a classically pastoral ideal of agrarian simplicity that nonetheless managed to incorporate a softened heart, refined sensibility, and benevolence.[22] In light of all of these ideological tensions – all of the nuanced and highly contextual meanings for republican civic ethics during this era – consider the Introduction to one of the most popular textbook histories of the United States, where its author justifies his work by claiming that "[h]istory sets before us striking instances of virtue, enterprise, courage, generosity, patriotism; and by a natural principle of emulation, incites us to copy such noble examples."[23] What did these words really mean in 1829?

The historical representation of Puritanism during this era inscribed cultural and ideological tension as well as rhetorical instability. Republicanism, as virtually everyone recognizes, gradually gave way to liberalism amid the modernizing changes of antebellum America, for the latter was better suited to market capitalism, social diversity and mobility, and interest-group democratic politics.[24] As I show in the next section, however, during this era of change a conservative milieu of predominantly New England history-writers invoked the Puritan fathers as a historical metaphor for an outmoded – and yet resilient – model of classical republican consensus and hierarchy.[25] The gendered implications of masculine republicanism I address later on, but for now we might focus on the politics of an expanding industry of history-writing dominated largely by a New England elite. The natural affinities between the Puritan commonwealth and classical republic (apparent, for example, in the many classical allusions Cotton Mather provides in the *Magnalia Christi Americana* to buttress the communitarian ideal) recast Puritanism in the image – and language – of contemporary New England conservatives (and kindred spirits like the South Carolinian David Ramsay) who wrote didactic histories to ensure social and political order. What I call "metaphorical Puritanism" constituted a political–cultural act of recuperation of a traditionally conservative ideology. This historical subject, however, registers as well the entangled relations between republicanism and liberalism in the early American republic. The language of Puritanism testifies to a great historical irony, since it reveals how a conservative project of historiography was itself inflected with modern affinities for self-interest, commercial growth, and national prosperity.

The process of cultural transformation created a linguistic situation in historical writing about Puritanism that might be called a "double-voiced discourse." Bakhtin's theories of the social construction of language and the multivocality of any "utterance" aptly characterize the rhetorical interplay of classical and liberal ideologies within the textual subject of Puritan New England. Early national histories – the didactic productions of ministers, antiquarians, and legislators – ostensibly appear to fall within the category of the "epic," as Bakhtin defines it, the monological discourse of the status quo meant to ensure hierarchical power relations by repressing society's diversity of languages. These histories certainly are epics in the sense that they are premised upon an elite's resilient cultural authority. Yet the subtleties of language within them reveal how the very dynamics of cultural change disrupt even their most conservative intentions, and allow the presence of alternative languages to appear and dialogize a premodern discourse of republicanism. Language "refracts," according to Bakhtin, varyingly through the voices of narrators and characters, thus creating an unstable state of "double-voicedness." The dialogic relationship between classical and liberal ideologies in these histories parallels that envisioned by Bakhtin between author and character in the novel, where two languages simultaneously speak:

> Heteroglossia, once incorporated into the novel . . . is *another's speech in another's language,* serving to express authorial

intentions but in a refracted way. Such speech constitutes a special type of *double-voiced discourse*. It serves two speakers at the same time and expresses simultaneously two different intentions. . . . In such discourse there are two voices, two meanings, and two expressions. And all the while these two voices are dialogically interrelated . . . it is as if they actually hold a conversation with each other.[26]

The imbedded conversations about the nature of republicanism taking place in early national discourse reveal a complex, ambivalent response by conservatives to a modernizing world around them. Puritanism becomes the site where different intonations of the same words – "virtue," "liberty," "property," "industry," "enterprise" – all of the key words of the Revolution – confront one another and become dialogized. The utterance of ancestral memory in early national New England enacted this kind of double-voicedness, as early nationals conversed with readers, with history, and with themselves over the nature and future of the republic.

The Discourse of Puritan Order

For all their reservations about intolerance in colonial New England, early national history-writers had no qualms about calling the Puritans "republicans." One could find in New England's historical journals the characterization of the typical Puritan as a "republican in politics, but sour and bigotted in religion."[27] Even a regional outsider such as the South Carolinian David Ramsay believed that Plymouth Plantation was founded "on a truly republican principle" and that "New Englanders [of Massachusetts Bay] were advanced a century a-head [sic] of their contemporaries, in the school of republicanism and the rights of man."[28] Like Hale and so many other conservative nationalists during this era, Ramsay generally dissolved the whole issue of Puritan intolerance within the larger solvent of "those times of ignorance,"[29] demonstrating to us today how an Enlightenment vision of progress conveniently served the purposes of historical euphemism. One of Ramsay's colleagues, Abiel Holmes, Orthodox minister of the First Church in Cambridge, similarly claimed to both a Forefathers Day audience in 1806 and to general readers of his *American Annals* (1829) that the Plymouth Pilgrims, upon signing the Mayflower Compact, erected a "republic."[30] By simultaneously acknowledging Puritan "bigotry" and lauding New England's republican politics, these writers found themselves engaged in the difficult task of disentangling political and religious lessons from the historical record, implicitly asking their readers (or auditors) to at once embrace and reject an ancestral model of behavior. The medium of exemplary history, in other words, paradoxically compresses and distends historical time.[31]

But what did this word "republican" actually mean? Like the Constitution makers of 1787–8, early national history-writers negotiated both ethical and institutional meanings of a republic; the former context, however, bore most significantly on the representation of Puritan history. One way to demonstrate this is to compare the period's respective narratives of the foundings of New England and Virginia. Together they constitute something like an early national version of a medieval morality play. To Abiel Holmes, for example, Virginia was "planted in discord" by "vicious and profligate people"; the "wildest anarchy" of "dissipated and hopeless young men" initially made Virginia a failure, for "[s]uch persons were little capable of the regular subordination, the strict economy, and persevering industry, which their situation required."[32] Yet in these didactic histories, the capacity for "industry" revives just in time. Both John Smith and Governor Thomas Dale enforce order there, and eventually the settlers get smart and plant tobacco instead of digging for gold: "Thoughtless adventurers, assuming the sentiments of virtuous citizens and of provident fathers of families, became daily more solicitous for the prosperity of a country, which they now considered as their home."[33] But one can see that "virtue" in Virginia – what Ramsay calls the "more extensive laws of industry" – tellingly signifies the independence for greater means rather than merely the means to independence. Its industrious "labour" eventually pays off in a lucrative cash-crop economy, showing early-nineteenth-century readers how the common good is fulfilled by the aggregate pursuit of individual interests. This is the liberal credo.

Unlike Virginia, Massachusetts Bay and Plymouth were founded "by higher motives than the extension of agriculture or commerce."[34] The religious idealism, which Ramsay and others invested in colonial New England, refurbishes traditionally Whiggish republican values at the very least skittish of commercial sophistication and material gain. The Puritans, in Ramsay, "emigrated, not for the advantage of trade, but for religion, and the enjoyment of liberty of conscience."[35] They exemplified "an indefatigable industry in settling and cultivating a wilderness, to encounter which, no worldly motive could have been an adequate

inducement."³⁶ As the borders between religion and politics significantly blur (an ironic maneuver, given the tendency at other
moments to rationalize Puritan religious intolerance by disentangling it from political norms), the very nature of "liberty" itself
becomes problematic. What kind of "liberty" was colonial New
England intended to model for early nationals? A Fourth of July
oration given in 1815 by the Massachusetts jurist and politician
(and later father-in-law to Herman Melville) Lemuel Shaw, begins
to suggest the capacities of Puritanism to serve as a historical
trope that might refurbish a deteriorating politics of hierarchy
and deference:

> The early emigrants to America, were actuated by no ambi-
> tious views of aggrandisement; their sole design was to
> found a state, in which they and their descendants [sic]
> might enjoy their civil, social and religious liberties in secu-
> rity and in peace. They, however, were no levellers, no advo-
> cates for licentious doctrines, which, under the specious
> name of liberty, have since been so prolific a source of
> misery and crimes.³⁷

This imagined place of pristine origins is, in effect, early national
New England's version of the Machiavellian *ricorso:* the return to
moral and political origins. As William C. Dowling has shown, the
currency of Augustanism among the Connecticut Wits in late-
eighteenth-century Connecticut led such poets as John Trumbull
and Timothy Dwight to idealize the "settled life of the original
Puritan colonies, and in particular Connecticut . . . as nothing
other than the *ricorso* demanded by classical republicanism in
its post-Machiavellian mode."³⁸ This historical antidote to the
inevitable doom of cyclical history to which all republics theoretically succumbed endured well into the nineteenth century and
well beyond the Calvinist proving grounds of Yale. Restoration, or
return, was enacted through historical representativeness – in the
Emersonian sense of the word.

   Colonial New England was invoked, or reimagined, by early
national conservatives as a premodern ideal which could forestall
cyclical time. Puritan "virtue" serviced a larger cultural project of
social and political containment. One can thus begin to see how
a New England elite grappled with the embarrassment of Puritan
"bigotry," only to subsume it within the larger context of an
ancestral stability, which metaphorically eased their own anxieties
in a changing world. At its core lay an apologia of hierarchy in
the name of national health (or "constitution" in its antiquated

sense). The implicit correlation among physical, moral, and political health, as the Revolutionary physician and politician Benjamin Rush had theorized in the 1780s, underwrote post-Revolutionary narrative of Puritan "virtue."[39] Early nationals, for example, consistently praised the numerous measures with which the commonwealth legally enforced an anticapitalistic brand of civic ethics: the 1647 ordinance mandating (in a "republican manner") local funds for public education, sumptuary laws against luxury preventing "the costliness of fashion," public records of profligates, the attempt to control prices and wages.[40] "Care was . . . taken," as Holmes put it, "to prevent, or punish, idleness, luxury and extortion."[41] All of these legal and legislative measures were part of a larger effort to maintain a communitarian, agrarian order of middling, fee-simple propertyholders, who were shepherded firmly (yet benevolently) by a patriarchal order of ministers and magistrates vigilantly fastened upon the public good. Puritan virtue demonstrated the full potential of civic personality (in the classical sense) and was duly cast in a republican lexicon of code words that demonstrated the presumed affinities between commonwealth and republic. New England's "vigorous and active" settlers, early national readers were told, "were generally industrious, temperate and healthy . . . they were careful to contract no debts, and to live within their income. They indulged in no luxuries, or unnecessary expenses of living or dress."[42] Here is conservative politics teaching by example.

Such an ideological imperative could be translated from historical subject to historian. Like concentric circles, David Ramsay's account of the Puritans parallels the brief biography of Ramsay himself that prefaces his posthumously published *History of the United States* (1818). The anonymously printed "Biographical Memoir of David Ramsay, M. D." (a sketch which had appeared in the *Analectic Magazine*) was much kinder to Ramsay than later reviewers and historians would be.[43] Quoting the authority of Benjamin Rush, the author proclaimed that Ramsay's " 'abilities are not only good, but great; his talents and knowledge universal.' "[44] Even in Ramsay's upwardly mobile climb, these talents tellingly are couched in an ethos of selflessness. Like the Puritan fathers themselves, Ramsay shows "uncommon industry" as he works "for the common welfare"; his entire life is "devoted to the service of his country" and promotes "the cause of virtue."[45] As a frame for the entire *History*, then, the *Analectic* sketch creates a biographical subject whose virtues gloss the historical subjects within. Ramsay's "[w]ant of judgement in the affairs of the [business] world" only further confirms his exemplary status, since he risks his financial neck and incurs losses of $30,000 for the construction of a "public utility." His losses paradoxically prove his worth.

Such an ideological project affects the medium as well as the message of didactic history. After Ramsay, for example, notes that Connecticut's migrants "settled their vacant lands on principles of the wisest policy . . . [of selling] the soil in small farms, to those who personally cultivated the same," he goes on to recount the colony's progress:

> In proportion to their respective numbers, it is probable that no other country in the world contained more sober, orderly citizens, and fewer who were profligate and abandoned. . . . Their less fertile soil disposed them to a spirit of adventure, and their victorious industry rose superior to every obstacle. In carrying on the whale fishery, they not only penetrated the deepest frozen recesses of Hudson's Bay, and Davis's Straits, but pierced the opposite regions of polar cold. . . . [T]hey carried on this perilous business to an extent exceeding . . . the vigour of English enterprise. . . . The country was settled with yeomanry, who were both proprietors and cultivators of the soil. Luxury was estranged from their borders. Enervating wealth and pinching poverty were both equally rare.[46]

As the passage ranges across the entire face of the globe, it also traverses the historical and ideological space of the early republic. It moves almost mellifluously from communitarian order to an entrepreneurial capitalism in which Yankee whalers span the globe from the Arctic to "the coast of Africa" to "the shores of Brazil." New England's vigorous association of egalitarian propertyholders can still beat the English in the "perilous business" of seafaring and trading. Hence the passage dialogizes republican manhood according to competing (and yet reconcilable) cultural norms. Still, the rhetorical logic here circumscribes the restless energies of competitive risk-taking within a communitarian ideal, the passage's final repugnance for "luxury" disinfecting the theoretical danger of the market itself.

The resiliency with which conservatives clung to an outmoded conception of the republic helps to explain the historical reputation during this era of John Winthrop, the first governor of Massachusetts Bay colony. As Lawrence Buell has noted, Winthrop's reputation was so prolific in this period that even Unitarians momentarily laid down their weapons in the sectarian wars against Orthodox Calvinists.[47] This is because in Winthrop an early national conservative elite found an apostle of republicanism. He is *the* representative man, for example, in Jeremy Belknap's *American Biography* (1794–8). Belknap, the liberal-minded minister of Boston's Long Lane Church, and one of the principal founders of the Massachusetts Historical Society, generally has been viewed as an "Enlightenment" figure of reason, tolerance, and historical progress.[48] And so his disdain for that supposed villain of the Salem witchcraft trials, Cotton Mather, is no surprise. Yet even as he mocked Mather's superstitions in his private correspondence with his friend and fellow antiquarian, Ebenezer Hazard, Belknap nonetheless borrowed heavily from Mather's portrait of Winthrop in the *Magnalia*.[49] This is because the Matherian Winthrop (which in itself derived in large part from Winthrop's own *History of New England*) offered both an actor and a spokesman for the consensual and hierarchical politics of republicanism. As the "father, as well as the governor" of Massachusetts Bay, Winthrop's absolute devotion to "the public service" legitimates *any* authority based upon republican ideals of self-denial and disinterested patriotism.[50] Belknap's ad nauseam insistence upon such representativeness subtly contains a political message for early national readers:

> He was exemplary in his profession as an upright and impartial magistrate, and in his private character as a christian. He had wisdom to discern, and fortitude to do right in the execution of his office; and as a gentleman, was remarkable for his liberality and hospitality. These qualities rendered him dear to men of sobriety and religion, and fitted him to engage in the great and difficult work of founding a Colony.[51]

> He was an example to the people of that frugality, decency and temperance which were necessary in their circumstances, and even denied himself many of the elegancies and superfluities of life, which his rank, and fortune gave him just title to enjoy, both that he might set them a proper example, and be better enabled to exercise that liberality in which he delighted ... to the actual impoverishment of himself and his family.[52]

Through such a biographical subject, Belknap reconstructs the contemporary contours of leadership amidst a political world in which hierarchy and deference (led by men of "rank" and "fortune") was quickly waning. Winthrop, as Belknap notes elsewhere, did not think much of "democratical government." One observes as well traces of modern virtues of humanity and benevolence whose potential discordance with classical austerity is harmonized within the larger frequencies of self-sacrifice. Winthrop's severity coexists with his "liberality" and "hospitality"; his worthy denial of luxuries, moreover, is problematized by the implication that all gentlemen have essential rights to them.[53] Belknap's historiographic regard for Winthrop translates a politics of deference and aristocratic authority from subject to writer, and from commonwealth to republic.

This kind of representativeness contrasts with the biographical subjects of Columbus and Captain John Smith, which are formulated according to the liberal faith in enterprising individualism, an ethos far less conducive to preserving hierarchical stability. Time and again, Belknap casts Columbus as a "genius" whose intellectual superiority is linked to commerce, as though the progress of both reason and venture capitalism are inextricably bound. Columbus is an active and enterprising "genius" whose ambition "gave a new turn to [European society's] thoughts, to their spirit of enterprise and of commerce."[54] This kind of "reason" inculcates the virtue of self-mastery. Unlike the reason modeled by Puritanism, however, the self-regulation exemplified by Columbus manages to liberate the individual. The same holds true for Captain John Smith. "From the first dawn of reason," Belknap remarks, Smith discovered "a roving and romantic genius, and delighted in extravagant and daring actions among his school fellows."[55] One sees in the Life of Smith another version of the Franklinian myth of rags to riches, the poor boy who, as Belknap notes, "quitted his master and with only ten shillings in his pocket"[56] to make his way in the world. In the necessarily rational calculations of market relations – America's new field of battle – Columbus significantly outwits his mutinous crew, and Smith both the infidel Turks and Native Americans. When Smith trades King Powhattan two pounds of blue beads for two hundred pounds of precious corn for starving Jamestown, Belknap models the virtue of "enterprising spirit" for contemporary readers.[57] These lives fulfill the promise of progressive history, the civilizing progress of science and commerce that, in the historiographic logic of liberalism, Columbus's first voyage inaugurates.

Yet this apparent opposition between Puritans and adventurers is a tenuous one. Belknap's transmission of republican and liberal ideologies belies their convoluted intimacy at the time of *American Biography*'s production during the 1790s. In this regard, the litany of John Smith's virtues – industry, "ingenuity, prudence, patience, activity, industry and resolution"[58] – suggest protean meanings that continually confound facile oppositions. In the Life of Smith, Belknap cannot help but align Smith's acquisitive energies (and perhaps his own, as an aggressive literary business-man) with the sanctity of community. Smith relinquishes his own food and shelter for his compatriots; he wisely enforces the plant-ing of crops. Just when a synthesis, however, seems to be resolved, the ramification of Smith's "labour" far outreaches a vision of communal landowners. Smith sees Virginia "not only as a source of wealth to individuals, but as a grand national object."[59] To work industriously, the Life of Smith instructs, is to ensure na-tional prosperity; the aggressive individual, as liberalism has it, secures the common good.

This certainly is not the case, however, when Belknap considers the arena of politics. The text's appearance during the middle-1790s explains its aversion to what in post-Revolutionary America were still called "factions." It was at this time that America's first political parties began to form around the fissures between Jeffersonian and Hamiltonian fiscal and foreign policies. This posed a crisis to republican political culture. In Chapter 5, I discuss the historical subject of Puritan witch-hunting within this political context, but for now we might consider its importance to Belknap's treatment of Puritan political authority in general and Winthrop's representativeness in particular. In *American Biography* much of Winthrop's exemplary status derives from his pro-phetic warnings against partisanship. Republicanism simply could not conceive of modern interest-group politics where, it was be-lieved, only self-seeking demagogues (the prototypes to today's talk radio mouths like Gordon Liddy and Rush Limbaugh) as-sumed power by artfully manipulating the people's passions. For Belknap, the Antinomian crisis of 1637 unmistakably appeared as a case study in demagoguery. Anne Hutchinson, we might recall, avowed a highly spiritualized form of grace that forsook preparationist schemes and the patriarchal authority from which they derived. Winthrop is heroic to Belknap because he "saw the pernicious influence of this controversy with regret, and feared, that if it were suffered to prevail, it would endanger the existence of the Colony."[60] Although Belknap declaimed Anne Hutchinson as a woman of "masculine understanding," he actually placed the principal blame on Governor Henry Vane, the political parvenu who, along with "his party," conspires "to throw all into confusion."[61] Even the Whiggish fear of standing armies is apparent in this scene where, after Vane is defeated for reelection, the "serjeants, who had waited on Vane, to the place of election, threw down their halberds, and refused to attend the newly elected Governor."[62] At the ensuing church synod, only Winthrop's "wisdom and gravity" manage to control the "heat and passion" of the opposition.[63]

Here, then, lie the natural affinities between commonwealth and republic. From Winthrop's own "A Defense of an Order of Court" (1637), which defends the exclusion of English Antinomians in the name of "the welfare of the body," to the *Magnalia*'s defense of Winthrop's handling of the Antinomian crisis, to its ventriloquized expression in Belknap, Puritan fears for a Bible commonwealth have been translated into early national ones for a consensual order of politics. Yet this transmission involves translation as well, an important change in the understanding of historical process. Sacvan Bercovitch has argued that the reappearance of Mather's *Magnalia* in 1820, largely owing to the efforts of the antiquarian Thomas Robbins, received an unexpectedly popular reception because of "the general fascination with the growth of America [and] ... the persistence of the redemptive meaning of America."[64] A thinly veiled version of the *Magnalia*'s Life of Winthrop, however, appeared more than two decades before Robbins's landmark republication of Mather's monumental text. Moreover, the translation of Mather's Winthrop as "Nehemias Americanus" to Belknap's "great and good man" suggests a larger historical and ideological translation of the Puritan covenant to the American republic. Puritan exceptionalism is now displaced by Whiggish fears of the cyclical decay republics inevitably face.

Is the "great and good man" of *American Biography* John Winthrop or George Washington? Winthrop's example in the text offers political instruction uncannily similar to Washington's "Farewell Address" (1796), which warned Americans against the bane of factions and entangling foreign alliances. But how, one might ask, does Winthrop's "goodness" affect his metaphoric presence as classical republican patriarch? Jay Fliegelman has argued that Washington's "goodness" actually encoded the antipatriarchalism that culminated in the late eighteenth century: "The new understanding of greatness as goodness reflected an essential theme of the antipatriarchal revolution that would replace patriarch with benefactor, precept with example, the authority of position with the authority of character, deference and dependence with moral self-sufficiency, and static dichotomies with principles of growth."[65] Yet the authority of benevolence should not mystify its role in preserving in this case patriarchal power. Early national conservatives deftly deployed modern, affective forms of virtue with the intention of refurbishing their own status amid contemporary realities corrosive to deference and hierarchy. Example: John Davis, a conservative jurist and member of the Massachusetts Historical Society. On its surface, Davis's eulogy to Washington in 1800 effectively updates republican virtue to the enlightened benevolence of a good heart, since Washington's "martial and manly virtues" rhetorically give way to the "sentiments" of an "enlightened friend of man," "[t]he tender sympathies of humanity," and a "delicate and refined moral sense."[66] Authority by example instead of precept, however, buttresses a distinct hierarchy upon which society and politics would seem to depend:

> Modelled by [Washington's] great example, the [military] camp became a school of virtue, as well as of military science. There were seen unshaken fidelity; unsullied honor; humane and social sympathies; pure love of country; *respect for the magistracy, and reverence for the laws.* He sustained the standard of American Liberty with energies suited to her character: tempering authority with mildness, bravery with discretion.[67]

As in Belknap's claim for Winthrop's representativeness, this account of Washington registers the affective changes in republican virtue. Yet its feminization is still made to service the same "standard of American Liberty" informing Shaw's oration and, indeed, all of this era's conservative discourse of Puritanism. The microcosmic world of Washington's military camp makes vertical distinctions between people and rulers; respect for laws and magistrates follows on the heels of any mention of "liberty." The conservative project to preserve the status quo (Davis, after all, was a Washington appointee as a U.S. attorney) becomes even clearer at the oration's end, where Davis reminds his audience to uphold the "sober paths of practicable good" and the "old and approved truths" meant to prevent the "Lords of Anarchy and Misrule."[68]

    Fear of democratic libertarianism allows for a significant reconsideration of the relations among historiography, politics, and theology in early republican New England. Much has been made – and with good reason – of the sectarian rivalries during this era between Unitarian and Orthodox camps, which mediated contemporary animosities through historical evaluations of Puritanism. Religious liberals, as Lawrence Buell has shown, sniped particularly at the superstitious figure of Cotton Mather in order to distance contemporary New Englanders further from a "bigotted" past, while conservatives set up the Founders as a model of piety against which to measure the present generation's shameful backsliding.[69] But the political anxieties characterizing this era permeated sectarian borders. Amid all the crossfire of theological and cultural animosity – Jedidiah Morse's and James Freeman's sparring over Morse's *American Geography* (1789), the battle over Cotton Mather's reputation by Charles Wentworth Upham, William Poole, and others, as well as the ongoing competition between the orthodox *Panoplist* and the liberal *Monthly Anthology* – amid all of this squabbling, Orthodox and Unitarian elites often found themselves speaking the same political language of rational liberty and social control.[70]

What Puritanism offered was a historical reservoir of a language that could be marshaled effectively by transforming chronology into trope. This language derived in part from Winthrop himself; it shaped much of his modern reputation. For both Orthodox and liberals, Winthrop's status resulted, oddly enough, from a rather difficult episode where he was reproached by the General Court in 1645 for exceeding the bounds of his authority as lieutenant governor (Winthrop had squelched a dispute in Hingham, where a certain group of citizens had opposed the election of militia officers). The famous speech he gave to the General Court in response to its proceedings distinguished between "liberty of corrupt nature" and a "civil, moral, federal liberty." Rather than jettison such a potent, albeit Calvinist, rationale for a well-ordered society, religious liberals merely subjected it to ideological surgery, pruning conservative republicanism of the supposed necessity for religious uniformity. In the process, liberals showed their own class-driven fears of democracy, anxieties that politically allied them with their Calvinist adversaries. Belknap, for example, who became increasingly sympathetic to religious liberals' objection to the central doctrine of innate depravity, reveals this kind of maneuver in his commentary on Winthrop's speech: "However true [Winthrop's] principle may be in point of morality, yet in matters of opinion, in modes of faith, worship, and ecclesiastical order, the question is, who shall be the judge of right and wrong?"[71] This distinction aimed to preserve

Puritanism as a political model only so far as "the peace of the Commonwealth" did not become confused with "liberty of conscience."[72] But such a distinction also could lead to historiographic contradictions. When did religious liberty endanger social and political stability? And so in *American Biography* Belknap finds himself awkwardly memorializing communitarian order and debunking religious bigotry, praising the Puritan banishment of Anne Hutchinson and assailing the Puritan persecution of Quakers. His distinction, then, which was aimed at his zealously orthodox contemporaries, actually unconsciously reveals his own narrative predicament.

Religious liberals' particular interpretation of Winthropian "liberty" was due in large part to the Orthodox insistence on equating religious uniformity with a virtuous republic. Staunchly Orthodox divines like David Tappan, for example, manipulated both biblical typology and affectional ideology to argue that, like Moses and Aaron, only a "harmonious compound" of church and state in contemporary New England could prevent "the scoffs and the sophistry of libertinism": "The divine appointment, then, and concurrent agency of the civil and ecclesiastical ruler, in leading the ancient people of GOD, naturally invite our attention to the importance and utility of political and religious guides in a christian state, and to that union of affection and of exertion for the common good, which ought to characterize and cement them."[73] As Tappan repeatedly returns to this idea, his religious polemics based on the biblical model increasingly become an issue of contemporary society and politics; he is, in effect, considering the terms of a virtuous republic, just at the moment the French Revolution was heading toward the excess of Jacobinism. The Orthodox difference with liberals devolved upon an issue that at first looks like mere semantics. Was the Puritan commonwealth a "republic"? Or was it a "theocracy" modeled on the Old Testament patriarchs? As we have seen, Abiel Holmes could call it a republic, but Belknap dubbed it a "theocracy" to distinguish colonial from contemporary times. Other liberals did so as well.[74] Hannah Adams occasionally slipped and called colonial Massachusetts a "republic," but she generally extricated the two by claiming that its government was founded "on the plan of the Jewish theocracy" where "the clergy acquired . . . a vast ascendency over rulers and people."[75] In this light, the historian Mercy Otis Warren, whose resistance to Calvinism fell short of embracing Unitarianism, hedges somewhat about the nature of the Bay colony, calling its government "a mixture of Jewish theocracy, monarchic government, and the growing principles of republicanism."[76]

The political semantics of sectarian politics, however, obscures those crucial political assumptions shared by liberals and Orthodox elites. Perhaps no more hostile front to New England's sectarian warfare during this era existed than the literary and legal battles between Hannah Adams and the Orthodox diehard who bemoaned the loss of Harvard to religious liberalism, the inimitable Jedidiah Morse.[77] However much this protégé of the *Monthly Anthology*'s Unitarian literati and her Orthodox nemesis became embattled with one another over Puritanism (and plagiarism), they interpreted social and political disorder in much the same way. There are, of course, important differences between their two histories. For instance, Morse doggedly defended the Fathers from the crime of persecution by casting their Quaker critics as "enemies to government" and "raving fanatics."[78] More poignantly than Morse, Adams located the paradoxes of Puritanism, highlighting (as did others) both the Puritans' "ardent love of liberty, an unshaken attachment to the rights of men"[79] as well as their reprehensible treatment of these very same Quakers and also of Roger Williams, the apostle of religious freedom in Rhode Island. By at least acknowledging the potential merits of the Puritan quest for liberty, Adams was placing colonial history into a nationalist, progressive schema that later would find its fullest articulation in the work of George Bancroft. Her implied optimism derives in part from Revolutionary historicism, for as Nathan Hatch has shown, the association of civil liberty with millennial promise for America had been a common theme of Revolutionary-era preachers. Adams certainly places Puritanism, albeit ambiguously, within such a historical eschatology.[80] But how could one locate Puritanism both within and without this paradigm of the historical progress of liberty? Perhaps unsurprisingly, she finds herself making the claim that Puritan New England was founded on the principle that " 'all men are born free, equal, and independent.' "[81] Yet she simultaneously invokes phrases such as "at present," "the ... present age," or "[t]o us, who live in an enlightened age" as a way of distending historical time for contemporary readers.[82] This ambivalence reveals the intersection of politics and theology, the perception that Puritanism's political virtues were compromised only by its narrowly sectarian view of who constituted the *res publica*.

What might be called the era's republicanization of Puritanism, however, collapses much of the ideological differences between liberal and Orthodox historiography. At certain crucial moments both groups could agree on the contemporary relevance of colonial history, moments where the parameters of "liberty" were subject to strict construction. Compare, for example, Morse's and Adams's respective assessments of the Hingham episode that, as we have seen, led Winthrop to offer his famous speech:

> Inextinguishable zeal for liberty was a prominent feature of their character. Not the mad democracy of modern growth, but a rational and safe enjoyment of civil and religious privileges, was the great object of their pursuit.[83]

> The affairs of New-England were at this period in so flourishing a situation, that the people were intoxicated with prosperity, and the liberty they enjoyed threatened their ruin.[84]

Here Puritanism is inflected more directly with class-driven interests than with those of theology. Morse's association of disorder with "modern growth" and Adams's with "modernity" both belie the importance of Puritanism in general and Winthropian liberty in particular to elite New Englanders who were witnessing the erosion of deferential politics, especially during the Jeffersonian era.

In this part of the *Compendious History*, Morse culls from John Adams's "Dissertation on the Canon and the Feudal Law" (1765), composed during the Stamp Act crisis. Adams places the Puritan fathers in context of the progress of enlightenment, putting the theory of *translatio studii* (the Western course of civilization and enlightened learning) to the service of Revolutionary politics. Ventriloquizing Adams, Morse is able to claim boldly that Puritan "policy" generally was consistent with the " 'principles of the best and greatest and wisest legislators of antiquity.' "[85] Michael Warner rightly notes how Adams "treat[s] enlightenment republicanism as the latent meaning of Puritan history,"[86] and yet he underestimates how "republicanism" itself during this entire era functioned as an utterly ambiguous sign subject to myriad interpretations. It could be used as a sort of dirty word, a fact underlying John Adams's admission, "It may be thought polite and fashionable by many modern fine gentleman, perhaps, to deride the characters [of the Puritan founders] as enthusiastical, superstitious and republican."[87] For conservatives like John Adams and Jedidiah Morse, Puritan history fastened regulatory control upon

a concept fraught with devilishly entropic and chaotic implications – in the hands of, say, Thomas Paine – of "rights" and
"liberty." In one sense, I suppose, the more liberal Hannah Adams
actually does invert Orthodox interpretations of Winthrop by
concluding that the General Court showed a "republican spirit"
in making *Winthrop* accountable for his actions. Yet this slightly
different negotiation of the meaning of colonial – and early
national – "liberty" was in itself premised on the historical metaphor of the commonwealth for the republic. Adams, no less than
Morse (or, for that matter, Cotton Mather in the *Magnalia*),
lauded Winthrop's "noble speech," which checked, she believed,
the recklessness of mobs.

The comparison between Morse and Adams measures the extent to which Thermidorean politics reshaped sectarian rivalries.
What I am calling the period's discourse of Puritan order inhabited the Unitarian pulpit as well. One should recognize that for
years, literary critics consistently have associated Unitarianism
with the intellectual development of romanticism because of the
influential work of both Perry Miller and F. O. Mathiessen.[88]
This, however, obscures the conservative politics of liberal theolo-
gians, the breadth of a cultural discourse meant to put history in
the service of a masculine, hierarchical politics. Liberal treatments of Puritanism, of course, depended on the contexts of
occasion and audience. William Emerson, for example, could
excoriate Jedidiah Morse's *Compendious History* in the highly partisan pages of the *Monthly Anthology and Boston Review*. Yet Emerson's subtle distinction between Morse's blemishes of "sect" and
the "much interesting matter" in his history suggested that Puritanism itself might have nuggets of redeeming material.[89] This
was certainly apparent only a few years earlier, in 1802, when
Emerson gave a Fourth of July oration in Boston's sweltering
summer heat. He informed his audience that its ancestors, "from
whom you boast your descent . . . entertained no romantick notions. They neither sought nor wished the freedom of an irrational, but that of a rational being."[90] Puritanism in this case metaphorically models a conservative fantasy of "American manners":

The planters of this western world, especially of New-
England, were eminent for the purity and lustre of their
morals. They were industrious from choice, necessity and
habit. Their mode of living rendered them abstinent from
enervating pleasures, and patient of toil. The difficulties of
subduing a rough wilderness . . . and the rigour of paternal

discipline, were almost alone sufficient to preserve in their offspring this simplicity of life.[91]

Colonial New England was indeed a seminal age, in both its ideological power to re-create republican simplicity in its "offspring" and in the exclusively masculine character of such a generative act. Likening the decline of the republic to the barbarian invasions of Greece and Rome (both of which were culpable of "luxury and vice"), Emerson claims that the "besom of innovation" in New England similarly threatens "the customs of our forefathers."[92] Only a masculine republicanism equated with patriarchal order ("the rigour of paternal discipline") can forestall "[l]ibertinism and lethargy, anarchy and misrule"[93] – in other words, the inevitable decay of cyclical history.

Such an invocation of Puritanism as a masculine ideal was particularly ironic for Unitarians, given their affinities with more modern – and feminized – forms of affective, benevolent virtue. Faith is "as intimately and inseparably connected with the social virtues, and with domestick and personal duties," Harvard's first liberal Hollis Professor of Divinity, Henry Ware, Sr., declared, "as with those of piety to God."[94] In 1821, Ware gave an election day sermon that tried to redefine republican patriotism in terms of a more modern, humanist understanding of virtue. Taking his text from Acts 17:26 ("And hath made of one blood all nations of men, for to dwell on all the face of the earth"), Ware's initial project would seem to have been to promote a kind of Christian humanism transcending national boundaries in the name of a universalized ethos of community. Indeed, midway through the address Ware distinguishes between a "Christian" patriotism based on "universal benevolence" and its false imitator: "The patriot of this school loves his country; but it is only because it embraces all his own interests ... its prosperity is his own prosperity."[95]

Ware's inability to maintain this distinction, however, registers the enduring resonance of an anachronistic, masculine republicanism that narrowly defined the purview of civic attention. In light of the feminization of virtue during this era (the subject of the next two chapters), the use to which Ware puts Puritanism in this sermon begins to illuminate crucial differences between men's and women's historical writing about colonial New England. This involves very different treatments of affectional norms. Just as the value Emerson places on "civilized and social man" and "the elegancies and joys of polished life"[96] ultimately gives way to the Roman *virtu* of 1776, so too is Ware's affective humanism displaced by an older ideology of republicanism. As his discourse progresses, Ware significantly abandons his original thesis of the primacy of Christian love as a model for the contemporary United States. The Christian patriot tenuously combines "a more pure and elevated and disinterested character . . . [with] *an ardent zeal for his country's good.*"[97] This tension becomes even more pronounced as the sermon's real agenda emerges. Apparently apprehensive about a society in which it is "the competition of each class of citizens to gain some advantage over other classes, and of each individual over other individuals of the same class,"[98] Ware turns to ancestral origins as a model for the new republic. To defuse present social dangers he recasts Puritan history in the image – and language – of Whig republicanism where one could find the "habits of industry, frugality, sobriety, and temperance" meant to secure "rational liberty and good government."[99] Such values originate in the Founders:

> It is to be found in the principles and habits of the people; in the religious and moral character of the inhabitants of this state; in a state of society, derived originally from our ancestors; brought with them when they came to this country; preserved and improved by the institutions which they established . . . for religious instruction, for general education, and for the general diffusion of knowledge and virtue.[100]

For Ware the republic is just as much an ethical as an institutional phenomenon, the "state" of Massachusetts correlated to the abstract "state" of republicanism. Like his 1826 funeral sermon for John Adams, where he praised Adams's "patriotic and disinterested spirit" as well as his "benevolence,"[101] the election day sermon oscillates between the gendered meanings of republican virtue. Given Ware's tendency in other settings to equate a modern republic with Christian virtue,[102] his sermon's inconsistencies suggest in effect the ghost of John Winthrop – the need, that is, to refurbish the republic in strictly communitarian, masculine terms.

That the very status of the "Puritans" in these texts is problematic suggests the metaphoric quality of historical language during this era. Those historical affinities between commonwealth and republic made colonial New England an apt metaphor for a masculine political fantasy. There is a moment in Abiel Holmes's Forefathers Day oration of 1806 where the linguistic ramifications of didactic historiography become fully apparent:

> Why should I detain you, either to prove or to illustrate the disinterested philanthropy and paternal condescension of CARVER; the profound wisdom and exemplary moderation of BRADFORD; the unaffected modesty and patriarchal simplicity of BREWSTER; . . . the preeminent abilities and inflexible integrity of WINSLOW; the daring intrepidity and heroic achievements of STANDISH? These illustrious names, and the merits attached to them, are entirely familiar to you. . . . To a tablet, however, less perishable, than either [historical tradition or records] are those names committed; and it ought to heighten the pleasure of the day to reflect, that a biographer, worthy of them, has at length been found.[103]

The biographer to whom Holmes refers is of course "BELKNAP," a name whose capitalization suggests both his equivalent exemplariness to colonial forebears and the metaphoric nature of historical writing itself. As Holmes portrays it, this is an issue of naming. Presumably, the "merits attached" to these names are unnecessary because Holmes's audience is "entirely familiar" with them anyway. The implication here is crucial, for it means that the language of Puritan history – in this case, the name of each Puritan Father – actually signifies more than it strictly denotes. The names of the Fathers signify as tropes, indicating in each instance clusters of republican virtues for orator and audience alike, Holmes suggests, whether he takes the trouble to recount them or not. In this complex iconography the very act of naming enacts a republican code of civic ethics.

Like the Constitution itself, then, the discourse of Puritan order aimed to preserve the fundamental republican principles of liberty and property. Perhaps less ambiguously than the Constitution, however, these tenets were formulated in wholly conservative ways. Praise for the Fathers' refusal to exchange agrarian simplicity for what Holmes calls "the lucrative pursuits of commerce"[104] was premised on a notion of property as *only* the means to preserving personal independence. No less anachronistic was the "liberty" that Puritanism exemplified for early national Americans. In its own way, the discourse of Puritan order aimed to codify the distinction between "natural" and "civil" liberty, which Webster made in the 1828 *Dictionary*. The latter, as Webster explained it, was "expedient for the safety and interest of the society, state or nation."[105]

The remainder of this chapter, as well as the succeeding ones reevaluating historical belles lettres, explores the highly manipulable nature of republican language. Its unique elasticity is apparent in the comparison of operative key words within this discourse of Puritanism – words like "industry," "frugality," "vigor," "manliness" – with their meanings later on in the nineteenth century. In the first number of *The United States Magazine and Democratic Review,* for example, the editor John L. O'Sullivan pays lip service to traditional republican fears ("those corruptions and those hostile influences, by which we see its beneficent and glorious tendencies . . . perverted and paralysed [sic]"); but he then goes on to champion the democratic spirit of the nation: "We believe, then, in the principle of *democratic republicanism,* in its strongest and purest sense. We have an abiding confidence in the virtue, intelligence, and full capacity for self-government, of the great mass of our people, our industrious, honest, manly, intelligent millions of freemen."[106] As opposed to a post-Revolutionary elite, later democratic enthusiasts like O'Sullivan could deploy republican language without a hint of the jeremiad. History, in other words, was disengaged completely from cyclical time.

The Discourse of Puritan Enterprise

The premodern politics underlying this discourse of Puritanism, however, does not really tell the whole story. The early republic's representation of Puritanism registers as well an emergent liberalism in the early republic, the increasing fascination with modern market capitalism, which lends a poignant instability to republican language. Encoded within the key words of Puritan virtue were modern meanings that equated civic behavior with enterprising individualism. Words like Puritan "industry," "labour," and "zeal" encoded ideologies of capitalism, and inflated the Lockean intellectual inheritance of "natural" property rights into a full-fledged rationale for individual acquisitiveness. This phenomenon, then, demands close attention to the ideological texture of civic and political language. For what Bakhtin has claimed for novelistic discourse describes just as accurately historical discourse about Puritanism during this era: "Even in those places where the author's voice seems at first glance to be unitary and consistent, direct and unmediatedly intentional, beneath that smooth single-languaged surface we can nevertheless uncover prose's three-dimensionality, its profound speech diversity."[107]

Bakhtin's understanding of double-voicedness is in keeping, I think, with the highly elastic nature of early republican discourse, a phenomenon to which scholars have become increasingly sensitive.[108] In the most comprehensive analysis of linguistic and political representation in early America, Thomas Gustafson has argued that early national Americans became increasingly anxious over the fact that the language of the Constitution could be manipulated, construed, almost arbitrarily reshaped by anyone with virtually any kind of political predispositions. Noting that "the arbitrariness of the linguistic sign" was no original discovery of poststructuralism, Gustafson goes on to summarize the cultural anxieties of linguistic politics in the early republic: "After the ratification of the Constitution, and especially in the midst of the constitutional crises over nullification in the 1830s, and slavery in the 1850s, Americans confronted in their politics and explored in their literature the benefits and liabilities that arise from the freedom of words from a fixed sense."[109]

However true linguistic self-consciousness was in antebellum American culture, it should not obscure the ways in which early nationals often engaged the instabilities of language *unconsciously*. The "virtue" of the Puritan Fathers demonstrates exactly this. For in the didactic medium of historiography, the same set of republican signifiers managed to absorb new, liberal meanings. Yet the traditionally premodern meanings of this language, which derived from the cultural experience of the Revolution, actually defused its newer meanings' potentially negative connotations of luxury and corruption. As one historian of the early republic has noted, "The farther the classical ideal receded from the dynamic reality of the nineteenth-century American economy, the more Americans liked to think of themselves in its terms."[110] Early nationals used a language that was laden simultaneously with modern and premodern implications, suggesting both the reality of modern markets and the fantasy of the nation's pristine origins. By examining this language, as it was inscribed in the historical literature of Puritanism, and noting the ways in which it signified both classical and liberal meanings, we might see not only how intimate these ideologies actually were during this era, but also how language itself helped to mediate cultural change. One sees, in other words, not only how early nationals shaped republican language but also how it shaped them.

The potently ambiguous quality of American civic language

bears this out. As we have seen, history-writers consistently politicized Puritan spirituality to narratively make religious idealism in
colonial New England the sign of social and political order. The
"zeal" behind the great Puritan "enterprise" of migration signaled
New England's transcendence of the common greed propelling
so many other colonies such as Virginia. Yet the very meaning of
Puritan "enterprise" encoded the growing affinities of early national conservatives – many of whom were conservative National
Republicans and proto-Whigs who supported national economic
development – with the risk-taking and rugged individualism associated with venture capitalism. In *Lectures on American Literature*
(1829), for example, Samuel Knapp called Plymouth's first governor, John Carver, "a man of enterprise, intelligence, and great
benevolence, and quite a business man."[111] Likewise, to David
Ramsay, the great crime of Sir Edmund Andros's tyrannical treatment of Boston during the 1680s was that it temporarily stymied
economic activity: "[A]ll the motives to great actions, to industry,
economy, and enterprise, were, in a great degree, annihilated."[112]
The founding of Plymouth, as Abiel Holmes put it, was an "enterprise [in which the Pilgrims] aimed to erect themselves into a
republic . . . 'which the true spirit of liberty inspires.' "[113]
    What did "enterprise" and "liberty" mean in these instances?
One can hear their modern, liberal resonances during those
infrequent moments when these rather staid histories actually try
to liven up. One of the more exciting passages of both Holmes's
American Annals and Charles Goodrich's *History of the United States*
concerns the first Pilgrim movements into the frontier. Both historians laud the Plymouth "enterprise" in establishing a trading
post in Windsor in 1633, an anecdote that becomes in these
texts a lesson in that same American can-doism that salvaged
the reputation of Ollie North during the televised Congressional
hearings on the Iran–Contra affair. Goodrich gives this episode a
bit of flash when the commander of the Pilgrim ship "gallantly
disregarded the order" [to retreat in the face of Dutch cannon
fire];[114] in Abiel Holmes "the commander of the enterprise . . .
went resolutely forward."[115] In both cases the languages of martial valor and liberal enterprise synthetically form an inchoate
version of nineteenth-century American manhood premised on,
as Charles Sellers has put it, "a market world that takes the
competitive ego for human nature and rationality for revelation."[116]
    The modern norm of entrepreneurial risk resonating in Puri-
tan "enterprise" begins to reveal Puritanism's double-voicedness.

The historical word becomes the site of an ideological confrontation and exchange between liberal and classical ideologies. Historical writing, then, highlights the ambiguities of civic discourse with which conservative Americans delicately mediated cultural change. The capacity of republican language to accomplish this is apparent in Timothy Dwight's prolific *Travels in New-England and New-York* (1821–2), a massive, four-volume survey of the contemporary scene that unsurprisingly reaches back into the past to define a moral geography of the present. In Letter XIII, Dwight devotes an entire letter to Puritan "industry" and "enterprise." Here the narrative tellingly oscillates between "the [Puritans'] inseparable connection between liberty and good order" and the "spirit of commerce" that was sown into New England character, he claims, from the voyage of the Mayflower.[117] This kind of cultural dialogic informs as well Belknap's ambivalence about the essential nature of the Puritan migration. New England, he says in the *History of New Hampshire* (1784–92), presented the first settlers with "a country full of woods, to subdue which required immense labour and patience," and yet it also promised "the full liberty to pursue their own inquiries, and worship God according to their consciences."[118] Similarly, Morse showed contemporary backsliders that the "enterprising" Fathers "possessed a firmness of spirit and a zeal for religion bordering on enthusiasm"; but such virtue paradoxically fulfills the secular destiny "to plant and subdue a wilderness ... to lay the foundation of a great empire."[119]

The entanglement of these discourses produces an abundance of rhetorical irony. In *The History of New Hampshire*, for example, Belknap refers to the "business on which [the first generation] had come into this wilderness."[120] Note how in Morse's hand piety unconsciously is subjected to modern canons of individual initiative: "Religion was always the first object in all their calculations and arrangements."[121] In these instances, linguistic meaning "refracts," as Bakhtin conceives of it, to show the unintended presence of dual voices, which, I think, reveals much less the clichéd passage "from Puritan to Yankee" and more the cultural tensions inhabiting a conservative elite faced with the rise of modern capitalism. Moreover, the infrequent attempt by some early nationals to sort out these discourses only further confirms their rhetorical and ideological intimacy. In the abridged version of the *Summary History*, Hannah Adams attempted to do just that for her younger readers. She called attention to the real meaning of the word "industry," stating, "To industry we owe the comforts of civilized life. By industry the wilderness of the new world was converted into a fruitful field." She immediately recoils, however, from its liberal implications by instructing young boys and girls that "[w]e ought however to be excited to industry from nobler motives, than merely to gain fortune and reputation in this world."[122]

The elasticity of republican language thus marks the limits of authorial intention and produces highly nuanced meanings of "republicanism." This linguistic situation reflects the larger cultural situation of Federalist/Whig New England. The discourses of Puritan order and enterprise rub up against one another, each component symbiotically changing the other in their rhetorical engagement, and ultimately serving to erase stable boundaries of meaning. Linguistic instability in turn helped actually to palliate a cultural transformation that might otherwise have been more painful, since emergent ideologies of the market safely resided within the trope of Puritan "virtue," a signifier whose real power lay in disinfecting modernity with associations (in the Scottish sense) deriving from the mythologized purity of the American Revolution. This is the highly dense, even duplicitous, language of nineteenth-century capitalism. It is a language that would be subjected to merciless exposure over the next century by diverse American writers who would make it the cornerstone of cultural critique: Thoreau's merciless debunking of it in the "Economy" section of *Walden*, Twain and Warner in *The Gilded Age*, Sinclair Lewis's parodies in *Babbitt*. As we shall see in later chapters, writers such as Catharine Sedgwick, Lydia Child, and Cooper engaged – and reconstructed – this civic discourse via their fictions about Puritanism.

Not only rhetoric but also characterization itself in these histories succumbed to the pressure of liberalism. Perhaps the leading candidate among colonial New Englanders as the prodigious man of enterprise was Sir William Phips, the Mathers' hand-picked governor after the loss of the charter between 1684 and 1691 (and later villain of the Salem witchcraft trials). Mitchell Breitwieser brilliantly has shown how Phips offered a biographical subject in *Magnalia Christi Americana* upon which Mather projected his own conflicted impulses for godliness and worldliness.[123] I would add that this phenomenon has its parallel in early republican culture. In Charles Goodrich's *History*, for example, Phips oscillates between the selfless republican and entrepreneurial genius, a figure who in many ways recollects Belknap's John Smith or Christopher Columbus. Phips exhibits "the powerful spirit of personal enterprise which the peculiar circumstances of the colonies called forth."[124] Following much of *Magnalia* – Phips's exploits at sea, the recovery of sunken treasure, his ability to outmaneuver mutinous seamen – Goodrich recycles a man whose "enterprising genius" is nonetheless carefully reconstructed in terms of the public good. Like a vigilant republican, Phips declines an offer to be an officer in the British navy because "he had too great an attachment for his native country to think of a permanent residence other than that of New England."[125] His "generosity and patriotism, integrity, and piety" circumscribe the potentially reckless energies of the American success story, the poor boy from the backwaters of the Kennebec River country in Maine, who later rises to become governor of Massachusetts Bay. Indeed, Goodrich is thoroughly self-conscious about the requirements of an exemplary life:

> The life of a man is always replete with instruction. It reveals to those in the humble walks of life, the means by which they may not only arrive at distinction, but to that which is of far higher importance – an extended sphere of usefulness in church and state. Enterprise, exertion, integrity, will accomplish everything.[126]

Phips's life, then, via the *Magnalia* (which Goodrich footnotes), would seem to confirm for early nationals the openness of American society, the exceptional fluidity in which one thrives or falters according to willful initiative and personal greatness. At the same time, however, it attenuates this ethos of "distinction" through the lingering imperative of civic good. Goodrich, in other words, recycles Phips to master the potentially frightening logic of American liberalism signified by Phips's "enterprise." He both loves and fears him.

Puritan representativeness, then, rhetorically assimilates the colonial *ricorso* as the site of civic personality and the reality of modern America where that personality is now expressed through the calculating powers of the atomized individual. Most significantly, this dialogic poses dual understandings of historical time. Puritan "industry" simultaneously was premised on cyclical time and on a liberal, post-Enlightenment faith in progressive history and national prosperity. As the cultural value of aristocratic leisure increasingly gave way to bourgeois mores, the virtue of work came to accompany a radically modern conception of the republic which, as one should suspect by now, prefigures the later, antebellum ideology of Manifest Destiny. Consider in this context the opening of Morse's *Compendious History* and a telling moment in Dwight's *Travels:*

> If any country has merited the notice of history, New England has her strong claims. . . . [F]rom the bosom of uncounted tribes of savages, from feebleness, poverty and contempt, she has risen in might, and numbers, and resources, till she may bid defiance to invasion from any power by land or sea. Her virtues, her industry, her frugality, her piety, her valor, in the hands of God, have been the means of this unexampled prosperity. Her soil is not the most fertile, her climate is forbidding, yet her wealth is greater, and her population more numerous, than any other portion of the United States.[127]

> Were you an American; and had you with me traversed the several settlements made by the people of New-England in its immense forests; had you traced the hardships and discouragements, with which these settlements were made; had you seen the wilderness converted by them into fruitful fields; had you surveyed the numerous, cheerful, and beautiful towns and villages, which, under their forming hand have sprung up in a desert; you would regard this mighty work as an unanswerable and delightful proof of both the Enterprise and Industry of this extraordinary people.[128]

In both cases the contours of republican masculinity are etched from a historical model. But the change in historical eschatology here is telling. Those crucial code words, made famous by the American Revolution, now have been resituated in the context of prosperity (the "wilderness converted," of "might" and "unexampled prosperity") and the progressive concept of history underlying it. All of this, of course, is cloaked safely under the aegis of providence. Old words, laden with new meanings, describe a new sense of time that, at least momentarily, has sloughed off fears of inevitable corruption.

But not for very long. The competing notions of historical process that shape early national narrative about Puritanism were unstable enough to allow for almost schizophrenic visions of progress and decline. Perhaps the major factors contributing to this doubleness of vision were the period's changing ideologies of "luxury." From the very moment that David Dagget and Jedidiah Morse debated at Yale the need for sumptuary laws in the new republic – a debate really over the danger of luxury – early national Americans ambivalently viewed the effects of luxury on society's moral fitness.[129] As Peter Onuf and Cathy Matson have argued, traditional republican fears of luxury, as both the symptom and the agent of selfish indolence and political corruption, was accompanied by a more modern view of commercial goods as an important civilizing agent; this view, of course, was in keeping with modern understandings of sociability, gentility and refinement as the new standards of republican life.[130] New forms of consumption and ideology, as Charles Sellers has shown, permeated America's middling classes during the early antebellum period.[131] Perhaps inevitably, then, historical discourse about Puritanism uneasily negotiated these ideologies. When Charles Goodrich, for example, summarized colonial history for his readers, he simply gushed over the "smiling fields and cheerful villages" of a successfully domesticated wilderness, but his subsequent commentary reveals the tortuous attempt to separate American bourgeois capitalism from European, aristocratic luxury: "We have indeed seen the hardy spirit of enterprise [in] leaving the luxuries of Europe, and plunging into the forests of America."[132] The year that Samuel Knapp published *Lectures on American Literature* he also gave the annual oration of the New England Society of New York. Here Knapp imaginatively, if only momentarily, freezes time – both in colonial New England and, one might even say, in 1829 – by locating a moment where commerce was not accompanied by luxury.

> For the first century their growth was slow, but solid and hardy. . . . The whole community were like that class in other countries in which it has been said, that nearly all virtue and intelligence centres [sic]; in the class which has not reached opulence and is yet above want. – Our forefathers put in no claims for ancestral honors or splendid alliances, but they were justly proud of pure, honest blood; there were no left-hand marriages among them, and none of the poison of licentiousness, or the taint of crime.[133]

As in Belknap's portrait of an exemplary John Winthrop, Knapp renegotiates the terms of political authority by reconfiguring the meaning of "blood" from an ancestral name to a civic ethos flourishing in an imagined Puritan land poised exceptionally between primitivism and "opulence." If this historical schema is reminiscent of Thomas Cole's famous series "The Course of Empire" (1836), the theory of luxury underpinning it is compromised in almost the very next breath, when Knapp praises a

burgeoning network of intercolonial commerce: "[T]he intercourse they had encouraged with each other had been mostly
commercial, and commerce brings with it the best courtesies of
life."[134] Luxury, in other words, can just as readily signify the
virtue of civilized refinement as it can the dreaded plunge into
corruption.

These ethical uncertainties at once derive from and fully express the ambivalence to historical process underlying virtually all
of the period's histories of Puritanism. As this chapter draws to a
close, I think it important to note that this cultural ambivalence
has important consequences for contemporary intellectual historians. From George Bancroft's *History of the United States,* to the
contemporary work of Bercovitch and others, Puritanism has
been situated consistently in context of a progressive/millennial
model of historical process. Scholars have tended to overlook the
fact that, in the aftermath of the Revolution, *both* republican and
progressive conceptions of time coexisted.[135] For quite some time
after the Revolution, the more sober vision of Whig history accompanied (and problematized) the post-Enlightenment liberal
faith in progress and national exceptionalism that eventually
gained ascendency in nineteenth-century American culture. One
sees this historical dialogic everywhere in the discourse of the
post-Revolutionary period. In an oration celebrating the end of
the war of 1812, for example, John Lathrop, minister of Boston's
Second Church, claimed that America represented "a new state
of things in this quarter of the world, – a new empire, which, in
process of time will probably be equal in extent, in power, and in
wealth, to any nation in the world."[136] He soon warns, however,
that "In an uncorrupted state of society, men will not be seen
making interest for places of honor and profit. . . . God grant that
we may live to see a return of something like that golden age of
purity and simplicity, which our country once enjoyed!"[137]

These dual imperatives of republican and liberal historicism
create erratic rhythms at the end of Mercy Warren's famous *History of the Rise, Progress and Termination of the American Revolution*
(1805). At one crucial moment Warren calls upon Americans to
embrace the "sobriety, economy, industry, and perseverance in
every virtue"[138] to ensure national destiny. As she models virtue
on the same Puritan *ricorso* suggested by Lathrop, however, her
nationalist fervor tellingly begins to wane:

But if the education of youth, both public and private, is
attended to, their industrious and economical habits main-

tained, their moral character and assemblage of virtues supported . . . there is not much danger that they will for a long
time be subjugated by the arms of foreigners, or that their
republican system will be subverted by the arts of domestic
enemies. Yet, probably some distant day will exhibit the
extensive continent of America, a portrait analogous to the
other quarters of the globe, which have been laid waste by
ambition. . . . But this will not be done, until ignorance,
servility and vice, have led them to renounce their ideas of
freedom, and reduced them to that grade of baseness which
renders them unfit for the enjoyment of that *rational liberty*
which is the natural inheritance of man.[139]

The obvious oscillations of this passage testify to a confusion
about the nation's historical trajectory. Warren may have quib-
bled with John Adams over the relative merits and dangers of the
federal Constitution, but she, no less than Adams, internalized
the residual fears of Whig history that posited the inevitable decay
of all republics. The hope that public education (a trait for
which the Puritans were everywhere praised) will secure America
explodes suddenly with the phrase "Yet, probably." By rehearsing
these republican fears, however, Warren is able to pronounce
euphorically the promise of America. Drawing upon Christian
parable, she figures America "as a fair and fertile vineyard, which
requires only the industrious care of the laborers to render it for
a long time productive . . . in the full harvest of prosperity and
freedom."[140] This translation of time involves a translation of
metaphor as well, for the biblical vineyard now becomes a cultivated field made productive by the virtue of Puritan industry,
which itself has become transformed to signify the liberal energies that turn "western wilds" into "that stage of improvement and
perfection."[141] God becomes the "Divine Economist" who brings
forth the American New Jerusalem in "this last civilized quarter
of the globe" through the most prolific translation of all: the
rewriting of the Book of Revelations into a liberal tract on American political economy.

　　Warren's conversion of cyclical time into millennial time obviously pursues the formal logic of the Puritan jeremiad. As one
historian has put it, "Reformation prophecy allowed the millen-
nium to be seen as a progressive historical period into which the
reformed world was about to enter, and the Puritan errand had
moved the scene of that hope to the New World. When independence was won, fervent Protestants identified the American re-

public with the advent of the millennial period, which was to usher in the final salvation of mankind and the end of history."[142] The syncretic brand of biblical prophecy and liberal ideology ringing out at the end of Warren's history is indicative of the design of a good deal of early national histories.[143] Their affirmation of American destiny marks the continued currency of a Puritan jeremiad whose simultaneous imperatives of a return to origins and of an exceptionalist promise "naturally" fit the early republic's synchronicity of cyclical and progressive time. Yet the legacy of the Puritan jeremiad actually obscures the metaphoric significance of Puritanism during this era. If the jeremiad provided a seductive *form* for conservatives with which to both chastise and affirm a "chosen" people, the *substance* of metaphorical Puritanism derived just as much from a republican as a millennial/progressive model of historical time. In large part, Puritanism exemplified an outmoded conception of masculine virtue to combat enduring fears of cyclical history. The difference between form and substance describes, as I suggested earlier in this chapter, the difference between Winthrop the American Nehemiah, and Winthrop the American Cincinnatus. The latter disinfects the dangers of prosperity lurking within millennial euphoria. Yet this new Puritan-Republican man was ultimately a modernized one more suited to a liberal republic, his virtuous work ensuring much more than his "independence," his freehold of property spilling across the Appalachian divide and into the Ohio valley, his republican cant of "liberty" and "property" speaking two convoluted languages at once.

The New Ebenezer

Images of monuments fill Cotton Mather's *Magnalia Christi Americana*. Their metaphoric potential for textually memorializing New England's founders is simply immense. Nowhere is this more salient than in Mather's allusion to the Ebenezer, the "stone of help" (1 Samuel 7:12), which Samuel erected between Mizpeh and Shen to remind the Israelites of God's role in their victory over the Philistines.[144] Like the Ebenezer, *Magnalia* is intended to regulate behavior through the agency of memory, to remind a contemporary – and backsliding – generation of the stamp of grace upon the souls of the Fathers.[145] No less than Mather himself, early national history-writers memorialized the New England Fathers to shore up the civic bonds of community, erecting their own versions of the Ebenezer, a monument constituted in language whose facade was shaped and reshaped by the various self-appointed stewards of the early American republic. If sectarian differences created distinctive faces for this monument, its foundation was nonetheless built upon a corporate vision of hierarchical politics that necessitated a "rational" liberty ensuring social order. But this foundation was itself constructed upon the precarious ground of early republican ideology and language. This double-voicedness of Puritan "virtue" was ultimately empowering. As a traditional lexicon absorbed modern meanings, its older connotations provided a means – if only rhetorical – by which conservatives could find expression for a growing fascination with the market while still avoiding naked avowals of materialism and self-interest. As in *Magnalia,* history-writing at once unleashed and contained emergent ideologies of modernity.

So what does all of this have to do with historical fiction? It is my argument in the following chapters that historical romances, as well as sketches, tales, short stories, poems, and plays about Puritanism, all were similarly engaged with *contemporary* history. As I discussed in the Introduction, the social, cultural, and literary conditions shaping the production of both historiography and historical belles lettres made them intimately connected, sometimes even collapsing generic distinctions altogether. It is important to keep in mind that historical romance emerged during the 1820s at a time when historiography had already established itself. *Both* genres self-consciously aimed to fulfill the didactic project of teaching good citizenship. In light of their similarly didactic ends and cultural positions, it is no surprise that historical fiction engaged in dialogue with other forms of historical discourse over the contemporary terms of "republicanism." Highly elusive as it may be, this term significantly allows one to go about reconceptualizing the operative categories and resonant languages with which historical novelists took up the issues of liberty, property, virtue, and authority.

For women's historical writing, these political issues were inflected particularly with ideologies of gender. From the Revolution on, as many have noted, the feminization of virtue increasingly associated it with qualities of benevolence, affection, and sentiment.[146] This even affected notions of republican manhood. The polished manners and benevolent heart for which David Ramsay is praised in the *Analectic Magazine*'s biographical sketch begins to show this. On the other hand, the very premises of the classical tradition were at best exclusive and at worst downright misogynistic. Those, like the progressive-minded author of "The

Legal Condition of Women" (1828), who argued for changes in
coverture laws (but *not* voting qualifications) noted the inherent
limitations that classical ideology placed upon a modern, enlightened republic:

> Roman austerity was too near akin to unsocial rudeness, at
> least in the days of the republic, Roman courage too fond of
> camps, conquest, and free quarters, Roman ambition of too
> exclusive and selfish a character, to admit woman to the
> elevation by the side of man, which is the surest evidence of
> genuine public refinement.[147]

As the next two chapters demonstrate, these gendered changes
in republican virtue actually enabled women writers to address
politically significant issues in their works. What was the status of
masculine patriotism vis-à-vis Christian humanism? What kind of
virtue were republican wives and mothers supposed to inculcate
in male citizens? How tenable was an exclusively masculine form
of republican *virtu* in a self-consciously modern world of benevolent sociability?

This last question is crucial for understanding the gender politics of women's historical fiction. One should recognize that in
nationalist histories the subject of Puritanism helped to codify an
exclusively masculine understanding of republican citizenship.
This is the "patriarchal" context for women's historical writing
about New England. Metaphorical Puritanism implied the legitimacy of contemporary patriarchal authority under the guise of
"virtue," "wisdom" and "the public good," epithets that retained
rhetorical and cultural currency in the aftermath of the Revolution. Women writers such as Catharine Sedgwick and Lydia Child
contested the contemporary terms of republican virtue within the
medium of history, exploiting a central paradox in nationalist
histories that at once acknowledged the primitiveness of colonial
times and still invoked the Fathers as a contemporary model of
republican self-denial, sacrifice, and simplicity.

Nowhere were the exclusively masculine contexts for republican behavior more saliently drawn than in early national narratives of the Pequot War of 1637, a subject explored in the following chapter. Here the ideal of Roman *virtu* pervaded early
national historical writing, and celebrated the "vigorous" and
"manly" American yeoman who, like that of 1775, had temporarily left the plow to save the republic. "Our Fathers have been
ridiculed as an uncouth and uncourtly generation," Lyman Beecher noted. "And it must be admitted, that they were not as

expert in the graces of dress, and the etiquette of the drawing room, as some of their descendents. . . . [But] had none stepped upon the Plymouth rock but such effeminate critics as these, the poor natives never would have mourned their wilderness lost . . . the Pequots would have slept in safety that night which was their last."[148] The year before Beecher gave his Forefathers Day oration at Plymouth, the Massachusetts Historical Society republished the most famous firsthand Puritan account of the war, by Captain John Mason. The year of Beecher's oration Catharine Sedgwick offered her revisionary history of the war in *Hope Leslie*. In doing so, she revised not only those Puritan histories that were being reprinted abundantly in her day but also contemporary histories appropriating the event as an instance of republican manhood. The subject of the Pequot War, in other words, begins to demonstrate the contemporary historicity of historical romance, the gendered negotiations of those values upon which the new Ebenezer was built.

CATHARINE SEDGWICK'S "RECITAL" OF THE PEQUOT WAR

I hope my dear Mrs. Embry [sic] you will go on to enrich your native country and to elevate the just pride of your country women.
  – Catharine Sedgwick to Emma Embury, January 29, 1829[1]

It has been the fate of all the tribes to be like the Carthaginians, in having their history written by their enemies. Could they now come up from their graves, and tell the tale of their own wrongs, reveal their motives, and describe their actions, Indian history would put on a different garb from the one it now wears, and the voice of justice would cry much louder in their behalf than it has yet done.
  – "Materials for American History," *North American Review*
  (1826)

Shortly before Catharine Sedgwick published her third novel, *Hope Leslie*, in 1827, she wrote a letter home to her brother, Charles, recounting a recent trip to Boston that she had made by stagecoach. Along the way, as Sedgwick described it, she encountered an aged veteran of the Revolutionary War who somehow charmed her. To Sedgwick the incident was worthy of detail:

One old soldier I shall never forget. He was not like most of our old pensioners, a subject of pity on account of (perhaps) accidental virtue, but everything about him looked like the old age of humble frugal industrious virtue. And then he was so patient under the severest of all physical evils . . . so cheerful and bright, so confiding in kindness, and so trustful in his fellow-creatures. . . . [He wore] famous green mit-

61

tens, knit as he said, with a tear in his eye, "by his youngest *darter*," leaning on his cane, the horrid cancer decently dressed and sheltered, talking with a benign expression of his old friends, but his eye kindling, and his form straightening with a momentary vigor as he spoke of the heroic deeds of his youthful companions, and the serenity and meekness, and philosophy with which he spoke of the sufferings and the progress of them.[2]

On its surface, Sedgwick's encounter seems to be nothing more than a sentimental account of an endearing old man. Yet her narrative of the incident, I would argue, suggests her relation – specifically through *writing* – to a living, cultural symbol of Revolutionary republicanism. What kind of "man" is this? Or better yet: What kind of manhood does Sedgwick manage to re-create here? By claiming both his unique and ordinary qualities, Sedgwick locates this "old soldier" both within and without the fold of a identifiable type. This immediately raises the issue of his representativeness. As a masculine legacy of the Revolution, he is transformed, albeit subtly, by Sedgwick's pen into an androgynous ideal. The passage's rhetoric welds together his meekness and vigor, his tears and heroic deeds, figuring a new symbol of republican manhood whose classical virtues are subsumed by his capacity for feeling. His daughter's mittens – a domestic production, after all – literally and symbolically cover his hands. So the scene translates power from male subject to female writer, from classical vigor to sentimental pathos, and devilishly suggests that the very icon of Revolutionary manhood is itself diseased, and perhaps on its last leg. This is the theme of *Hope Leslie*'s "recital" of the Pequot War.

The successful revision of this icon depends on the negotiation of the masculine language and ideology we examined in the preceding chapter. As I began to show, republican language of "virtue" was layered densely with gendered meanings during the transitional era of the early republic. "Virtue" signified not only the tenets of classical republicanism and liberal individualism but also the precepts of affect, benevolence, and pious, universal love that descended in large part from eighteenth-century Scottish Common Sense philosophy. As the word began to signify new, modern republican adhesives of sociability and Christian benevolence, these traits became increasingly associated in early national America with women themselves and evolved into an ideology of domesticity during the antebellum era. The crucial point here is that during this era the gendered meanings of republican virtue could lend instability to the nature of "masculine" and "feminine" behavior. And as Sedgwick's letter to her brother shows, such instability afforded the chance to refashion the terms of civic ethics in a republic. By manipulating language, one could redefine along the lines of gender the very meaning of a "republic."

In the next two chapters I take up the issue of gender politics in women's historical romance by situating two of the era's most popular historical romances, *Hope Leslie* and Lydia Child's *Hobomok* (1824), in this cultural and historical context. As I argued at the outset of this study, literary critics of all sorts have placed women's historical romance of the 1820s in context of the American Renaissance. In this schema, these texts are either failures that mark Hawthorne's later success or credible novels that should be considered part of the nation's literary flowering. In each case, the critical trajectory points forward, ignoring the specifically *post-Revolutionary* nature of the language and thematics of women's writing. Moreover, women's historical romance emerged during the 1820s in the context of an established, masculinized genre of nationalist history. Historians like Hannah Adams and Emma Willard were extraordinary women even to cultivate literary careers for themselves at this time. Yet there was little room for "revisionist" historiography at this time. Why, then, we should ask, did women writers even take up the subject of Puritanism? How do their historical productions about Puritanism compare to those of male "historians"? How did they engage contemporary, nationalist histories – and what were the cultural stakes of writing revisionary history via the medium of historical romance?

Virtually everyone recognizes the "antipatriarchal" nature of women's historical fiction. Yet this theme is made even more significant when recast as part of a larger gendered struggle over the nature of the republic, a struggle, I would argue, taking place in part through the medium of Puritan history. The transitional nature of the early republic, with all of its cultural and rhetorical instability, made such a struggle particularly resonant. Indeed, it made it possible. In this chapter and the next, I unravel the languages of republicanism in women's historical romance as a way of demonstrating that the political nature of Sedgwick's and Child's novels descends from the cultural experience of the American Revolution. This chapter demonstrates the immediate significance of *Hope Leslie*'s revisionary history of the Pequot War, where Sedgwick thematizes the incompatibility of gendered forms of "republican" virtue. It provides a segue to Chapter 3, a more comprehensive reconsideration of the literary "conventions" of women's historical romance in the context of this period's changing political culture. Puritanism provided an arena in which to debate the protean, gendered meanings of republican "virtue," a debate that directly involved a struggle over language itself.

Hope Leslie, the Pequot War, and Republican Virtue

The Pequot War has produced more than its share of historiographic controversy. This, as we shall see, is much more the case with present-day interpretations of the war than those current in early national America. In the aftermath of Watergate and the Vietnam War, revisionist historians began with renewed fervor to question the reliability of Puritan accounts of the attack on the Pequot in 1637. Francis Jennings led the charge during the mid-1970s by pointing out a regional bias that supposedly had distorted an entire historiographic tradition: "During the nineteenth century and much of the twentieth, the whole historical profession was dominated by historians who were not only trained in New England but at the same time were steeped in the accepted traditions of that region. Our histories generally show their imprint."[3] The revisionist refusal, however, to treat Puritan sources "as gospel" (as Jennings puts it) has itself come under attack. For instance, one critic of the revisionists' "radicalizing polemics" has argued that they tend to oversimplify ambiguities in Puritan histories and thereby unfairly assail Puritan military tactics and political motives alike.[4] These historiographic debates are characterized by deep animosities, but more importantly, they reduce themselves to two crucial questions: Did Captain John Mason's attack on one of the two Pequot forts at Mystic constitute a "massacre"? And did the leaders of Connecticut and Massachusetts Bay undertake a defensive operation, or a war of conquest? This debate continues to occupy early Americanists, presenting the vexing problem of how we interpret Puritan sources.[5]

As critics of Hope Leslie have noted, it is just this issue that lies at the heart of Catharine Sedgwick's revisionary history of the Pequot War. In the novel's crucial fourth chapter, which recounts the war from the point of view of Magawisca, a young Native American woman who witnessed the Puritan attack, Sedgwick interrogates seventeenth-century accounts of the conflict found in William Hubbard's A Narrative of the Troubles with the Indians in New England (1677) and John Winthrop's The History of New

England (1630–49), both of which had been reprinted in the decade before *Hope Leslie*'s publication.[6] Mary Kelley rightly admires Sedgwick for strategically "[m]ining the early histories": "Sedgwick simultaneously turned the [Puritan] witnesses against themselves and introduced an alternative interpretation."[7] Sandra Zagarell similarly has concluded that *Hope Leslie* "challenges the official history of original settlement by exposing the repositories of the nation's early history, the Puritan narratives, as justifications of genocide."[8] More recently, Dana D. Nelson has extended and complicated antipatriarchal approaches by claiming that, taken together, Puritan and Native American versions of the war in *Hope Leslie* testify to "the political aspect of [all] historical representation": "Thus through a sympathetic frame of reference, Sedgwick is able to establish a historical dialogue that had been suppressed from the Puritan accounts."[9]

Whether *Hope Leslie* contains, then, a radical attack on Puritan histories or an uncannily prescient exercise in historical dialogics, the line of continuity in these readings locates Sedgwick vis-à-vis seventeenth-century historiography. None considers the novel primarily in an early republican cultural context – that is, by reading its history of the war in the context of post-Revolutionary discourse about the conflict. What were, in other words, the contemporary political and cultural issues imbedded within early national narratives about colonial military history? By comparing Sedgwick's history to those of her own era, rather than simply to the likes of Hubbard, Winthrop, and others, we might reconceive of *Hope Leslie* as an exercise in contemporary cultural criticism. This significantly lends new meanings to its "antipatriarchal" theme. In the context of contemporary histories, *Hope Leslie* both critiques the viability of masculine, classical republicanism and participates in a larger cultural debate over the nature of citizenship in the early American republic.

This debate was facilitated by the potently ambiguous meanings of "virtue." As several historians of Revolutionary America have noted, during the eighteenth century numerous intellectual-historical pressures transformed the traditionally masculine meanings of "virtue." Its classical context, of course, was *exclusively* masculine. "Virtue" derived from the Roman concept of *virtu* (the source of "virility"), signifying the austerity, patriotic vigilance, and martial valor theoretically requisite to republican life. Citizenship, as the ancient Romans conceived of it, was the ideal medium for men to express their collective personalities; the *vivere civile* – the ideal of active citizenship – generally described a situation whereby rulers served dutifully in politics and the

masses in military defense. However, in a landmark essay exerting
wide influence on scholars of women's history, Ruth Bloch has
traced a number of intellectual developments during the eighteenth century that gradually feminized traditionally masculine
meanings of virtue.[10] "Virtue," Bloch concludes, "if still regarded
as essential to the public good in a republican state, became ever
more difficult to distinguish from private benevolence, personal
manners, and female sexual propriety."[11] Gordon Wood similarly
has argued for the modern forms of love and benevolence that
gradually emerged as the new adhesives of a republican order:
"Virtue became less the harsh self-sacrifice of antiquity and more
the willingness to get along with others for the sake of peace and
prosperity. Virtue became identified with decency. Whereas the
ancient classical virtue was martial and masculine ... the new
virtue was soft and feminized and capable of being expressed by
women as well as men; some, in fact, thought it was even better
expressed by women."[12]

Changes in eighteenth-century civic culture later coalesced
into what one historian has called the "discernible social theory"
of domesticity.[13] The view that women were the "natural" stewards
of national morality helped to create what Linda Kerber has, in a
now famous (and debated) phrase, called "republican motherhood."[14] From its Revolutionary-era genesis, as Kerber noted, this
role imposed upon American women "the contradictory demands of domesticity and civic activism."[15] The republic's new
guardians of civic ethics were at once politically valued and politically disenfranchised. While historians today have come to view
with suspicion the gendered dichotomy of "private" and "public"
spheres,[16] the home theoretically became the site of inculcating
republican virtue.[17] For example, Benjamin Rush, the Revolutionary generation's most prolific writer on republican education,
specifically stated that American women (and by this, of course,
he meant white, middle- and upper-class women) "must concur
in our plans of education for young men, or no laws will ever
render them effectual."[18] One should recognize as well that
Rush's gendered construction of republican morality and pedagogy (a subject I pursue at greater length in the next chapter)
was premised on the same understanding of cyclical history as the
New Ebenezer of Puritanism: "In the ordinary course of human
affairs," as Rush put it, "we shall probably too soon follow the
footsteps of the nations of Europe in manners and vices. The first
marks we shall see of our declension, will appear among our
women."[19] Hence republican womanhood derived from those

anxieties in Whiggish thinking that cast the republic as a fragile, fated thing.

Born from such anxieties, the cultural role of the republican woman helped to legitimate women's writing during this era. The image of the republican woman writer, however, pen in hand, righteously invested in America's civic and political health, was only tenuously empowering. Writers like Catharine Sedgwick certainly carried the "political" authority of moral propriety into the public sphere. Even as a very young woman, a decade before she wrote her first book, *A New-England Tale* (1822), Sedgwick appeared to be aware of the personal, literary, and ideological leverage that republican womanhood afforded. In 1812 she wrote a letter to her father, Theodore Sedgwick, the Speaker of the U.S. House of Representatives, which declared with ostensible humility, "You may benefit a nation, my dear papa, and I may improve the condition of a fellow being."[20] Despite her use of the metaphors of "cottage" and "palace," to distinguish her sphere from her father's, Sedgwick subtly implied a gendered equivalence of their roles: "Wisdom and virtue are never at a loss for occasions and time for their exercise, and *the same light* that lightens the world is applied to individual use and gratification."[21] Throughout her literary career, Sedgwick's moral role, with its enabling and sometimes radical possibilities, was premised on the "light" that symbolically marks the beginnings of the evolution of republican womanhood into domesticity. Years later, an anonymous writer for the *North American Review* began his evaluation of *Hope Leslie* by legitimating women's writing in much the same way. "We hold it to be a fortunate thing for any country, that a portion of its literature should fall into the hands of the female sex; because their influence, in any walk of letters, is almost sure to be powerful and good."[22] In "the interests of virtue," women's writing "nurture[d] the growth ... of youthful intellect and feeling."[23] At the same time, however, he delimited women's writing to the "proper walks" – "the lighter kinds of literature"[24] – thereby circumscribing its politics within domestic space.

This newfound "political" role for women, however, raised a troubling question buried within the cant of republican motherhood. Which kind of "virtue" were women supposed to teach husbands and sons at home? This issue crucially involves the substance of republican citizenship. Male political theorists, of course, glossed over it, recognizing little problem in ideologically reconciling classical and domestic virtue. Men, after all, ideally incorporated benevolence and love into their social relations, even if times of political crisis demanded an exclusively "masculine" response of patriotic duty and martial courage (a subject taken up in Chapter 5). But the opposite was not true. Women had no access to the classical norms of republican citizenship. One should recognize that a lingering ideology of austere manhood contained misogynistic overtones (the abhorrence of "effeminacy," for example, or the negatively feminine connotations of "luxury" and "indolence"). Moreover, masculine republicanism undervalued the *affective* ways in which women could forge truly political identities. How, then, did women writers treat a masculine ideology that in large part underwrote their own legal and political disenfranchisement? Divested of true representation, if not always political expression, women writers waged a cultural and ideological struggle within the republic by exploiting the contradictions in their political role.

Nowhere in early national culture was masculine republicanism more pronounced than in the heroic subject of military history. To put it simply, military history was meant to "inspire virtue" and "instill patriotism" in male citizens.[25] Exploits of the American Revolution, the many frontier conflicts with Native Americans, and, to come to the issue at hand, the Pequot War, all helped codify a narrowly masculine understanding of citizenship that effectively heightened the difference between men and women as political beings. This is the cultural politics of *Hope Leslie*'s revisionary history. Soaked in a rhetoric of Roman masculinity, the subject of the war in Sedgwick's own day served to memorialize classical *virtu*. Her novel, then, addresses decidedly contemporary issues of the republic by debunking an entire tradition of masculine iconography derived immediately (though not exclusively) from Revolutionary-era political culture. *Hope Leslie*'s fourth chapter is just what she calls Magawisca'a narrative – a "recital," or performance, of history, which competed with other contemporaneous performances over the meaning of virtue in early America.

The "Story" of 1637

Hope Leslie's "recital" of the Pequot War confronts a long-standing historiographic tradition. Puritan versions of the conflict tell the larger story of God's Providence in New England, and they typically begin with the murders during the 1630s of three Englishmen – John Stone, Walter Norton, and John Oldham – as a way of justifying Mason's expedition against the Pequot in what is

now Mystic, Connecticut, in the spring of 1637. New England's
early historians virtually ignored the fact that these three men
were anything but saintly figures (Stone, for example, pirated a
Plymouth ship, nearly stabbed Plymouth's governor, and was exiled from Massachusetts Bay for adultery and threats of violence;
Oldham, as Bradford's *Of Plymouth Plantation* attests, was quarrel-
some enough to be called "Mad Jack" by the likes of Thomas
Morton).[26] Instead, they turned these three rogues into martyrs
in order to confirm Native American "savagery" and thereby
justify the war. In one of the most important firsthand accounts
of the war, John Mason himself unwittingly confirms this rhetorical strategy by claiming that "the Beginning is the Moiety of
the Whole."[27] Even providential history, Mason suggests, is manipulable: "If the Beginning be but obscure, and the Ground
uncertain, its Continuance can hardly persuade to purchase belief: or if Truth be wanting in History, it proves but a fruitless
Discourse."[28]

From the seventeenth to the nineteenth century, this narrative
framing device for the war aimed "to purchase belief" and hold
the moral high ground. The four histories by the actual participants in the war – Mason, John Underhill, Lion Gardiner, and
Philip Vincent[29] – deftly contextualize the Puritan massacre in
this way. Mason, for example, begins by recounting the fate of the
"cruelly murdered" John Stone, who fell into the "bloody Design"
of the Pequot,[30] while Underhill similarly laments Oldham's
death: "The Indians [the Eastern Niantics, a tributary of the
Narragansetts] . . . knocked him in the head, and martyred him
most barbarously, to the great grief of his poor distressed servants."[31] Gardiner and Vincent focused instead on Pequot "mischief" in Connecticut at Fort Saybrook and Wethersfield, but the
narrative effect remains the same.[32] Later Puritan historians, such
as William Hubbard, easily adopted this narrative strategy because it worked so well in casting the war as a defensive operation
against a most "fierce, cruel, and warlike People" who "treacher-
ously and cruelly murthered Captain Stone, and Captain Norton."[33] Ever since the nineteenth-century antiquarian James Savage disparaged his abilities as a historian, most critics have noted
how Hubbard's *A General History of New England* borrows extensively from John Winthrop's *Journal*. But what better way to stir up
passions than the gruesome account of Oldham's murder that
Winthrop provides: "[The Puritans] found John Oldham under
the seine stark naked, his head cleft to the brains, and his hands
and legs cut as if they had been cutting them off, yet warm."[34]
Founded upon the dichotomy between "saint" and "savage," the

sensationalist rhetoric of Puritan narrative would seem to belie
John Mason's claim that reliable history need not "stir up the
affections of men."[35] Puritan history works affectively, consuming,
like the flames of Mystic Fort, whatever sympathy readers might
later have for the Pequot themselves.

Early nationals easily appropriated this narrative scheme. The
deaths of these three "martyrs" later served the nationalistic bias
of early republican historiography quite well. Connecticut's premier history-writer, Benjamin Trumbull, merely reinscribed the
Puritan line as it was found in Mason and Hubbard by beginning
his chapter on the war with the accusation that the "Indians in
general were ever jealous of the English, from the first settlement
of New-England, and wished to drive them from the country."[36]
The "brutal" murders of Stone and Oldham soon follow, as they
do in Abiel Holmes, Jedidiah Morse, and Epaphras Hoyt.[37] Moreover, the subject of the war further demonstrates ways in which
sectarian rivalries of post-Revolutionary New England collapse
under the pressures of nationalist piety. No less than her orthodox adversary, Jedidiah Morse, Hannah Adams argued that the
New England Fathers "had still an arduous task to secure themselves from the malevolence and jealousy of the natives . . . [tak-
ing] every precaution to avoid a war."[38]

The perpetuation of this rhetorical frame for the war helps
to explain the historiographic design of *Hope Leslie*. One might
otherwise overlook Sedgwick's inversion of the chronological sequence of an entire historiographic tradition, as she transplants
what she realizes are the embellished "stories" of the deaths of
Norton, Stone, and Oldham to a moment *after* the massacre has
occurred.[39] In the preface to the novel, she manipulates uncertain generic distinctions and gender stereotypes by assuming with
all humility the persona of the inadequate historian. Yet this
very act devilishly signals her historiographic maneuver: "The
antiquarian reader will perceive that some liberties have been
taken with the received accounts of Sir Philip [or Sir Christopher]
Gardiner, and a slight variation has been allowed in the chronology of the Pequod war" (5). By dislodging these stories from their
traditional placement, Sedgwick is able to emancipate readerly
sympathy for the Pequot, and thereby recover that element of
pathos – that humanitarian impulse at the core of domestic ideology – which both Puritan historians and their early national
descendents successfully suppress.

In lieu of the murders of the Big Three, Sedgwick reframes
Magawisca's narrative with a scene between Everell Fletcher, a

Puritan boy who is the novel's future hero, and Digby, an actual veteran of the war, which functions to invalidate masculine historiography. Indeed, as Digby dutifully guards the Fletcher freehold against the possibility of Indian conspiracies, he stands as a trope for the virtue of Puritan and republican vigilance. And as he begins to rehash the war for Everell, he becomes a living metaphor for a historiographic tradition with which *Hope Leslie* now competes:

> The subject of the Pequod war once started, Digby and Everell were in no danger of sleeping at their post. Digby loved, as well as another man, and particularly those who have had brief military experience, to fight his battles o'er again; and Everell was at an age to listen with delight to tales of adventure and danger. They thus wore away the time till the imaginations of both relater and listener were at that pitch, when every shadow is embodied, and every passing sound bears a voice to the quickened sense. (43)

In this instance Sedgwick wryly criticizes the historical reliability of status quo historiography, since even eyewitness accounts (what William Hubbard called "the mouths of some faithful witnesses")[40] derive from romantic imaginations. At stake here are the Horatian tenets that history offer both pleasure and instruction, the cultural foundations for historical print that Sedgwick problematizes by transferring supposedly "female" faculty psychology to male sensibilities.[41] Both Digby and Everell are stirred up by the "adventure and danger" of a romantic, masculine history, which places them in an imaginative "pitch" distorting "sense" itself.

The ambiguous meaning of "sense" here exploits thematic possibilities arising from the complex legacies of Lockean epistemology and Common Sense morality. Sensation signifies a number of things: immediate impression, the (failed) capacity for reason, and sensibility as the affective source of moral behavior. After pontificating to Everell on the vulnerability of the senses, Digby is unable to recognize Magawisca as she emerges from the forest shadows – a fact that parallels his inability to recognize the ethical implications – because of his lack of moral feeling – of the Puritan massacre at Mystic. Digby fails, then, on simultaneously moral and epistemological counts: Magawisca he mistakes for a man and the Pequot for "a kind of beast" (42). Confounded by his own misperception at the moment Magawisca emerges from the woods, Digby asks, completely dumbfounded, " 'Could I have been so deceived?' " (44). As a representative male historian, his inadequacy devolves upon a deformed moral sense. Sedgwick thus dramatizes a larger defect in masculine historiography by destabilizing the rigid categorical oppositions (reality and illusion, male and female, history and romance) upon which it is founded. Both Everell and *Hope Leslie*'s contemporary reader clearly need another historian.

Republicanism and Revisionary History

But what kind of historian? And what was at stake in rewriting this kind of history?

These issues involve the nature of the war's representation in Sedgwick's own era as well as the historiographic and ideological relations between commonwealth and republic. Certainly early national antiquarians, both textbook writers and more "original" historians, naturally borrowed from Puritan sources. The theory and method surrounding their historiographic practice, however, should be understood in its immediate context, for too often critics mystify how and why nineteenth-century historians borrow from their predecessors. George H. Callcott, for example, has argued for the increasing scholarly rigor and sophistication with which nineteenth-century historians approached primary sources, suggesting that the ideal antebellum historian was a "lawyer" or a "judge" of historical evidence: "To use the sources was a simple dictum, but to criticize them, weigh their authenticity, and use them discretely was an art."[42] But Callcott simultaneously admits that the historian "felt no need to argue for originality, and he would not have understood why he should make a fetish of reworking material when what he wanted to say already had been better said by another."[43] Together, these two assessments only muddle the issue of historiography as a cultural and political practice. Why, one might ask, did early national history-writers assume that the narrative of the war "had been better said" by their Puritan ancestors?

Early nationals thematized the war principally in two ways, both of which involved important ideological relations between Puritan commonwealth and early American republic: the validation of American exceptionalism and the recovery of Revolutionary *virtu*. Didactic historians during Sedgwick's day co-opted the Puritan theological concept of "special Providences," the rare intervention of divine agency to determine events, which was in this case apparent in Mason's success despite being greatly outnumbered. To dramatize the divinely miraculous nature of this underdog victory, they followed their Puritan forebears in misleadingly casting the Pequot as a rising power.[44] Hannah Adams, for one, marveled at the "interposition of Divine Providence [that] was visible in restraining the savages from their [the Puritans'] infant settlements."[45] Trumbull emphasized the day of thanksgiving that the Puritans held afterward, noting that "in all the churches of New-England devout and animated praises were addressed to him, who giveth his people the victory, and causes them to dwell safely."[46] Such rhetoric deliberately blurred the meaning of the "people," transferring its eschatological promise from commonwealth to republic.

Such a transferral involved translation as well. Much more dramatically than in Puritan histories, early national narrative of the war occasioned the opportunity to instruct readers in the political necessity of republican *virtu*. Early nationals mediated the Pequot War through a cultural discourse of Revolutionary republicanism. Even as Americans gradually sloughed off the atavistic codes of classical republicanism, they still periodically invoked it as a source of masculine identity. Its cultural use, of course, was contingent on rhetorical context. Even a proponent for a wholly "modern" Constitution, such as James Madison, could resort to it, declaring, for example, in the *Federalist* #57 that the "vigilant and and manly spirit" of the people must safeguard the republic against the power of the House of Representatives.[47] This masculine ethos also informed Andrew Jackson's cultivation of the persona of "Old Hickory," the hero of the War of 1812 who had saved the republic at the Battle of New Orleans. Timothy Dwight's handling of his ancestors' run-in with the Pequot begins to show how the period's historical discourse was shaped by a resilient ideology of masculine republicanism. In *Travels in New-England and New-York,* Dwight concluded:

> Few efforts, made by man have been more strongly marked
> with wisdom in the projection, or with superior courage and
> conduct, in the execution. Every step appears to have been
> directed by that spirit, and prudence, which mankind have,
> with one voice, regarded with admiration and applause in
> the *statesman and the hero.*[48]

In this same vein, Benjamin Trumbull's history reveals an affinity with an older ideal of republicanism, where the selfless virtue of volunteer yeoman-citizens (as opposed to standing armies) ensures political survival: "The importance of the crisis was now come, when the very existence of Connecticut, under providence, was to be determined by the sword, in a single action; and to be decided by the good conduct of less than eighty brave men."[49] This is more than the clichéd patriotism it might initially appear to be. Trumbull's rhetoric mediates syntactically between passivity and activity, between the agencies, in other words, of divine providence and republican heroism. The phrase "by the sword" allies this militarism metonymically with a distinctly premodern mode of warfare.

The political logic of this historical metaphor is apparent as well in the association of colonial New England with an ancient myth of republican purity. In a Forefathers Day oration of 1820, for example, an Orthodox minister from Connecticut concluded that the "valour" of Mason's expedition prevented "an extermination of the rising colonies."[50] In his *History of the Indian Wars* (1824) Epaphras Hoyt employs a similar language: "Finding war unavoidable, the Connecticut people acted with vigour."[51] As we have seen, in the aftermath of the Revolution these words lent an exclusively masculine resonance to the historical trope of Puritanism. Here, specifically within the context of military history, their meanings draw upon an Anglo-Saxon mythology of manhood. In the 1828 *American Dictionary,* Noah Webster significantly noted that "vigor" derived from the Saxon word *wigan,* which meant to "carry on war," and that (to recall Dwight's emphasis above on both wisdom and fortitude) it meant both "[s]trength of mind" and "force of body."[52] At least theoretically, then, these masculine qualities ensured one's ability to preserve one's property and hence one's independence. Moreover, the word's lexical origins place Puritan militarism within a larger mythology of the ancient purity of the Anglo-Saxon constitution, which to many American Revolutionaries had provided the historical roots of American "liberties" and hence a justification for independence. Revolutionary theorists as diverse as Thomas Jefferson (in "A Summary View of the Rights of British America" [1774]) and Noah Webster (in his conceptualization of the relation between politics and a national language) looked to the mythic purity of the ancient Germanic tribes as the source of English liberties. The Norman invasion in 1066 disrupted Saxon liberties which the American struggle of 1776 in effect recovered.[53] The submerged lexical associations between Puritanism and Saxonism thus further place colonial history within the framework of Whig ideology.

Surprisingly enough, in light of the period's overt racism, what might be called the valor/ization of Puritanism was paralleled by the Pequot themselves. As Neal Salisbury has noted, to Puritan historians "the Pequot's most offensive traits were their 'pride' and their 'insolence.' "[54] Early nationals easily marshaled these racist epithets to reinforce the saint/sinner dichotomy upon which the narrativity of the war was constructed.[55] Lion Gardiner was careful to include a scene where, during an interlude in the fighting, the Pequot approached the Puritan patrol outside Fort Saybrook and asked "if we did use to kill women and children?" Gardiner's blunt reply, "We said they should see that hereafter," supposedly elicited a moment of Pequot bravado: "We are Pequits, and have killed Englishman, and can kill them as mosquetoes, and we will go to Conectecott and kill men, women, and children."[56] The subtext of contesting masculinities in these Puritan histories (apparent, for example, in Winthrop's and Hubbard's account of John Gallop's heroism, or Mason's bristling over the Narragansett slights upon Puritan valor) endured into early national discourse. Jedidiah Morse, for one, noted how the Pequot became cocky with their initial successes and mocked the Puritans, calling them " 'all one sqaw.' "[57]

Paradoxically, however, the Pequot stood as a model of republican virtue. Juggling their admiration for the Pequot's "manly resistance," and the obvious benefit of the war's outcome, historians refashioned the Pequot according to conflicting imperatives of gender and race. After narrating their utter defeat, historians such as David Ramsay uncannily refashioned savage pride into civic valor: "In this first essay of their arms, the colonists of New England displayed both courage and perseverance; but instead of treating a vanquished foe with the respect due to an independent people, who made a gallant effort to defend their property, the rights and the freedom of their nation, the victors urged upon them the desolations of war."[58] In this context, the Pequot sachem Sassacus could be transformed from the most ignoble of savages to the paragon of patriotism. "In an enlightened age and country," Timothy Dwight maintained, Sassacus "might perhaps have been a Charles, or an Alexander."[59] Once they were defeated, the Pequot exemplified, according to Hannah Adams, "the spirit of a people contending for their country and existence."[60] And Abiel Holmes's claim that the Pequot refused "dependence"[61] suggests more than one might at first expect. This code word derives specifically from Revolutionary political assumptions juxtaposing liberty and enslavement, and signals the need for arms to ensure freedom. Such an odd configuration of Native American republicanism was, of course, not restricted to the Pequot alone. Cadwallader Colden, after all, had done virtually the same thing in his *History of the Five Nations* (1727), and the praise Washington Irving heaped upon the Wampanoag sachem, Metacom, in "Philip of Pokanoket" was typical (as I discuss in Chapter 4) of post-Revolutionary histories about King Philip's War. Most important here is the double bind into which the Pequot were narratively placed by early republican history-writers. Alternatively cast as satanic savages and vigilant republicans, the Pequot were "othered" in simultaneously countervailing ways, bearing the early national inscriptions of both an ideal of citizenship and a foil for civilization.

This context helps explain the structural and rhetorical design of *Hope Leslie*. The novel's "recital" of the war consists of twin massacre scenes dramatizing a cyclical pattern of history in which gendered equivalences model a pattern of "savagery" transcending race. The symmetry of the two massacres – one Puritan, one Pequot – crucially works to subvert an ethos of masculine republicanism, specifically in the equivalence history-writers drew between Puritan and Pequot *virtu*. The novel's parallel massacre scenes invert this equivalence, disfigure it by redefining republican valor as male "savagery." *Hope Leslie* shows that it is self-consciously engaged with the masculine cultural formulas surrounding narratives of the war. I should at this point distinguish my reading of this section of *Hope Leslie* from those who have noted Sedgwick's revision of racial stereotypes.[62] Others duly have suggested the limitations of such a revision but have overlooked or simply ignored the ways in which Sedgwick substitutes gendered stereotypes for racial ones. Native American men in this instance become no less "savage" than their Puritan counterparts; they show that "masculine savage quality" Sedgwick attributed to Indian nature in her autobiography written later in life.[63] Gender, in other words, distills race. And the context of republicanism in early national culture helps to explain why.

The issue is this: *Hope Leslie*'s dual massacre scenes thematize the incompatibility of the gendered forms of republican "virtue." The Puritan attack on Mystic, and Mononotto's revenge against the Fletcher household at Bethel, constitute analogous violations of the *home*. Sedgwick takes her cue from the repressed guilt in both Puritan and early national accounts about the killing of innocent women and children (Mason's tortuous insistence, for example, justifying his decision to attack that particular fort; or Jedidiah Morse's paradoxically titillated disgust with "a scene of sublimity and horror indescribably dreadful").[64] In this context, Magawisca describes the fort as a "nest, which the eagles of the

tribe had built for their mates and their young" (47). She speci-
fies that the torch used to light it on fire "was taken from our
hearth-stone" (49), thus lending the massacre a particularly dark
irony rooted in an emergent antebellum ideology of the home.
More importantly, since the historical record located Sassacus
and the rest of the ruling elders at another fort nearby, Sedgwick's placement of them at a council of chiefs implicitly argues
that the public sphere of political duty (the *vivere civile* in classical
terms) leaves the home tragically unprotected. Only the maternal
figure Monoco can sense its imminent destruction. There is no
middle ground here: The twin republican tenets of valor and
duty together precipitate an inevitable disaster for domestic life.
Later, as Pequot fugitives flee to a Connecticut swamp for protection, the final Puritan attack culminates in an explicit violation of
sacred domestic space, as "the wailings of the dying children"
resound after the English "penetrated the forest-screen" (53).

Virtually the same domestic idyll becomes the victim of the
Pequot attack on Bethel. "All was joy in Mrs. Fletcher's dwelling"
(60), the narrator notes as the family prepares for the arrival of
Mr. Fletcher and Hope Leslie. Even as Sedgwick in this scene
suggests that a wife's vanity may result from an unhealthy desire
to please her husband ("in obedience to matrimonial duty, or, it
may be, from some lingering of female vanity . . ." [61]), Sedgwick still idealizes the moment distinctly in terms of familial
harmony: "A mother, encircled by her children, is always a beautiful spectacle" (61). Sedgwick here deploys a romantic trope
whose sentimental surface almost obscures its political potency:
"like diligent little housewives," the minstrel birds seek "materials
for their housekeeping" (61). The affinities between the "natural"
and the domestic, however, are complicated by the scene's emphasis on the cultivated order of Anglo domestic space – a trait
that significantly distinguishes the Fletcher home from the
Pequot one. In light of what we have seen as the period's discourse of Puritan enterprise, Mrs. Fletcher's house tellingly reflects "the neatness of English taste"; "a rich bed of clover that
overspread the lawn . . . *rewarded the industry of the cultivators*" (61,
italics mine). What appears to be a series of replicating images,
then, is subject to slippage, as the Pequot fort, Fletcher home,
and house of Nature vary in degrees of cultivation, together
demonstrating both the sanctity of domestic space and a liberal
mythology of property rights.

In Chapter 4, I take up the importance of this ideology in
reading James Fenimore Cooper's novel of the Connecticut fron-

tier, *The Wept of Wish-ton-Wish* (1829), but for now we might recognize that similar details surrounding these two massacre scenes reinforce this gendered equivalence and suggest its empowering claims to universality. First of all, both patriarchal heads are significantly absent during the respective massacres. Second, Magawisca's desperate plea during the murder of Mrs. Fletcher and her child – " 'the mother – the children – oh they are all good – take vengeance on your enemies – but spare – spare our friends – our benefactors" (63) – strikes the same cords of domestic pathos ringing out earlier at the attack on Mystic. Moreover, there is a biographical context for all of this. In her autobiography written to her niece, Sedgwick admitted as much: "There was a traditionary story of my mother's childhood which used to affect my imagination, for in my youth, dear Alice, the dark shadows of the Indians had hardly passed off our valleys, and tales about them made the stock terrors of our nurseries."[65] The real terror (the vulnerability of the "nurseries") lies in the imagined violation of domestic space that *Hope Leslie* dramatizes in symmetrical scenes of massacre.

The difference here between Puritan and Pequot men dissolves almost entirely. Although the Pequot sachem Mononotto experiences a momentary pulse of feeling for his victims, his "obdurate heart" only really awakens at the "courage of the heroic girl." At this moment, the Native American sachem significantly bears one of the early national era's most common epithets for the Puritan Fathers when he silences his daughter "sternly" (75).[66] Sedgwick thus inverts the equivalence which her own culture drew between Puritan and Pequot valor, recasting republican manhood as a "savage" code of civic ethics.[67] This thematic maneuver implicitly mocks those ethical and racial discrepancies in status quo historiography which failed to see the obvious equivalence between "white" and "red" savagery. For if Puritan histories unwittingly dramatize vengeful behavior on both sides, early nationals were unwilling to recognize an equivalence that would have shaken their moral high ground. David Ramsay in this respect merely parroted the Word of the Fathers on Pequot "nature": "Revenge is the darling passion of savages, to secure the indulgence of which, there is no present advantage that they will not sacrifice, and no future consequence they will not totally disregard."[68] "When determined upon revenge," Charles Goodrich assured his readers in 1829, "no danger would deter them; neither absence nor time could cool them."[69] Morse shuddered at the image of five Pequot heads perched on poles at Fort

Saybrook, a result of vengeance taken by Lion Gardiner's men: "So contagious are malignant passions."[70] The hollowness of this racist dichotomy between saint and savage, which Morse cannot bear to admit but cannot completely hide either, gets a biting rebuttal by Sedgwick in an earlier scene in the novel where Digby and a Mohawk are traveling together to deliver Sassacus's scalp to the Puritan magistrates. In a moment of unforgiving irony, Sedgwick has Digby comment that the dried, bloody scalp " 'is an abomination to the soul and eye of a christian' " (25). Transporting the badge of Puritan triumph, Digby and the "fierce savage" are indubitably equated.

The gendered project of *Hope Leslie*'s revision of military history is coterminous with a critique of America's millennial destiny constructed upon the smoldering ashes of Mystic Fort. Sedgwick's exposure of masculine republicanism subverts a theory of exceptional, progressive history by, oddly enough, invoking the Whiggish concept of cyclical time. If Puritans relied on typology (in Hubbard's reading of New England, for example, via the Israelites' victory over Amalek) to explain the war's meaning, early nationals perpetuated the theory of providential destiny. In this context, the symmetry of *Hope Leslie*'s narrative design suggests a view of cyclical history that disrupts the historical teleology of nationalist narrative. Male vengeance occurs and reoccurs in inexorable cycles of retribution that parade falsely as republican virtue. The macabre image of Mrs. Fletcher's blood "trickling, *drop by drop,* from the edge of the flooring to the step" (67, italics added) not only gothically refigures the true nature of Revolutionary *virtu* but resonates as well, especially in light of these quid pro quo retributions, with a sense of inevitability. Historical process is key to gendered revision. As we have seen, the subject of Puritanism during the early republic was emplotted to fulfill both cyclical and progressive history. In this regard *Hope Leslie*'s revisionism at once inscribes and redeploys this ambiguity. The novel bears the markings of its own historical emergence at the very moment it displaces progressive with cyclical history – at the very moment, in other words, when the trope of the home's destruction displaces that of the American Israel.

The novel's treatment of race, however, complicates its gendered intentions. Consider, for example, a moment during *Hope Leslie*'s preface:

The Indians of North America are, perhaps, the only race of men of whom it may be said; that though conquered, they

were never enslaved. They could not submit, and live. When
made captives, they courted death and exulted in torture.
These traits of their character will be viewed by an impartial
observer, in a light very different from that in which they
were regarded by our ancestors. In our histories, it was
perhaps natural that they should be represented as "surly
dogs," who preferred to die rather than to live, from no
other motives than a stupid or malignant obstinacy. Their
own historians or poets, if they had such, would as naturally,
and with more justice, have extolled their high-souled courage and patriotism. (6)

The first part of the passage could be culled from the period's
nationalist historiography. (How similar, for example, is Salma
Hale's claim that Pequot "resistance was brave and obstinate" and
that "for bravery in battle and fortitude in suffering [the Pequot]
were not surpassed by any of the English troops.").[71] At this
moment *Hope Leslie* participates in the cant of Revolutionary
America by arguing in effect that the Pequot chose, in the words
of New Hampshire's state motto, to live free or die. The new
historian whom her reader presumably needs – the "impartial
observer" – thus humanizes the Pequot within the sanctioned
terms of masculine republican heroism. Her self-conscious departure from Puritan racism (in the brief but stinging allusion to
William Hubbard in quotation marks in the excerpt above) res-
cues the racial other in a way that partakes in a cultural apotheosis
of "republican" Native Americans.

What, then, one might ask, is the ethical status of the two
massacre scenes? A close reading of Magawisca's history shows
that this trope of Pequot valor actually problematizes the thematic trajectory of these scenes, their subversion of classical republican virtue. First of all, Magawisca refers to the Pequot as
a "proud and prosperous" tribe (56). As a wavering heroine in
the tradition of Sir Walter Scott, her unwillingness to inform
Mrs. Fletcher of Mononotto's presence results from kinship ties,
specifically because her "pride" is "enlisted on the side of her
people" (55). Most importantly, Magawisca's actual account of a
massacre of domestic innocents loses its initial intention. What at
first looks like a "home" inhabited by women and children uncannily becomes a battleground where the Pequot braves "fought
as if each man had a hundred lives" (48). William Bradford,
Sedgwick argues to reinforce this point, mistook Pequot "courage" and "fortitude" for savagery. Interestingly enough, these

textual inconsistencies actually create a parallel to issues raised by today's historians about the Pequot War. Sedgwick in effect prepares her reader for the kind of massacre that Francis Jennings and other revisionists have argued, but then quickly changes frequency during the conflict to emphasize the "manly spirit" of Samoset, who defends the home "with a prince-like courage" (49).[72] Why?

The contradictions surrounding *Hope Leslie*'s history of the Pequot War – the simultaneous appropriation and subversion of classical republicanism – derive from Sedgwick's complex relationship both to her immediate audience and to her period's prevailing ideologies of race. Her revisionary history belies the difficulty of carrying on simultaneous revisions of gender and race. A historiographic and ethical problem faced her: How does one both critique republican manhood and fully humanize the Pequot for a potentially dubious audience? In *The First Settlers of New England* (1829), Lydia Child faced a similar dilemma and marshaled the trope of Pequot manliness to similar ends. In Child's series of domestic dialogues, a mother/historian informs her children/readers that had "the Pequods quietly submitted to have their country ravaged, and fortresses built in their immediate vicinity to awe them into immediate subjection, they must have been less than men."[73] Both Sedgwick and Child in these instances resort to a culturally specific brand of ethnocentrism, which if they did not at least partly embrace, they nonetheless deployed to sway their readers *on their readers' own terms*. Revolutionary republicanism was apparently too misogynistic an ideology to embrace as a modern standard of civic behavior, and yet too powerful a polemical tool to resist. Hence the Pequot warrior himself emerges from this era as a protean text, a sign of cultural and gendered ambivalence, and the object of psychological and ideological projections of Anglo authors. The Pequot War becomes the fictive site of a thematic fracture between gender and race revealing in this case the cultural legacy of the American Revolution.

Romantic History and Historical Romance

These thematic inconsistencies in *Hope Leslie* coincide with theoretical issues surrounding the very status of historical narrative. Indeed, this section of the novel raises the issue of the representational status of all history-writing; it does so within the context of the changing relations between "history" and historical "fiction" during this early republic. Sedgwick's narrative strategies obviously fulfill her objections to an exclusively masculine form of republicanism. But these strategies also expose an irrepressible (and yet unacknowledged) sense of the impossibility of composing "objective" history. The ideological disruption Sedgwick creates as a historian, of sorts, actually complicates her claims to authenticity. Her revisionary history, after all, manipulates narrative to defamiliarize readers. To put this in present-day theoretical terms, Sedgwick "reemplots"[74] the Pequot War, divesting the deaths of Stone, Norton, and Oldham of their narrative power (which Jennings and others have recognized) to rationalize the later massacre at Mystic. By reframing the massacre at Mystic, and constructing parallel massacre scenes, Sedgwick's engagement in gender politics ultimately exposes the metahistorical status of *Hope Leslie*. Her novel's fourth chapter is exactly what she calls Magawisca's narrative – a "recital," or performance, of history. So despite her intentions to award Magawisca narrative authority, the text's performative qualities suggest the inevitability of historical relativism.

A close look at the relationship between Magawisca's and Digby's histories bears this out. From the outset of Magawisca's narrative, Sedgwick complicates the subject of historical truth by suggesting that her Indian angel's history is an enumeration of events *and* an artistic performance. "[Magawisca] paused for a few moments, sighed deeply, and then began the recital of the last acts in the tragedy of her people; the principal circumstances of which are detailed in the chronicles of the times by the witnesses of the bloody scenes" (47). Through her own eyewitness, Sedgwick aims to compete with Puritan ones like John Mason and John Underhill, who, via William Hubbard and others, influenced early national discourse about the war. Yet she creates at this moment uncertainties about the status of "history." Is it a dramatic performance – or merely an enumeration of facts? Magawisca's performance is implied by her need as an artist to pause and capture the moment, to marshall her resources before she stands and delivers. Magawisca's description recalls the generic ambiguity established in the novel's Preface when Sedgwick states that hypothetically either Pequot "historians or poets" (6) could have defended their people's cause.

Magawisca's performance further suggests the power of historical romance as a medium for revisionary history. The crucial point here is that Digby's and Magawisca's histories metaphorically express an increasing competitiveness (and familiarity) between history and historical romance, a subject that I addressed in the Introduction. In this instance the text of *Hope Leslie* inscribes its own context – that is, the discursive practices surrounding the production of all history-writing during this particular era. Everell Fletcher thus can be situated as the early republic's implied reader for whom the genres of history and historical fiction are competing. And this implied reader, *Hope Leslie* suggests, already has been corrupted by masculine nationalist historiography. The reader (perhaps unknowingly) comes to historical romance in need of help.

Like *Hope Leslie*'s reader, Everell becomes easily seduced into the scene's paradoxically liberating and debilitating pathos: " 'Did they so rush on sleeping women and children?' asked Everell, who was unconsciously lending all his interest to the party of the narrator" (48). As Magawisca's story progresses, Everell unwittingly loses his capacity to object to her "version," and helplessly asks instead for more details about the fate of Sassacus. So the power of historical narrative would seem to lie along the axis of feeling and imagination. Yet the logical extension of such thinking destabilizes the authenticity of Magawisca's history. Sedgwick's apparent desire to authorize Magawisca is frustrated by language belying an irrepressible sense of the artificiality (as in "art" or "artifice") of historical romance:

> It [the war] was an important event to the infant colonies, and its magnitude probably somewhat heightened to the imaginations of the English . . . and Everell had heard [the events] detailed with the interest and particularity that belongs to recent adventures; but he had heard them in the language of the enemies and conquerors of the Pequods; and from Magawisca's lips they took a new form and hue; she seemed, to him, to embody nature's best gifts, and her feelings to be the inspiration of heaven. This new version of an old story reminded him of the man and the lion in the fable. But here it was not merely changing sculptors to give the advantage of one or another of the artist's subjects; but it was putting the chisel into the hand of truth, and giving it to whom it belonged. (53)

The metaphor of the chisel at once legitimates *Hope Leslie*'s artistic achievement and undermines the historicity of such a performance. The language surrounding this achievement suggests its purely representational quality: Magawisca's account is "a new *version* of an old story," possessing only a new "hue and form" rather than a new substance. Compare this language to the epigraph at the start of this chapter. The reviewer of an early national history defending the Pequot (which tellingly equates the Puritans to the Ancient Romans) rhetorically raises the same theoretical problem: a "different garb" suggests form rather than substance, the inevitable dressings and redressings of language that we inevitably bestow upon the past. Historical narrative would seem to face the problem that the claim to "the hand of truth" is complicated by the lurking sense that only new "versions" can be told.

Sedgwick's intentions here would appear to be open to debate. Dana D. Nelson recently has argued against the notion that Magawisca's history simply subverts the patriarchal Word. In her view Sedgwick juxtaposes Digby's and Magawisca's histories in order to show the inevitably dialogic character of historical narrative.[75] My argument coincides with Nelson so far as both of us recognize the representational nature of the two histories. But her understanding of Sedgwick's intentions ignores the cultural and historiographic contexts in which *Hope Leslie* emerged. First of all, the ideological stakes of writing history in this case – the gendered meanings of republicanism during this era – make it difficult for one to believe that Sedgwick stood so theoretically detached from Magawisca's account.

Moreover, the view that Sedgwick self-consciously upholds historical relativism depends on Everell's unreliability (because of his excessive emotionalism) as a standard for judging the "truth" of Magawisca's history. Yet to read Bakhtin backward, as Nelson does, in order to find an avatar of dialogism in Catharine Sedgwick herself, elides early national assumptions about the nature of historical writing. The romanticization of historiography during the antebellum era is crucial to gauging the relative status in *Hope Leslie* of Digby's and Magawisca's narratives. Early nationals increasingly understood historiography to be an affective and imaginative process. "You will struggle in vain," Samuel Knapp declared in the preface to *Lectures on American Literature* (1829), "to make American history well understood by your pupils, unless biographical sketches, anecdotes and literary selections, are mingled with the mass of general facts. The heart must be affected, and the imagination seized, to make lasting impressions upon the memory."[76] Reviews of nationalist histories increasingly called for a works of "genius" that could buttress the nation's artistic reputation at home and abroad.[77] The year of *Hope Leslie*'s publication, a writer for the *American Journal of Education* defined a new American history in just these terms: "Our country is the monument of our great men. Our history is our national poetry. . . . If we are an intellectual people, it is to be hoped we are not merely so. It is hoped that we have [in the composition of history] imagination and feeling. Then let this history have an interesting form . . . let those parts of it appear which address the moral sentiments."[78]

In this emergently romantic era Sedgwick herself understood Everell's response to Magawisca's "history" to approximate an affective ideal that she elsewhere endorsed. Indeed, the exchange between Magawisca and Everell actually models a dynamic of *all* history-writing that Sedgwick espoused in a letter (written the year after *Hope Leslie*'s publication) to the renowned Swiss historian Jean-Charles-Leonard Simonde de Sismondi, author of the multivolumed *History of the Italian Republics in the Middle Ages* (1809–18):

> But, after all, you cannot estimate the benefit, for you are not aware of the homage your writings have inspired . . . that you infuse into them a moral life, that you breathe your own soul into them, impart to them . . . a portion of your own identity. This seems to me to be one of their attractive and attaching peculiarities. It is this that makes us feel them to be the production of a being, whose affections and sympathies are kindred to our own.[79]

The passage marks an ostensibly odd moment where a writer of historical fiction tells a historian that she admires him *as* a historian because his work appeals to faculties associated with imaginative writing. Sedgwick situates history-writing's didacticism within a psychological, emotive dynamic allying the "affections and sympathies" of both reader and writer. The net result not only blurs the genres of history and romance (as we saw in the earlier scene with Digby and Everell) but also obviates the idea that, in Sedgwick's view, Everell's response somehow problematizes the reliability of Magawisca's historical narrative. Just the opposite: It further validates it.

An affective epistemology helps to explain the equivalence *Hope Leslie* draws between Digby's and Magawisca's "histories." *Hope Leslie* registers both the performative nature of *all* history-writing and the increasing competition between the genres of history and fiction expressed in the juxtaposition of Digby's and

Magawisca's accounts. Both historical narratives have the same audience; they produce essentially the same effects. Moreover, *Hope Leslie* reveals the instability of generic borders. The reasons for this lie in the convergence of two, important trends during the early republic: the proliferation of historical romance in the 1820s and the gradual romanticization of history. Chapter 5 explores the politics of faculty psychology in histories of the Salem witchcraft trials, and locates the uncertainty with which early nationals viewed the imagination, but here I wish to emphasize that during this transitional era historiography was increasingly subjected to romantic literary standards.

The similar cultural space that these dual genres inhabited in the early republic is metaphorically apparent in the equivalent receptions that Digby's and Magawisca's narratives elicit. If we recall the scene between Digby and Everell, where masculine war stories produce only "heightened imaginations," revisionary history in the form of female romance produces much the same thing: "Everell's imagination, touched by the wand of feeling, presented a very different picture of those defenseless families of savages . . ."; he "did not fail to express to Magawisca with all the eloquence of a heated imagination, his sympathy and admiration of her heroic and suffering people" (54). Moreover, the power of imagination (as in the letter to Sismondi) involves both historian and audience. For the "wand of feeling" with which Magawisca touches Everell ambiguously refers to their mutually affected sensibilities. Through Magawisca, then, Sedgwick anticipates a principle of romantic historiography which valued the historian's passionate involvement in historical subject matter.[80] The interaction leaves Magawisca and Everell in the same kind of "romantic abstraction" (54) that Digby and Everell earlier had experienced. And so if Digby's history manages to invalidate itself as nothing more than a specifically masculine romanticism, its feminized revision in Magawisca's performance similarly relies upon the purely manipulative function of language. As history and romance metaphorically vie for authority in *Hope Leslie*, they expose only an equivalent performativity.

In this context, then, *Hope Leslie* stages dual modes of history-writing whose epistemological claims inevitably are compromised by the very qualities of affect and imagination that lend them narrative power. Yet *Hope Leslie*'s "recital" at least suggests the problematic implications of history-as-performance that early national histories generally suppressed. Most history-writers used the term simply to signify an enumeration of historical facts. The title of Jeremy Belknap's *American Biography*, for example, includes the phrase, "Comprehending a Recital of the Events connected with their Lives and Actions." Those, like Belknap, who claimed historical accuracy refused to acknowledge how nationalist pieties may have complicated those claims. "Where is the American," one orator asked in 1826, "who has not felt a glow of enthusiasm in listening to a recital of those events that led to our national emancipation?"[81] David Ramsay similarly claimed a scrupulous fidelity to the facts: "The history of a war on the frontiers can be little else than a recital of the exploits, the sufferings, the escapes and deliverances of individuals, of single families, or small parties."[82] Ironically, the *North American Review* found that Ramsay was too close to the contemporary materials treated in the third volume of his history "to admit of a cool, philosophical recital."[83] Yet even here its signification slips as the reviewer in the next breath calls Ramsay's history a "performance." Thus, predominantly male writers and reviewers alike deployed the term to denote a scrupulous fidelity to the facts, the kind of research that enhanced one's narrative and political authority.[84]

Hope Leslie's performance calls attention to yet another meaning of "recital." The first entry for the word in Webster's 1828 *American Dictionary* defined it as a "Rehearsal; the repetition of the words of another or of a writing; as of the *recital* of a deed; the *recital* of testimony." This suggests an act of ventriloquy. Certainly, as we have seen, this process aptly characterizes the transmission of Puritan narrative into early national historical discourse. Early nationals, in effect, followed the biblical epigraph to William Hubbard's *A Narrative of the Troubles with the Indians*, taken from Exodus 17.14, after God had granted the Israelites a victory over the tribe of Amalek: "And the Lord said unto Moses, Write this for a Memorial in a Book, and rehearse it in the ears of Joshua, for I will utterly put out the Remembrance of Amalek from under heaven." From John Mason's account of the assault on Mystic Fort, through William Hubbard's paraphrasing of it, to its virtual ventriloquy in Benjamin Trumbull and his contemporaries, the Puritan story of the Pequot War continuously was "rehearsed." Like Joshua himself, early nationals were reminded of the sacredness of national destiny and the purely secular means by which the republic would survive. In the very act of engaging the subject of the Pequot War, then, Sedgwick confronted – and disrupted – the word of the Fathers as it was "rehearsed" from the commonwealth to the republic.

Women's Writing and Revisionary History

The appearance of the Pequot War in *Hope Leslie* is thus no accident at all. The subject of the war in early national culture was laden with the masculine ideologies of Revolutionary republicanism, and it carried, like the Y chromosome, the genetic inheritance of a misogynistic understanding of the "republic," which presumably would be passed on (through narrative) to future generations. Sedgwick's treatment of the war was impelled by a gender-specific republican politics of exclusion rooted in classical ideology, which understood the republic in terms of the capacity of male citizens to express their identities fully through active citizenship. Sedgwick's manufacturing of domestic pathos, and her redefinition of "savagery" along the lines of gender – as opposed strictly to race – should be understood in this context. Classical republican ideology merely highlighted the political and ethical inconsistencies in the Revolutionary settlement of 1787–8, ones that excluded women from citizenship and yet still asked them to contribute to the making of good citizens. Women had a political role with no political rights.

So the thinly veiled contest taking place in *Hope Leslie* between nationalist history and historical romance actually shows Sedgwick interrogating the ethical viability of her culture's association of Puritanism with "republicanism" – a word she already is beginning to redefine in the early part of the novel. This crucial section of *Hope Leslie* signals her controversy with a political and cultural metaphor, her dismantling of what I have called the New Ebenezer of the early republic. In the next chapter, I explore this process of historical revision as cultural criticism, a process that further brings into focus the contemporary historicity of the "Puritans" in women's historical romance.

The representational status of Puritanism has important consequences for redefining the very terms of the debate about women's history-writing in general. In *The Feminization of American Culture* (1977), Ann Douglas argues that nineteenth-century female romance represented an "escape" from masculine history.[85] Douglas noted that ministers like Jared Sparks turned away from the feminized province of the Unitarian pulpit in order to pursue the more masculine avocation of history. As Douglas saw it, this was a way for men to escape feminine "influence" and reassert their masculinity. Recent critics justifiably have argued that Douglas failed to see the seriousness of domestic politics in antebellum women's writing.[86] Yet the typical corrective that women's history-writing represented anything but an "escape from history" misses the point. A contemporary reviewer of *Hope Leslie* rightly claimed that Sedgwick "has had the industry to study the early history of New England,"[87] but today we should not define the novel's historicity so narrowly. *Hope Leslie* represents its own emergence in post-Revolutionary culture. And this explains why Douglas objected to Sedgwick's anachronistic language, which presumably reflected an "apostasy from history" and a "confused conscience,"[88] – traits characterizing, for Douglas, women's historical writing in general. What she (and many others) fail to see is the secondary importance of Puritanism in *Hope Leslie*. The novel's anachronistic language and thematics of "virtue" testify to its preeminent concerns with the status of civic ethics in the republic.

The "recital" that *Hope Leslie* offers begins to suggest the competition between alternative forms of "history" during this era. Published in 1827, the very year in which Massachusetts legislated the study of history into the public school curriculum, *Hope Leslie* registers a hyper self-consciousness about the discursive field of history-writing into which it enters. Much later in life, in her autobiography addressed to her niece's daughter, Sedgwick would time and again juxtapose the state and the home as contending spheres of education, emphasizing, of course, the superiority of the latter: "I believe, my dear Alice, that the people who surround us in our childhood, whose atmosphere infolds us, as it were, have more to do with the formation of our characters than all our didactic and preceptive education."[89] The antagonistic power relations between the state and the home are inscribed in *Hope Leslie* in the contest between Digby's and Magawisca's tales, or, in effect, masculine nationalist historiography and women's historical romance. Eight years after *Hope Leslie*, Sedgwick again suggested this tension in *The Linwoods* (1835), a historical novel set in Revolutionary America. While lightly chastising the "duty" that the meekly obedient Bessie Lee performs by "so virtuously" reading histories, the novel's heroine, Isabella Linwood, asks her, "If history then is mere fiction, why may we not read romances of our own choosing? My instincts have not misguided me, after all."[90] Isabella's iconoclasm toward status quo historiography expresses ex post facto Sedgwick's own in *Hope Leslie*. Isabella here testifies to Sedgwick's underlying assumptions about the competition for an immediate reading audience. The story of the Pequot War introduces narrative strategies that work ideally to emancipate the implied reader of the day who, like Everell, presumably has been corrupted.

Like Hope Leslie, who, we should remember, nearly married William Hubbard, Catharine Sedgwick vented herself "upon the ungainly ways of scholars" (154). But these scholars were not really the dead ghosts of John Mason and William Hubbard, but the very real, living spectres of Benjamin Trumbull, Jedidiah Morse, and others who exerted significant cultural power in early-nineteenth-century New England. In the next chapter I explore the narrative strategies with which both Sedgwick and Child conduct cultural criticism, articulating along the way the ambiguous ideological relations between republicanism and domesticity. Such criticism was made possible by the very instability of "virtue" itself during this transitional era. What did it mean – masculine vigilance or affectional benevolence? Who were the real stewards of republican virtue? Like the old war veteran of her letter to Charles, the "republican" heroes of *Hope Leslie* and *Hobomok* are subjected to complex surgical procedures in which the language and ideas of republicanism are forever changed.

REFASHIONING THE REPUBLIC:

GENDER, IDEOLOGY, AND THE POLITICS OF VIRTUE IN HOBOMOK AND HOPE LESLIE

———

The great object of history is to teach us how we may become good citizens, not only as the ancients understood the word, but as its present broad and comprehensive meaning denotes – considering every individual as a member of the great human family, and as such bound to acts of kindness and charity to every other . . . in a word, it inculcates a liberal philosophy . . . a wide philanthropy . . . whether of a political nature or belonging to the gentler connections of social life.
    – "The Philosophy of History," *North American Review* (1834)

In general, it may be said, that the proper end of all reading is to make *"good men and good citizens."* But by what particular steps is History to subserve this end?
    – Charles Goodrich, *History of the United States* (1829)

Hope Leslie's story of the Pequot War begins to reveal both the problems and the possibilities for those women writers of the early republic who wrote (and rewrote) Puritan history. Yet Sedgwick's novel raises a prickly issue concerning its own reception in the 1820s. How could a historical work, which discredited those masculine ideologies of "republicanism" rooted in the American Revolution, still be a popular and critical success?[1] This chapter takes up this issue with regard to the whole of *Hope Leslie* and its counterpart, Lydia Maria Child's first novel, *Hobomok*, published a few years before, in 1824. The key to their revisions of gender-ideology and their simultaneous popularity lies in the transitional nature of the early republic itself. The very instability of republican "virtue" during this era allowed women writers to engage in (and be praised for) a kind of cultural criticism that was if not "radical," at least revisionary in its reshaping of a historical Ebenezer whose cultural work was to define the republic in exclusively masculine terms. Such revisions of civic ethics were launched from the moral foundations of republican womanhood, a form of authority riddled with political and psychological ambiguities, which I explore further on. So this chapter is as much about tensions within ideologies of American womanhood in the aftermath of the American Revolution as it is about historical writing. The former, as I show, are written into the fabric of historical romance.

Since their appearance in the 1820s, *Hobomok* and *Hope Leslie* have undergone a history characteristic of a lot of antebellum women's writing: initial popularity, then critical erasure, and finally a revival of their importance to the American canon. Obviously, my ability even to discuss these novels results in large part from their recuperation by contemporary feminist critics such as Carolyn L. Karcher and Mary Kelley, who wrote the important introductions to the American Women Writers Series' editions. Their efforts, as I suggested earlier, took place in context of a critical erasure waged largely by postwar critics who devalued writers like Sedgwick and Child in order to solidify Nathaniel Hawthorne's reputation. Indeed, Hawthorne's proficiency in moral psychology and historical irony provided a literary foil for women writers whose popularity the New Left associated with mass culture and hence cultural totalitarianism. Much of the modern complaint about Sedgwick and Child has targeted their supposed inability to render Puritan history convincingly. Their work, it is said, along with that of a host of other incompetent amateurs, is filled with "anachronisms, improbabilities, and overwriting."[2] As one can see, the aesthetic project of ensuring Hawthorne's reputation was wedded to a historical formula assuming the essentially colonial concerns of these texts. By reconsidering historicity, however, one begins to see the very issue of literary aesthetics in a whole new (early republican) light.

Even when more traditional critics have managed to place women's historical fiction in contemporary contexts, they generally divest the genre of its disruptive potential. In the early 1970s, for example, Michael Davitt Bell tried to place the antipatriarchalism of *Hobomok* and *Hope Leslie* in contemporary context by invoking the historiographic context of that well-known apostle of democratic nationalism, the historian George Bancroft. Not unlike the historical and political vision of Bancroft's monumental, multivolumed *History of the United States* (1834–76), these romances presumably express rather standard views of progressive history. "To understand Hawthorne's relation to his more conventional contemporaries," Bell concluded, "we must understand the importance to them of their conventions."[3] Just as Bancroft had seen in colonial New England the ambiguous origins of American liberty, which would organically mature over the course of American history (and culminate in his own era), so, too, the argument goes, did Child and Sedgwick construct heroines who function as "political symbols": "Hope Leslie *is* liberty, she *is* progress."[4] Two problems here. First of all, this paradigm dissolves difference in the name of Bancroftian historicism. Apparently contented with the state of things in nineteenth-century America, women writers – politically disenfranchised, after all, and still living under the laws of coverture – blithely become the acquiescent mouthpieces of the consensual mythologies of nineteenth-century democracy. And second, there is the problem of "liberty" itself. As Chapter 1 demonstrates, the "civil" or "rational" liberty metaphorically inculcated by Puritanism in early republican culture – and that which writers like Sedgwick and Child engaged in their historical work – was of a more conservative bent than Bell and others have realized.

Even in its departures from these views, the recuperation of *Hobomok* and *Hope Leslie* has mistakenly universalized the politics of women's writing. This chapter clarifies their "political" significance by placing it thoroughly within the cultural aftermath of Revolutionary America – an act that allows reconsideration of generic conventions and aesthetic features. For decades, critics underestimated the political significance of the genre's "literary" conventions – the rebellious daughter, tyrannical fathers, convoluted marriage plots, racial conflict, and miscegenation – that make up the dramatic conflicts and plot movements of these texts. More recent admirers of Sedgwick and Child, however, often inscribe *their own* language and values onto texts of the 1820s: *Hope Leslie* "challenges an order based upon patriarchy, [and so] Hope's rebellion is far more challenging than any man's";[5] or, the Puritans of *Hope Leslie* couple the crimes of "gynophobia" and "genocide" inhering somehow naturally within the larger political rubric of "masculinity."[6] *Hobomok* elicits the same response. Child's "radical revision of the patriarchal script," her "revolutionary insight into the connection between male dominance and white supremacy," makes the novel an utter "defiance of patriarchy," which, moreover, links Puritanism to the patriarchal crimes of the Vietnam War.[7] In this schema Puritanism becomes a timeless metaphor, a self-contained, patriarchal mythology. Such a view – problematically – tends to equate the fictive world of seventeenth-century New England with the realities of nineteenth-century America (Sedgwick, in this sense, is said to offer a "subversive political commentary on the patriarchal assumptions of the Puritans *and* her contemporary male audience").[8] This chapter shows that the very act of drawing historical analogies was complicated by the shifting ideologies and unstable language of this period. Puritanism, in other words, was much more a protean metaphor than a stable analogue for the early American republic.

Contrary to this view, Nina Baym recently has argued against overstating the radical politics of antebellum women's historical fiction. "A critic of today therefore needs to think twice about ascribing revisionary motives to antebellum women who wrote historical novels. In context, it looks as though the project of the American women who wrote historical novels was not to challenge received history but to show that historical fiction, like other forms of historical writing, was not an exclusively masculine genre."[9] Yet if Baym places a cautionary, sobering challenge to feminist critics – indeed, to all of us – she nonetheless decontextualizes the historical novels of Sedgwick and Child from the historical writing produced by conservative men during this era. Like Baym's, my reading of these historical novels similarly finds a self-consciously "modern" project in their general thematic designs. In the context, however, of the exclusively masculine model of republicanism, which was being codified via Puritan history, one can say that these novels certainly *are* revisionary. Moreover, their complex ideological legacy to classical thought complicates their thematic promotion of such modern values as refinement and gentility.[10]

So who *are* the Puritans of these novels? All of the critical approaches I have been surveying in varying ways decontextualize women's writing about Puritanism. They tend to distort the peculiar frequencies of these women's voices. These are voices that emanate from women, we should recall, who were born shortly after the Revolutionary settlement, and who were steeped in the period's concerns with republican citizenship. Throughout this chapter I argue that *Hope Leslie* and *Hobomok* engage the republican ideologies of virtue and gender underpinning, as we have seen by now, their own culture's representation of Puritanism. These novels' most crucial subjects – the ethical nature of political authority, gender and political identity, the androgynous possibilities of civic selfhood, the norms of conjugality – reveal specifically early national concerns. All we have to do is listen to the language. In doing so, we realize the ways in which literary conventions of historical romance are inflected with political meanings. The genre becomes the site of a specific kind of cultural criticism in which women played upon the inconsistencies of republican political culture and re-created a republican language of their own.

Political Woman

Modern students of post-Revolutionary America sometimes over-simplify republican womanhood. Too many have seen it simply as a "co-opting ideology that [maintained] mothers were indirectly responsible for *everything* that was crucial in the society," or have argued that its rationale for an expanded educational program for middle-class American women only made them "good wives and mothers, not authoritative interpreters of public texts."[11] Dismissals like these underestimate the empowering ambiguities of republican womanhood, specifically the ways in which it potentially supported their cultural role – and writing. In post-Revolutionary America, the parameters of "republican" behavior and language were so precarious that they could be radically reinterpreted to expand, if only imaginatively, the role of women in the republic.

One tension in republican womanhood involved the relationship between virtue and citizenship. A good example of this problem may be found in an enlightened mind of this era on the issue of women's education, Dr. Benjamin Rush, who nonetheless elided the gendered contradictions at the heart of republican culture. These contradictions hinged upon the exact meaning of "virtue." Neither Rush nor anybody else ever really addressed the issue of whether or not one could reconcile masculine and feminized forms of virtue, the patriotic vigilance and benevolent love, which in theory were *both* necessary to republican life. In "Thoughts upon Female Education" (1787), Rush prescribed to his audience at the Philadelphia's Young Ladies' Academy a serious regimen of study. This was premised on a political utilitarianism that envisioned male citizens as the product largely of women's influence. "[F]ew great or good men," he claimed, ". . . have not been blessed with wives and prudent mothers."[12] Even Rush's capacity to legitimate female reason, which derived largely from Enlightenment assumptions about human intellect, occurred only within the context of a woman's "natural" affections. This is apparent in his objection to female novel-reading. Rush lamented that it displaced real with imagined sympathy by "blunt[ing] the heart."[13] Women wept all morning over *Charlotte Temple*, and then turned "with disdain at two o'clock from the sight of a beggar."

This anecdote, however, introduces a crucial tension within republican political culture. In this instance the object of female virtue – Rush's imagined beggar – lies *outside* the body politic. In a Lockean context the beggar lacks property, and so lacks any tenable political identity. He's not a citizen, only a human being. And so, one might ask, what are the limits of a republican woman's "virtuous" field of attention? On the one hand, women were to practice a form of virtue that, in the name of "universal humanity," effaced the distinction between citizen and noncitizen; on the other, they were supposed to cultivate a male political order that ultimately did make such a distinction. This is apparent in Rush's claim, "The female breast is the natural soil of christianity; and while our women are taught to believe its doctrines, and obey its precepts, the wit of Voltaire, and the style of Bolingbroke, will never be able to destroy its influence upon our *citizens*."[14] Yet if this were true, republican women theoretically could marshal Christian virtue in virtually any way they saw fit. In doing so, they would complicate the strictly masculine conception of "citizenship" implied by Rush's demand that women's education should inculcate "[t]he obligations of patriotism."[15]

Republicanism depended upon a clearly defined understanding of citizenship. Jay Fliegelman poignantly has noted that by 1800 "a species of Christian and Republican Universalism ... stood in opposition to American nationalism and the allegiance to the 'city on the hill.' "[16] Yet Fliegelman underestimates the lingering influence of Whig thinking on conservative pedagogy and politics, arguing, for example, that Rush's "A Plan for the Establishment of Public Schools" (1786) intended "to remove the stigma from patriotism."[17] Certainly, Rush's understanding of the American "republic" juggles classical and Christian concepts of virtue, which are best translated as the difference between the national and human families. For Rush, however, male citizens must be true to the *res publica*. "A Christian, I say again, cannot fail of being a republican," he confidently proclaims, "for every precept of the Gospel inculcates those degrees of humility, self-denial, and brotherly kindness, which are directly opposed to the pride of monarchy and the pageantry of a court."[18] Yet this tenuous synthesis soon collapses under those lurking anxieties which lead Rush to declare that the republican schoolboy must be taught, above all else, to "watch for the state":

He must be taught to love his fellow creatures in every part of the world, but he must cherish with a more intense and peculiar affection, the citizens of Pennsylvania and of the United States. . . . [W]e impose a task upon human nature, repugnant alike to reason, revelation, and the ordinary dimensions of the human heart, when we require him to embrace, with equal affection, the whole family of mankind.[19]

When push comes to shove, the bonds of citizenship transcend those of the human family. To complete this tortured negotiation of civic ethics, Rush resorts to classical exemplars, arguing that the "commonwealths of Greece and Rome show, that human nature, without the aids of Christianity, has attained these degrees of [patriotic] perfection." New Testament virtue would seem to be politically untenable for republican men – at least by itself.

So where does this leave women of the republic? Critics tend to use the phrase "Christian republicanism"[20] to describe the ethos of this era, but rarely point out the ideological inconsistencies inhering within this epithet. The crucial point here is that between the 1790s and 1820s the republic underwent gradual changes in its understanding of the behavioral prescriptions of citizenship. It is precisely the transitional nature of this era that makes women's writing now so politically resonant. For the instability of "virtue" lent itself to masterful refashionings. In the hands of women writers, male virtue could be so easily feminized because it already contained within it the legacy of eighteenth-century affectionalism. Similarly, women writers could export female virtue into the public sphere, so long as it was couched safely in the canons of benevolence and pious love. As one pedagogue declared in 1826, "[w]hatever concerns the culture of the female mind, extends ultimately to the formation of all minds."[21] But if this were true, then what kind of "virtue" were female citizens to teach their male offspring? How tenable in public, political life was a code of civic ethics that, after all, collapsed the distinction between citizens and noncitizens? These are the questions that *Hope Leslie* and *Hobomok* address.

A second tension within republican womanhood concerned the subject of female faculty psychology. As many have noted, the impetus that republicanism gave to women's education (that is, white middle-class women) provided the foundation for women's political activity much later in the nineteenth century.[22] "The tensions and contradictions," however, as Mary Kelley cautions, "that had been encoded in the idea of the educated woman persisted well into the 19th Century."[23] Such contradictions described a situation where the subject of female intellect was circumscribed by social and political inequities. Consider a woman's "reason" in this context. As we have seen, republican advocates of women's education like Benjamin Rush could endorse the power of female reason only by couching it within women's "natural" vessels of affective piety. In doing so, Rush could go on to exclaim exuberantly that "[mothers] should think justly upon the great subjects of liberty and government!,"[24] and list a regimen of rudimentary knowledge in languages and history as well as light doses of science to prevent "superstition." As Rush's words attest, female reason was itself an agent of a larger, politically utilitarian goal: "It will be in your power, LADIES, to correct the mistakes and practice of our sex on these subjects, by demonstrating that the female temper can only be governed by reason, and that the cultivation of reason in women, is alike friendly to the order of nature, and to private as well as public happiness."[25] Thirty years later, similar commentaries were premised on similar grounds. The second volume of the *American Journal of Education* was filled with articles on theories of female education and new female schools, including ones like "Intellectual Education" (for women) and "Education of Females – Intellectual Instruction."[26] Even so, male writers during this period saw the overly intellectual woman as a scary prospect. Too much reading either debilitated the mind or, in some cases, created a dangerously political woman. Jeremy Belknap, as we have seen, defended Winthrop's severity toward Anne Hutchinson because she was "a woman of masculine understanding and consummate art."[27]

Women writers manipulated the ideal of the *res publica* to expand the domain of female reason. No better case of this is that protofeminist of the post-Revolutionary era, Judith Sargent Murray. The extensions to which she subjected Rush's republican thinking are strikingly apparent in one of the more radical essays of its time, "Desultory Thoughts upon the Utility of encouraging a degree of Self-Complacency, especially in FEMALE BOSOMS" (1784). Writing under the pseudonym of "Constantia" (drawn ambiguously from the classical and Christian worlds), Murray forged her political voice out of traditional republican fears about the cyclical course of history.[28] She marshaled traditionally conspiratorial fears in Whig thinking to promote a radical version of female faculty psychology. Only educated and rational women could fend off "the snares of the artful betrayer" and "the deep laid schemes" of rakish seducers.[29] Playing upon the assumption that women were susceptible to the frivolities of double-tongued deceivers (like Clara, who succumbs to Carwin's vocal powers in Charles Brockden Brown's novel *Wieland*), Murray argued for the political necessity in a republic of nurturing female reason: "I would, from the early dawn of reason, address her as rational being."[30] Only a young girl's respect for her "intellectual existance" [sic] could protect her virtue. In "On the Equality of the Sexes" (1790), Murray indignantly asked, "Are we deficient in reason? We can only reason from what we know, and if an opportunity of acquiring knowledge hath been denied us, the inferiority of our sex cannot fairly be deduced from thence."[31] The precarious republic, in other words, needed sober and stable women to forestall the inevitable process of history.

Early-nineteenth-century American women inherited the ideological tensions of republican womanhood. One should recognize that this cultural discourse was highly contextual, contingent upon immediate purpose, audience, and genre. It could both add radical undertones to naturally conservative voices and constrain naturally radical voices within the conservative limits of republican propriety. The Introduction to an early volume of Sarah Hale's *The Ladies Magazine*, for example, called for "a systematic and thorough education" for women, and later boldly proclaimed (as Hale was not always inclined to do) "that females may not only *attempt* to acquire science, but that they may succeed, and that their knowledge may be alike honorable to themselves, and useful to society."[32] Alternatively, this discourse both empowered *and* circumscribed a naturally iconoclastic sensibility such as Lydia Maria Child's. One of Child's early domestic manuals, *The Mother's Book* (1831), admonishes readers that effective mothering did not require "book-learning": "Good judgment, kind feelings, and habitual command over one's passions, is necessary in the education of children; but learning is not necessary."[33] Child's language is telling, however, when she distinguishes between the irresponsible mother as someone "thoughtless, indolent" and the admirable one who is an "observing woman."[34] This distinction, it later becomes clear, paves the way for an argument aligning good mothering to literacy: "It is not true that intellectual pursuits leave no time to attend to the common concerns of life. . . . It is merely *attention* that is wanted to make the belle literary and the learned lady domestic."[35] Yet if "a real love of reading is the greatest blessing education can bestow, particularly upon a woman," there is still a danger in "the *excessive* love of books."[36] Indeed, throughout this manual there is ongoing, apparently irresolvable tension between the educated and the overintellectual woman. Like Murray, Child is able to promote the need to cultivate women's minds by playing upon fears that women naturally were susceptible to the corruptions of frivolity and fashion.

A third problem within the cultural construct of republican womanhood involves language itself. Traditionally, English Commonwealthmen had excoriated the sins of placemen, stockjobbers and paper credit, and all the while had declaimed "effeminacy" as the bane to republican life. Corruption and indolence, luxury and decay, all were associated with the feminine. Even if, as some have noted, early nationals showed an increasing proclivity for consumerism and material goods, they still simultaneously voiced the dangers of "luxury."[37] Commercialization may have engendered alternative ideologies vis-à-vis consumer goods,[38] but we also should recognize the possibilities for women writers of this older Whig discourse whose ethical oppositions facilitated the argument *against* the objectification of women.

Women writers often manipulated republican ethical dichotomies to masculinize republican womanhood. "Corruption" typically described personal forms of licentiousness, duplicity, indolence, sensuality, and inordinate self-interest that all carried political ramifications. Moreover, these republican sins were traditionally associated with European aristocracy. The importance of female reason derived in large part from the republican ethical dichotomy between the vigorous American republic and an effeminate, aristocratic Europe. To Murray, for example, the dangerous girl is a decidedly feminine one who disregards her "rational being" by fleeing the home for "the sweet perfume of adulation."[39] This kind of woman is nothing more than an aristocratic object ("a polished casket . . . calculated for advantage as well as ornament").[40] Moreover, the major complaint in "On the Equality of the Sexes" involves a skillful manipulation of politicized ethical oppositions to create a new American woman who is neither passive nor objectified:

> And, indeed, in one respect the preeminence seems to be tacitly allowed us, for after an education which limits and confines, and employments and recreations which naturally tend to *enervate* the body, and *debilitate* the mind; after we have from early youth been adorned with ribbons, and other

gewgaws, dressed out like the ancient victims previous to a sacrifice . . . we are introduced to the world, amid the adulation of every beholder.[41]

Consider the androgynous potential of this American woman. Her "natural" piety and affection is coupled with an intellectual sobriety culturally associated with the "masculine." Later women writers negotiated this republican discourse of effeminacy and corruption, manipulating its political implications, and arguing "vigorously" against the objectification of republican women. *The Mother's Book,* for example, expresses Child's disdain for the "fashionable lady, extremely fond of the glitter of dress and equipage" and "an intelligent and judicious woman."[42] Another of Child's domestic tracts, *The Frugal Housewife* (1831), warned against the "vanity, extravagance, and idleness" of women who sacrificed the virtue of domestic work for the finery and flattery of the ballroom.[43] Like many others, Child manipulated a republican vision of cyclical history to accomplish progressive ends for American women: "If the ordinate love of wealth and parade is not checked among us, it will be the ruin of our country, as it has been, and will be, the ruin of thousands of individuals."[44] "A luxurious and idle republic!," she remarked incredulously, "Look at the phrase!"[45] Once women truly embodied this vigorous republican spirit, Catharine Sedgwick suggested, they would begin to establish parity in the republic:

> Think you, my young friends, that if women could talk intelligently and agreeably on these topics [of history and politics], you would see, in a small social party, the men talking party politics on one side of the room, and the women on the other, discussing their domestics, their kitchen affairs, or talking over the fashions . . . ? No – the effect of the intelligent and well directed reading of females would be, to improve the other sex as much as themselves.[46]

But this entire republican discourse of "effeminacy" was nonetheless misogynistic in its construction of the feminine as a moral disease, a kind of absence. One entry for "feminine" in Noah Webster's *American Dictionary* (1828) was "effeminate" or "destitute of manly qualities."[47] In this regard, the *American Dictionary* is a prison house of language for women. "Effeminacy" denoted "womanish softness or weakness," and "effeminate" was associated with political decay: "Having qualities of the female sex; soft or delicate to an unmanly degree; tender; womanish; voluptuous." The accompanying quotation here metonymically connected women, voluptuousness, and luxury: "The King, by his voluptuous life and mean marriage, became effeminate, and less sensible of honor." For this reason, as Lori Ginzberg has shown, those middle-class women, who used the "ideology of benevolent femininity" to critique social relations in an increasingly competitive world, tried to redefine "vice" itself. They translated it from feminine to masculine terms. Licentiousness and luxury were now associated with a masculine greed at the heart of modern liberalism.[48]

Were women writers in any position to write dictionaries during the decades following the Revolution? One might answer this question with a resounding "no," but in what follows I view the "novels" *Hope Leslie* and *Hobomok* as self-conscious recodifications of republican language; dictionaries of sorts. They are political and linguistic projects in refashioning the contemporary republic via the medium of Puritan history, and they exploit the many gendered ambiguities within the office of republican womanhood: the relationship of virtue and citizenship, its possibilities for an androgynous selfhood muddling public and domestic space, the state of female intellect, and the norms of a virtuous marriage. The very instability of language and ideology in the early republic facilitated such revisions. The cultural potential for them was already there (One male critic, for example, admired women writers for their "intellect," "strength," and "judgement").[49] All women writers like Sedgwick and Child had to do was exploit it, recontextualize it, bring its tensions to the surface and tease out their radical implications. So rather than look at women's virtue in the context of the masculine world of capitalism, or retreat to the time-honored cliché that cites the conflict between "individual" and "community,"[50] we might analyze gender politics of the 1820s in the context of the legacy of republicanism. This was the decade, after all, in which Jacksonian politics helped revive masculine myths of the Revolution. In this context, women's historical romance becomes the arena of gendered politics, and literary convention the site of political revision.

Virtue, Community, and Humanity

The praise for *Hope Leslie* in the *North American Review* unwittingly suggests the source of virtually all of the novel's conflicts:

> [E]very patriot and every philanthropist, every well-wisher
> to his country or his kind, should rejoice whenever he sees

those [women writers] who, with the magic wands of poesy and fiction and the potent spells of genius, might lead the spirits of men almost whither they would, and who yet would rather snap their wands asunder . . . than wield them for a moment in league with the powers of darkness.[51]

If the metaphor of the magic wand harkens back to the spell Magawisca casts over Everell Fletcher while recounting the Pequot War, the tension between political duty and universal humanity (the "patriot" and "philanthropist") derives from a deeper (and repressed) conflict between the gendered meanings of virtue in early national culture. But for this reviewer in 1828, as for Rush in the 1780s, the gendered forms of republican ethics were apparently unproblematic.

The novel *Hope Leslie* is founded upon the desire to bring the inconsistencies of this cultural solution to the surface. It does so even before it surveys the American scene. William Fletcher's exodus from England introduces a thematic opposition between political duty (*virtu*) and affective relations. What is the relationship, the novel begins to ask, between political authority and one's social, or even humanitarian, attachments? What might initially appear to be the patented conflict between individual and community actually describes conflicting conceptions of community itself where the domain of the "natural" is contested. The first sacrifice to the classical standard of civic ethics is Alice Fletcher, whose "affection" for Fletcher cannot compete with Fletcher's "duty" to the "great and good cause" of New England, an epithet that, as we have seen in Belknap's *American Biography,* suggests a political typology linking John Winthrop and George Washington.[52]

Sedgwick's skillful debunking of this republican ethos occurs not only through Fletcher's immediate emotional debility but also through the deflation of a cultural myth of the Puritan fathers. Sedgwick contests Puritan otherworldliness. "Fletcher obeyed the voice of Heaven," she claims, and then immediately undercuts this by self-consciously adding, "[t]his is no romantic fiction" (12). The narrator's claim that "[o]ur fathers neither had, nor expected their reward on earth" again immediately is subverted by reference to Fletcher's "severe duty" regarding Alice (12). In other words, part of Sedgwick's investigation into republican civic ethics via Puritanism involves the dismantling of a crucial component of the Ebenezer that, as we have seen, contrasted Bay colony asceticism to Virginian worldliness. Historical revision here implies cultural critique.

The association of Puritanism with contemporary political issues is further suggested by the epithet of "religious republic"
(16) to describe the Puritan commonwealth. Once he is in New
England, however, William Fletcher's continual position on the
commonwealth's periphery makes him one of the many Scott-like
wavering characters (Hope, Everell, Magawisca) inhabiting the
text of *Hope Leslie*. This results as much from an irresolvable
tension between political duty and affection as from Fletcher's
ostensible idealism. That Fletcher is "depressed by some early
disappointment" (16) devilishly suggests *both* his dismay over New
England's shortcomings and his emotional scars derived from a
masculine code whose self-destructiveness he cannot bring himself to acknowledge. Wallowing in the malaise that results from
this unacknowledged conflict, Fletcher retreats from the classical
ethos of the *vita activa*. In Boston "he refused the offices of
honour and trust that were . . . offered to him" (16); in Springfield he "was at first welcomed as an important acquisition to the
infant establishment; but he soon proved that he purposed to
take no part in its concerns, and, in spite of the remonstrances of
the proprietors, he fixed his residence a while from the village"
(17).

Fletcher's sequence of withdrawals is symptomatic of the irrec-
oncilability Sedgwick perceives between the gendered meanings
of republican ethics. The dual modes of masculine self-denial
and feminized selflessness, which conversed so easily in early
national discourse, are set in an uneasy juxtaposition. William
Fletcher's dilemma thus signals the novel's central thematic concerns that call attention to divergent understandings of *communitas*, one marking a strict construction of citizenship and the
other "any branch of the human family" (6). Sedgwick makes
this clear in Magawisca's arrival at Bethel by contrasting William
Fletcher's "mingled feeling of compassion and curiosity" (23)
with his wife's eventual embrace: "This natural domestic reflection [her worry that Magawisca is unsuited for housework] was
soon succeeded by a sentiment of compassion" (24).

The gendered inconsistencies of post-Revolutionary culture
propel *Hope Leslie*'s disruptive plot movements. Politically rebellious acts of the heart move things along in the novel and gradually "center" the text's feminized theme in a way that ruptures its
ethical kindredness (as Rush and others conceived of it) with
Revolutionary *virtu*. Magawisca's sacrifice for Everell finds its parallel in Hope Leslie's liberation of Nelema, which in turn necessi-
tates Magawisca's reappearance in the white community. This

dichotomizing of virtue is expressed in Magawisca's admonition to Mononotto, " 'Oh, my father, has your heart become stone?' " Moreover, feminized virtue provides real political power. Like Antigone, Hope "took counsel only from her own heart, and that told her that the rights of innocence were paramount to all other rights" (120). Christian beneficence, which Hope and Magawisca so vigorously carry into the public sphere, legitimates acts of civil disobedience. This is particularly true for early national readers who were culturally attuned to modern modes of humanitarian republicanism.[53] Feminized virtue specifically gains its power from collapsing the status quo conception of "citizenship," the masculine, communitarian norm, in other words, underpinning the political typology between commonwealth and republic. Paradoxically apolitical and politically affective, female virtue enables Hope (and Magawisca) to function as viable agents of protest. Sedgwick did not really redefine "republican" behavior for women; rather she radically recontextualized it, manipulating its latent contradictions.

In light of the position John Winthrop maintained in the early republic's historical writing, his role in *Hope Leslie* significantly counters feminized rebellion with a communitarian ethos founded upon the distinction between citizen and noncitizen. Sedgwick's governor is implicitly a rewriting of Belknap's and others' political typology between Winthrop and George Washington:

> Our humble history has little to do with the public life of Governor Winthrop, which is so well known to have been illustrated by the rare virtue of disinterested patriotism. . . . On the whole, we must confess, the external man presents the solemn and forbidding aspect of the times in which he flourished; though we know him to have been a model of private virtue, gracious and gentle in his manners, and exact in the observance of all gentlemanly courtesy. (144)

The passage would seem to displace the public Winthrop with the private one of civilized sociability, thereby exemplifying a "modern" (and feminized) form of virtue appropriate to an enlightened republic. But the novel actually goes on to do just the opposite. Most important here is the rhetorical yoking together of "disinterested" and "patriotism." It parodies, in a Bakhtinian sense, the monologic discourse of Puritan virtue in nationalist historiography. "Patriotism," as Noah Webster defined it in 1828, "is the character of good citizens, the noblest passion that animates a *man in the character of a citizen.*"[54] Derived from "pater" (or father), a patriot is one who "loves his country" and "zealously supports and defends it in its interests." "Patriotic" similarly meant "[i]nspired by the love of one's country; directed to the public safety and welfare; as patriotic zeal." Much later on, I take up the problematics of such patriotic zealotry, but for now one should recognize how Sedgwick begins in the portrait of Winthrop to interrogate the meaning of "disinterestedness" that contemporary historians associated with aristocratic authority and communitarian politics.[55]

As in Belknap's *American Biography,* the John Winthrop of *Hope Leslie* exemplifies an outmoded communitarian ideal. The political authority Winthrop wields also involves the desire to control, to homogenize, language itself. He is, in the Bakhtinian sense, the chief centripetal force in the novel. One might read the conflict between Winthrop and Hope Leslie (and later Everell) in just these sociolinguistic terms. Hope's language attempts to destabilize and pull apart the monological language of *communitas* sustaining republican ideology. It is no surprise, then, that Hope is forced by Winthrop to reside at the center of community – the Winthrop household – a place even Fletcher admits is "the narrow path." This is both a linguistic and physical movement, revealing Winthrop's dual attempts to contain linguistic entropy and to get Hope married to the right man. Hope resists "unitary" or "correct" language, which is coterminous with "the processes of sociopolitical and cultural centralization." In subverting the Winthropian boundaries of disinterestedness, she exposes the "heteroglot national language" (the tongues of the Algonquians during colonial times, or the voices of Georgia's Cherokees who were being removed from their land during the Jacksonian era) beneath the monological cant of the commonwealth/republic. Hence the language of Christian benevolence in the novel and the actual jailbreak of Nelema (and later Magawisca) should be seen as parallel acts of emancipation. These competing notions of disinterestedness textualize themselves in the many arguments among Fletcher, Winthrop, Hope, Everell, and others as "a contradiction-ridden, tension-filled unity of two embattled tendencies in the life of language."[56]

Hope and Fletcher negotiate these conflicting discourses in very different ways. Hope's rebelliousness works to bring Winthrop into conflict with Fletcher, who in turn succumbs to Winthrop's appeal to his lingering sense of public reputation. (What would people say, Winthrop suggests to him, if Hope were to

marry Everell? Fletcher the golddigger!) Fletcher gets weepy, recovers, admits that ever since childhood "my path hath been
hedged up with earthly affections" (152), but eventually "surren-
der[s] to "the public good" (161). As the scene concludes, the
narrative loses its tense satirical irony when Sedgwick intrudes to
reappraise the tenets of "disinterested patriotism" for which the
Puritans in general and Winthrop in particular were praised so
consistently during her own era. "Whatever gratified the natural
desires of the heart was questionable, and almost every thing that
was difficult and painful, assumed the form of duty" (156).

Hope is indeed Sedgwick's last hope to oppose and expose the
early republic's discourse of Puritan order. Fletcher succumbs to
it; Everell only gradually escapes from it (making him a fit spouse
in the end); even Magawisca wavers in the face of its Native
American version of civic duty. Hope, on the other hand, is
distinguished from her main foil, Esther Downing, by her capacity
to reinterpret the political meaning of "duty," a capacity involving
both her affective *and* intellectual faculties. Unlike Esther, who is
"without one truant wish straying beyond the narrow bound of
domestic duty and religious exercises" (136), and whose "strict-
ness was a submission to duty" (272), Hope refuses to acknowledge the legitimacy of the Puritan/republican ethos. During the
scene where she has just met Magawisca, Hope returns "home" to
the Winthrop domain soaking wet and with no ready explanation
of where she has been. All eyes fall upon her in an image of
communal monitorship. But at this moment Hope resists Winthrop's argument that her behavior might besmirch Fletcher's
public reputation: " 'I care not how sternly – how harshly I am
judged; but I see not why my fault, even if I had committed
one, should cast a shadow upon you" (176). This scene later is
paralleled by her second confrontation with Winthrop, when she
pleads mercy for Magawisca. In context of Winthrop's metaphoric
status among early national conservatives, we can see that the
scene ironically creates political–cultural irony when Winthrop
tells Hope, "I am no king" (273). Hope's argument, moreover,
justifying her plea for Magawisca, politicizes Christian benevolence via a republican language that Sedgwick deftly manipulates.
Winthrop asks her on what grounds she defends Magawisca. " 'On
what?' exclaimed Hope. 'On her merits, and rights' " (273).

This redefinition of republican ethics in *Hope Leslie* simultaneously reinvents republican language. Indeed, the novel's
language is anachronistic, which renders problematic its representational status of Puritanism per se. Consider, for example,

Sedgwick's treatment of the objections both Everell and Hope offer in refusing to follow the "commonwealth" code of civic virtue. In the first passage Everell complains to his father about the proscription to marry Hope; in the second, Hope defends her rebellion against Winthrop to Esther:

> "But, once for all, I entreat you not to dispose of us as if we were mere machines: we owe you our love and reverence."
> (162)

> "As to advice, it needs to be very carefully administered, to do any good, else it's like an injudicious patch, which, you know, only makes the rent worse; – and as to authority, I would not be a machine, to be moved at the pleasure of anybody that happened to be a little older than myself."
> (180)

What would Benjamin Rush say in response? Both Everell and Hope have refused to become what he promised would be the "republican machine" of America, the pure, mechanically reliable embodiment of civic virtue produced in theory by the right regimen of education.[57] Rush's medical training in Edinburgh had exposed him to Common Sense epistemology and ethics, which he revised in largely nationalist terms, arguing essentially that citizens could be nurtured from an early age to divest themselves of personal concerns in conflict with the *res publica*. In this context, the language of the novel inscribes gendered tensions within the rubric of "republicanism." Through her mouthpieces, Hope and Everell, Sedgwick voices her own immediate fears of this mechanized ideal of civic ethics, the Revolutionary-era equivalent of the citizen-as-Timex. The citizen's moral, physical, and political health were inextricably related, Rush theorized, and a healthy citizen was characterized by an automatic civic selflessness. Those chronic complaints offered by Hope and Everell explore the darker implications of self-regulation in post-Revolutionary civic culture, a quality that Puritanism buttressed in its role as a cultural metaphor for rational liberty and corporate politics.[58]

Whatever influence Sir Walter Scott may have had on Sedgwick's work, her treatment of Magawisca as a "wavering" heroine should be understood in terms of its immediate cultural resonance. The novel's analysis of gendered forms of republican virtue tends to bifurcate what early national culture placed along a continuum. It accomplishes this by highlighting very different conceptions of *communitas*. Magawisca's crisis over loyalties during the massacre at Bethel introduces an unresolved dilemma between her "resolution" to her people and "the entreaties of her own heart." For much of the novel, even after she betrays Mrs. Fletcher's maternal love but atones for it in sacrificing an arm for Everell, Magawisca painfully embodies these multivalent meanings of "virtue." She is, in this sense, like the early republican word, a signifier of entangled political meanings. As if by osmosis, her constant companionship with Mononotto makes her susceptible to his "melancholy," and makes her "obedient to the impulse of his spirit" (194). The narrator's assessment of her double consciousness (not unlike Emily Dickinson's ambiguous relationship to "Father") further demonstrates the mutually exclusive nature of republican and humanitarian modes of relation: "Her tenderness for Everell, and her grateful recollections of his lovely mother, she determined to sacrifice on the altar of national duty" (194–5).

The novel's correlation of feminized virtue with female power is poignantly shown in an important scene where Magawisca confronts that aristocratic rogue Sir Philip Gardiner in prison. Faced with the dilemma of saving herself at the expense of Gardiner's concubine, Rosa, Magawisca's Christian altruism shows emancipatory power from both her real and symbolic prisons. " 'And dost thou think,' " she admonishes Gardiner, " 'that I would make my heart as black as thine, to save my life? – life! Dost thou not know, that life can only be abated by those evil deeds forbidden by the Great Master of life?' " (257). In the face of such an "unsullied" humanitarianism, Gardiner's "heart quail[s]," his skepticism about "the existence of uncorrupted virtue" (255) collapses, and he scurries away an emasculated figure. If Magawisca here expresses the sentiments of that well-known Calvinist apostate Catharine Sedgwick (" 'Good God! the girl hath truly spoken of life!' " [258], Gardiner admits), liberal theology in this case is in keeping with a realignment of power that feminized virtue affords. And this, we should recognize, is *political* virtue; it theoretically ensures the survival of the republic. Think about the events that follow: Only Magawisca's selfless love for Rosa manages to unmask the conspiratorial villain, Gardiner, dislodging his crucifix, which is a nifty plot device and the key factor that sinks him later in court. Moreover, in Sedgwick's mind, or at least in her novel, the consummate virtue of female chastity affords female power. It is a positive, active construction, not passive, defensive. In their relations with Gardiner, both Rosa, the fallen woman, and Magawisca are doubled as contrasting versions of women who confront the "baffled tempter" (262). The contrast suggests that the sanctity of the female body inextricably is linked to the power of selfless love.[59]

Gendered thematics shape as well the novel's disjointed narrative structure. Time and again, Sedgwick implicitly challenges her reader by laying epistemological traps. The implied reader of *Hope Leslie* constantly is led to misperceive, to judge too quickly, and, through this disorienting process, to reexamine the virtue of masculine vigilance itself. The text's narrative gaps and chronological ruptures consistently frustrate readerly cognition of both character and plot. Nelema's escape, Hope's behavior at church, the identity of Rosa, the reasons for Magawisca's reappearance, and the chase scene and explosion in the end, all destabilize the reading process by exposing our own limitations as readers. This is done not to fulfill any kind of Melvillean quandary of epistemology, but to subvert the conspiratorial paranoia at the heart of classical republicanism. Sedgwick has a lot of fun with this. At moments she assumes a deadpan narrative seriousness that lightly mocks her readers' confusion – "It would be highly improper any longer to keep our readers in ignorance of the cause of our heroine's apparent aberration from the line of strict propriety" (182) – and that defamiliarizes them of republican civic norms. Misperception erodes the value of vigilance. When Hope, for example, finally returns to the governor's mansion, the various characters' reactions to her "impropriety" (Cradock's and Mrs. Winthrop's compassion, Winthrop's stern but mitigated judgment, Esther's oscillations) stage our alternative choices as readers. Sedgwick compounds this by dramatizing as well her characters' misperceptions of events (Everell's judgment of Hope and Gardiner, Hope's of Everell and Esther, Magawisca's mistaken belief in Everell's abandonment of her) in order to advance the critique of a strict communitarian ideal. The implied reader is a duped one who self-reflexively witnesses his, or her, own misjudgments and thereby embraces the text's thematic offer of a humane benevolence.

Nowhere is the novel's indictment of whiggish communitarianism more ironically biting than in its representation of Gardiner. Whereas Belknap's Winthrop explicitly is praised for weeding out conspiracies, Sedgwick's cannot see them right in front of his face. Masquerading as "a self-denying puritan" (200), Gardiner temporarily succeeds in gaining the magistracy's "most confidential intimacy" (205). Here, again, *Hope Leslie* parodically engages the monological discourse of nationalist histories in order to deflate a traditional republican ideal of political leadership. The satiric role of Gardiner works on multiple levels. By contrasting Winthrop's naive trust in "this stranger" with his exclusion of his wife ("his trust-worthy partner") from political matters, Sedgwick debunks republican vigilance. In doing so, she interrogates classical political assumptions, specifically its understandings of masculine citizenship and separate gender spheres. Moreover, Gardiner's success with the magistracy results from his ability to manipulate these conspiratorial fears endemic to Whig thinking: "Sir Philip had heard the rumor of a conspiracy among the natives; and when he saw Magawisca's extreme anxiety to secure a clandestine interview with Miss Leslie . . . [he calculated that] he was in possession of a secret that might be of value to the state" (247). Gardiner succeeds because he manipulates this discourse so well: " 'Scruple not, honest master Tuttle,' " he tells the jailer, just as he has told Winthrop at the dinner table, and the magistrates in court, " 'duty takes no note of time and place' " (252).

But such satire has its limits. In many ways, *Hope Leslie* curiously inscribes the very ideologies it deflates, showing once again the political significance of literary convention. Its version of the seduction novel's rake is particularly politicized in that Gardiner represents those *European* forms of vice and corruption that Americans tenuously claimed they had purged. The language describing Gardiner's physiognomy is particularly resonant in this regard; as a text in itself, it signifies (to those like Sedgwick, and unlike Winthrop, who can read it clearly) "the ravages of the passions" and the "designing purpose" of some "bon-vivant" (124). His aristocratic status, sexual depravity, his "fine cambric ruff," all encode fears of cultural invasion – the threat of moral and political degeneracy – that Sedgwick mocks in the novel's Puritan authorities. Hope Leslie's potential rapists, Sir Philip and the drunken band of Italian sailors, are associated with European vice. Moreover, the text is soaked in Whiggish conspiracies. Native Americans (Miantunnomoh, Chicatabot) plot against the English. Gardiner's plan to abduct Hope is the product of "the wicked designs of the conspirators" (337). The verse quotation that encapsulates Sir Philip Gardiner's "designing purpose" – " 'That all his circling wiles should end / In feigned religion, smooth hypocrisy' " (249) – would seem, then, to confirm fears that are otherwise debunked. This paradox perhaps reveals the lurking anxieties characterizing the 1820s,[60] which made, for many early nationals anyway, the future of the republic an uncertain thing. In a world of Gardiners, republican vigilance would seem to be necessary.

The context I have been drawing in this chapter need not homogenize all of the era's women's writing. One might, as a point of contrast, compare Sedgwick's novel to Delia Bacon's *The Regicides*, a novella published in 1831 as part of *Tales of the Puritans*. Like Sedgwick, Bacon demonstrates the ways in which Puritan/republican vigilance persecutes the politically disenfranchised, in this case the tale's protagonist, Margaret Weldon, who actually spends her time secretly aiding the fugitive regicides. Bacon's treatment of the regicide theme (a subject to which I return in Chapters 4 and 5) not only creates a serious political role for Margaret but also notably adds a woman, Isabella Goffe, to the list of regicides. Bacon has one of them, Edward Whalley, legitimate Margaret's superiority as a political actor vis-à-vis Puritan community: " 'The magistrates of the colony have refused to furnish any concealment; and the kindness of a private individual, even if discovered, would never bring ruin upon this people.' "[61] As Margaret conscripts Henry Davenport into aiding the three, she and her sister, Alice, suffer the community's "subtle spirit of popular superstition," which, according to popular rumor, makes *them* agents of the Prince of Darkness. As in *Hope Leslie, The Regicides'* penchant for political irony reveals its dialogue with the early national equation between Puritanism and republicanism. Unlike Sedgwick, however, Bacon's line of argument suggests only the inadequacy of such an equation rather than its faulty premises. Bacon's Puritan women, in other words, better exemplify the republican spirit than colonial men:

> But it is not to be supposed that a confederacy of intelligent females was to be outwitted by a couple of unassisted strangers [the royal agents]; for, though the magistrates of the colony had refused to furnish further concealment of the regicides, the helpmates of said magistrates in the true spirit of republicanism, secretly declared that resolutions which they had no share in forming, should not be considered as binding upon themselves.[62]

Bacon effectively voices a complaint about female disenfranchisement, but does so within a more traditional framework. Puritan women, and especially Margaret Weldon, outdo their male counterparts at their game. Bacon makes virtue possible for good republican women, but in less creative terms than does Sedgwick.

The political connotations that republicanism lent to Puritanism inform as well the central image of the circle in Lydia Child's *Hobomok*. Throughout the novel the circle symbolizes the pathology of a masculine communitarian ideal and, as in Sedgwick, questions arbitrary constructions of citizenship. Like Miriam Grey of Harriet Cheney's rather pedestrian *Peep at the Pilgrims* (1824), Mary Conant is victimized by the monological extension of this thinking. The daughter of Roger Conant, one of Naumkeag's chief magistrates, Mary herself foreshadows her ambiguous exile/removal by symbolically drawing her own circle in the ground. She tellingly composes this text, of sorts, outside of the community's field of attention, in a wilderness into which she has ambiguously "plunged."[63] Later, her friendship with the capricious and less intellectual Sally Oldham directly results from "the disheartening influence of the stern, dark circle in which she moved" (36). A "circle" of elders, moreover, entraps her at home (36). In this vein, the exchanges of affection between Mary and Sally most often take place on the periphery of community. Later, when word of the death of Charles Brown (Mary's Episcopalian suitor who has been exiled by Conant) reaches New England, it moves "like an electric shock through an united circle" (117). This symbolic motif suggests Child's revisions of Puritan and republican order, an ethos that precipitates the downward spiral of the plot, forcing a series of exiles that lead Mary into a condition which, as we shall see, Child could not accept.

To summarize at this point: Women's historical romances reimagine political modes of relation within a republic. And one might conclude this section by noting an uncanny resemblance between early republican women and contemporary feminists vis-à-vis masculine constructions of "the public sphere." Both vehemently contest its viability as a hermeneutic tool. *Hobomok* and *Hope Leslie* assail the misogynistic ramifications of public, masculine citizenship. The interrogation and reconstruction of "public" and "political" behavior strikingly parallels the reevaluations by contemporary feminists of Jurgen Habermas's theory of the development of a bourgeois public sphere during the late-seventeenth and eighteenth centuries.[64] Mary Ryan recently has summarized this dissent: "Noting that theories of the public rarely take cognizance of gender differences and that classic republicanism was overtly disdainful of women, some contemporary feminist thinkers reject the concept itself as patriarchy parading as universalism. ... Feminist political theorists push at the boundaries of the public by holding that sphere to the highest standards of open-

ness, accessibility, tolerance of diversity, and capacity to acknowledge the needs of a heterogeneous membership."[65] Both early
national and contemporary complaints about classical ideology,
then, question the viability of a narrowly masculine understanding of the public. In this sense Hope and Magawisca are the
forebears of today's gender-based, progressive historiography.

The New Man

The revisions of citizenship in *Hope Leslie* and *Hobomok* are in
keeping with their reconsiderations of republican manhood. As
we have seen, classical *virtu* still retained currency during this era,
especially in tales of Puritan military heroism that anticipated
the Revolutionary War. Certainly Andrew Jackson exploited this
cultural phenomenon of frontier republicanism, as he cultivated
a political persona out of a series of private and public battles he
fought to secure both personal honor and political independence. But part of the reason that Jefferson and others saw Jackson as a dangerous man was precisely the crude, recidivist quality
of this persona. In many ways it violated the self-consciously modern notions of gentility to which the Revolutionary generation
aspired.[66] A proponent of this argument, however, admits that if
affection and benevolence became the new adhesives of republican life, "[t]he revolutionaries [still] went great lengths to fulfill
classical values and create suitable classical personae."[67] In other
words, these two behavioral styles accompanied and competed
with one another in early republican culture.

    This ambiguous legacy facilitated strategies of androgyny
which *Hobomok* and *Hope Leslie* undertake. Both Charles Brown
and Everell Fletcher ultimately emerge at the end of these novels
as rather androgynized (rather than simply emasculated) figures.
But if these heroes of romance recall the eighteenth-century man
of feeling (Pleyel in Brown's *Wieland,* for example), they do far
more than merely promote male sentiment. Sedgwick and Child
deftly manipulate the period's unstable discourses of virtue to
create androgynous reformulations of hero and heroine alike, at
once feminizing republican manhood and co-opting masculine
political languages to invent female figures who carry domestic
virtue into the public sphere. Such conflations were possible
because of the very instability of early republican language.

    The feminization of republican manhood takes place in these
novels within the larger cultural context of metaphorical Puritanism. The Founders' heroic migration, their industrious auster-

ity, their antimaterialist drives, their military valor: All these "virtues" were premised on a masculine domain of public behavior and hence a narrow understanding of republican citizenship. As we have seen, even the disparate likes of Henry Ware and Lyman Beecher, who preached in different ways the virtue of universal benevolence, still managed to find in Puritanism a masculine ideal of the *res publica*. An exclusionary understanding of republican disinterestedness is evident as well in Noah Webster's careful distinction between two types of republican "vigor": "Vigor and all its derivatives imply active strength, or the power of action and exertion, in distinction from passive strength, or strength to endure." The latter better described a virtuous and pious woman.[68]

Hobomok and *Hope Leslie* invert this political discourse and reconstitute the contexts for republican language. Early on in *Hobomok*, Child deftly manipulates the romantic marriage plot to suggest that Hobomok might be a suitable companion for Mary. In doing so, she suggests to her readers through a recognizable rhetoric that he, despite his race, is the right republican man. Before his ultimate dismissal from the text, Hobomok combines the manly vigor and capacity for feeling that Revolutionary culture had validated. The rhetoric that essentializes him in these terms – his "manly beauty" (36), "vigor and elasticity" (84), "vigorous elegance of proportion" (36), along with the sensitive "heart-strings" (33) for which Corbitant taunts him (" 'Hobomok saves his tears for the white-faced daughter of Conant"[33]) – pursue the unspoken logic of republican manhood to highlight the androgynous potential of a cultural ideal. Child manages to extricate Hobomok from Wampanoags and Narragansets alike, bringing him into a post-Revolutionary world now in itself transformed by the power of domestic love.

Yet this displacement reveals problems over how and where to place the androgynous Native American man. Child oscillates between her willingness to use Hobomok as a foil for Puritan/ republican manhood and her fear of where such a literary tactic may lead. Hobomok's representation thus oscillates between the unlettered savage (his near murder of Corbitant; the night deer-hunt that repulses Mary) and the "vigorous" man whose devoted love leads him to watch over Mary's home "with eyes that knew no slumber" (41). A strange occurrence devolves from this: When Hobomok recites to Mary the legend of Tatobem (the Pequot sachem torn between conjugal affections and political duty), he actually is narrating his own autobiography. His feminization, presumably like Child's male reader, results from exposure to the influence of the hearth: "His long residence with the white inhabitants of Plymouth had changed his natural fierceness of manner into haughty, dignified reserve; and even that seemed softened as his dark, expressive eye rested on Conant's daughter" (36). James Fenimore Cooper, as I argue in the next chapter, created Conanchet as a way of revising this androgynous formula.

Before Child is able to displace Hobomok, however, Charles Brown must undergo a similar feminization. What first emerges as a theological conflict between Brown and the magistracy eventually takes shape as a political struggle in which all of the male participants seem to suffer from the same sins. Both Charles and Mr. Conant are guilty, ironically enough, of that most egregious of Christian sins, pride; both fail to acknowledge worldly motives (e.g., Conant's religious conversion occurs amid "financial misfortune and poverty" [8], and Brown desires to see England's " 'antique grandeur and cultivated beauty' " [73]). Child decidedly grants them equivalence: "Men so entirely uncongenial as Brown and his companions could not long tolerate each other. . . . Perhaps he and his adversaries equally mistook the pride of human opinion, for conscientious zeal" (69). Readers typically understand these theological polemics as part of Child's (amorphously) Unitarian disdain for theological rigor. But they resonate politically as well: "You . . . are accused of fomenting disturbance among the people," Endicott tells Brown as he is cast outside of the circle of community (70).

Brown's exposure to the domestic hearth, specifically Mrs. Conant's brand of Unitarian ethics and domestic virtue, ultimately transforms him. By eventually embracing her belief that " 'a humble heart was more than a strong mind' " (76), Brown is significantly changed during the second altercation with Conant:

> Pride was struggling hard for utterance, as Brown moved towards the door; but for Mary's sake it was repressed – and before the old man was aware of his purpose, he stept back and took the hand of the mother and daughter, as he said,
> "God bless you both. To me you have been all kindness."
> (77)

Even if Child does not endorse Mrs. Conant as the contemporary norm for republican womanhood – her passivity is, after all, self-destructive – she significantly nurtures Brown's capacity for "chastened tenderness" (63). This makes him Hobomok's double, as Carolyn Karcher has noted, but the transformation occurs not during Brown's exile from New England, as Karcher claims, but here at the Conant hearth where Brown's "manly" nature (63, 71) is injected with a requisite dose of domestic virtue.[69] The change enables him later to forgive Mary, show kindness to her child, even weep. It frees him from the prison of *virtu*, as Child conceives of it, and the text of *Hobomok* from Hobomok himself.

Sedgwick's characterization of Everell similarly recontextualizes the republic's gendered values. From the moment Sedgwick dramatizes the success of Magawisca's history of the Pequot War to enliven Everell's moral sense, she inaugurates a reconstruction of the new republican man. This involves similar modifications of republican language as Child's. "The active hardy habits of life, in a new country, had already knit [Everell's] frame, and given him the muscle of manhood" (22). Everell's feminized traits, however, come to subsume and destabilize a recognizably republican type. He shows "instinctive [read: natural] sympathy for Magawisca" upon her arrival (26). Later, during his captivity, his "burst of natural and not unmanly tears" (87) offers a foil for Mononotto's patriarchal heart of stone.

Thus begins *Hope Leslie*'s redefinition of Revolutionary manhood. During Everell's captivity, it is only the biblical counsels of youth that now comfort him. This is contrasted distinctly with the failure of patriarchal *communitas:* "He might have been agitated by the admission of the least ray of hope; but hope was utterly excluded, and it was only when he thought of his bereft father, that his courage failed him" (88). The implied transitive logic here is crucial for sorting out the relative forces of gender, for it takes place in context of the larger rhetorical fabric in early America. Everell's manly "courage" oddly is associated in this case with passive and faithful submission – or, in other words, with female virtue. Such a maneuver in effect reverses the gendered distinctions for "vigor" that Webster drew in the 1828 *American Dictionary*. This strategy of pinning masculine signifiers on the signified of domestic ideals is continued later on during Magawisca's jailbreak. Here Everell (as opposed to Esther) is said to possess a "manly, generous nature" (329) specifically *because* he rebels against political authority in the name of Christian altruism. Sedgwick devilishly goes on to conflate the discourses of benevolence and republicanism by playing upon that consummate republican virtue of "gratitude," which would bind citizens to their leaders in a cohesive republican order. Everell wishes only to prove to Magawisca "the constancy of his friendship and the warmth of his gratitude" (329).

One might further collapse the status of "Puritanism" by comparing these texts to literary treatments of the American Revolution: Child's *The Rebels, or Boston Before the Revolution* (1825) and Sedgwick's *The Linwoods, or "Sixty Years Since" in America* (1835). Their strikingly similar thematic designs attest to the contemporary historicity of discourses of Puritanism and Revolutionary America. The Revolutionary romances only more obviously engage those cultural icons of masculinity that inhabit, for example, Royall Tyler's *The Contrast* (1787). Both *The Rebels* and *The Linwoods* pursue the androgynous logic of Tyler's representation of American manhood, the synthesis of manly vigor and humanitarian sentiment that distinguishes Colonel Manly and (albeit comically) Jonathan from their European counterparts Dimple and Jessamy. In *The Rebels* the Yankee yeoman does not so much lose his iconic status as accrue a wider range of meanings. The potential for androgyny emerges when John (a descendent of the Puritan Thomas Dudley) at one moment picks up his infant son, Hancock. "[T]aking the child from his mother, and rocking him gently in his arms," John hopes his boy will grow up to be as honorable as his namesake.[70] One might take this fictive moment as symbolic of changes in this era. The transferral of child from mother to father stands for the larger cultural feminization of republican virtue, which takes place in the home – or, to pursue this metaphor – in the domain of women's writing.

In *The Linwoods,* Sedgwick also performs ideological surgery on Revolutionary iconography. The transformation of the hero, Eliot Lee, a descendant of "one of the renowned *pilgrim fathers,*"[71] initiates the text's sweeping reappraisals of republicanism. What charts the patriot hero's necessary transformation is his growing sensitivity to his sister's sensibility. When informed of her grief over being jilted by Jasper Meredith, Eliot in his letter to Bessie admits that he has forsaken his "duty" to his sister because of "political subjects," thus implicating him in Bessie's madness. Despite his good intentions, however, Revolutionary politics preempt Eliot's ability to connect with Bessie, which only makes her worse. Eventually, his "sense" of her grief signals *The Linwoods'* evolving transformation of republican manhood: "Eliot's manliness was vanquished, and he wept like a child over his sister's letter. He reproached himself for having left home."[72] On her deathbed, this transformation becomes complete: "Eliot, left alone and quite unmanned, poured out his heart over this victim of vanity and heartlessness."[73] In the same vein, *The Linwoods* continues this process on the actual historical figures inhabiting the text. For instance the Marquis de Lafayette embodies an exemplary "measure of human benevolence,"[74] while Washington himself reaffirms "the imperative dictates of humanity" when he tells Eliot, " 'No, my friend, – no . . . war too often cuts us off from the humanities.' "[75]

The elasticity of republican language allowed as well for an androgynous form of republican womanhood. David S. Reynolds has suggested as much, noting that the typical liberal protagonist of these novels has " 'masculine' qualities [of] strength and perseverance . . . and [a] 'feminine' inclination to simplicity and warmth."[76] However, in light of the notably conservative strain, of so much Unitarian discourse (the orations we have seen, for example, by William Emerson and Henry Ware, Sr.), gender politics would seem to be a more germane context than sectarian differences for portraits of modern womanhood. In this sense, *Hope Leslie* engrafts a masculine-republican language on its female heroines, casting benevolence as an active virtue rather than a passive abstraction. Hope, who boldly tells Gardiner at one point, " 'I have no fears,' " demonstrates this in her uncompromising devotion to her sister: "The thought of danger or exposure never entered [Hope's] mind, for she was not addicted to fear" (186).

Similarly, in *The Linwoods,* Isabella Linwood's response to an innocent victim incarcerated in a Tory jail renders a republican heroine masculine qualities that sanctify her transgression:

> Some young ladies would have rested satisfied with dropping a few pitiful tears over such a mischance; but Isabella Linwood was of another temper; and having no male friend on whom she could rely, she went herself to the prison, and easily obtained access to the prisoner's cell.[77]

The classical allusions characterizing Hope Leslie and Isabella – Hebe, Camilla, Juno – empower female heroism through their associations with protection, youth, and "masculine" activities like hunting and warfare. Rather than questioning essentialist formulas of masculinity and femininity, Sedgwick brilliantly conflates them. This strategy informs the treatment of Magawisca during her trial where she quotes Patrick Henry (" 'I demand of thee death or liberty' " [293]) and is likened to Admiral Nelson. The drama and pathos of Magawisca's speech is exceeded only by the scene's shimmering political ironies. The parallel between Native American angel and patriotic hero implicitly recontextualizes the political typology between colonial and Revolutionary America. As the colonial type to Patrick Henry, Magawisca's Christian beneficence displaces *virtu* with the workings of the heart – a form of virtue no less political than its antitype.

By rehistoricizing America, women writers dialogically engaged masculine historiography. Their revisions sometimes openly model the histories that they aim to subvert. Just as explicit as Sedgwick's rewriting of Patrick Henry is Delia Bacon's direct response to Ezra Stiles's *A History of Three of the Judges of Charles I* (1794) – a text included in *Tales of the Puritans'* Appendix (and which I discuss in the next two chapters). In Bacon's *The Regicides,* the male fugitives become androgynous figures, while Isabella Goffe actually takes the most vigorously active role. Only the memory of home and hearth sustains Goffe in his darkest hours, and Whalley confirms that Isabella's tenderness and affection has sustained the regicides during their flight. Their feminization revises Ezra Stiles's attempt to credit Whalley's display of "real, rational, and manly virtue" as well as "valor and military knowledge."[78] Meanwhile, Isabella strengthens her father's resolve, daringly roams the mountain, spots the horses with which Whalley and she eventually escape the cavaliers, faints during their escape – but recovers! And she accomplishes all of this while still (ostensibly) remaining true to her domestic virtues (" 'I will kneel at the foot of [King Charles's] throne, and weary him with tears and prayers till he grants me your pardon' ").[79] *The Regicides* confuses the contexts for patriotism and benevolence, for public and private spheres of "republican" behavior. In the process domestic virtue becomes a political activity.

Even as women writers contested a classical tradition, they revealed their indebtedness to it. One sees the ambiguous relations between republicanism and domesticity in the subject of "effeminacy." Women played creatively upon this word, shaping it to their own immediate needs. They pulled a terrific rhetorical maneuver: By inverting republican associations of luxury and corruption with the "feminine" they were able to masculinize female heroism. Isabella Linwood, for example, defends her plan for civil disobedience in terms that at once confirm and confuse her cultural role: " 'God grant that the affections thus cast back upon me may not degenerate to morbid sensibility or pining selfishness, but they may be employed *vigorously* for the good of my fellow beings."[80] In *The Rebels* Child similarly notes that the unconventional Lucretia Fitzherbert has a mind as "vigorous as an eagle's wing."[81] As we have seen, this Revolutionary key word derived, as Noah Webster noted, from the Saxon *wigan,* and so its net effect in women's writing is to empower republican womanhood. It does so through a republican opposition between virtue and corruption. Women's writing in this case translates misogyny into androgyny.

This shows the pliable qualities of Revolutionary-era ethical oppositions. Women writers deployed classical discourse in unique ways that served to work against the objectification of woman; they did so by associating the passive, deintellectualized woman with European cultural degeneracy. If, as some have suggested, women's rights activists during the 1840s exploited a Revolutionary cant of liberty,[82] earlier women writers just as vigorously shaped an elastic language of virtue. The issue of luxury provides a salient case for this. In one sense, *Hobomok* comically debunks republican fears of aristocratic luxury. The scorn Roger Conant and John Oldham have for "French gew-gaws" (a term, we may recall, Judith Sargent Murray uses to argue against the objectification of women) is merely a self-serving means to secure patriarchal power. Yet *The Rebels,* much like the frontier captivity narrative, stages Lucretia's rites of passage, which entail her undergoing a temporary Europeanization in order to establish herself among the enlightened stabilities of republican life. In the English House of Fitzherbert, Lucretia is reduced to what she admits is "the prop of his house," and only on her return to America does she recover "her native firmness and energy."[83] Isabella Linwood's passage is no different: She moves from "the mirror of fashion" to "no thrall of fashion,"[84] the "discipline of life" ultimately establishing her superiority to Europeanized women like Helen Ruthven and Lady Ann Seton.

Hope Leslie's paradoxical treatment of luxury works in the same way. The novel obviously satirizes John Cotton's sermons against ostentatious displays of wealth, since he, like Winthrop, represents the centripetal forces of language and attention. Yet Hope's moral and intellectual superiority to Mrs. Grafton is cast in traditionally republican terms. This results from Grafton's preoccupation with refinement and dress – which, we should recall, requires Digby to accompany her on one of her shopping sprees and thus exposes the Fletcher home to massacre. Her readers, Sedgwick declares, should take note of Hope's judiciousness in this regard:

Neither could any thing in outward show, be more unlike a modern belle, arrayed in mode de Paris of the last Courier des dames, than Hope Leslie, in her dress of silk or muslin. . . .
Fashion had no shrines among the pilgrims; but where

she is most abjectly worshipped, it would be treason against
the paramount rights of nature, to subject such a figure as
Hope Leslie's to her tyranny. (121–2)

Hope's resistance to the "tyranny" of fashion is politicized deliberately to confuse the meaning of Jeffersonian natural rights. Are
they political rights, such as life, liberty, and the pursuit of happiness? Are they the rights of the heart, the expression of universal
benevolence? In politicizing fashion to mark the gap between
political citizenship and the human family under the eye of
Nature's God, Sedgwick nevertheless shows her indebtedness to
the Whiggish opposition between Old and New Worlds. The
same ideology of luxury, then, that patriarchal authority uses to
perpetuate itself, *Hope Leslie* refashions to destroy the idea of
woman as ornament. In this way she devilishly exposes the inconsistencies of America's sacred political texts.

Bakhtin understands the novel to be the site of social and
political contention, the place where multiple discourses destabilize and interanimate linguistic meaning. Early national culture
tried to stabilize the meaning of "virtue" along the lines of gender, which, coupled with the institutional balance established by
the Constitution of 1787–8, presumably guaranteed the republic's future viability. The textual world of women's historical romance, however, exposes the frenetic static barely audible on the
lower frequencies (as Ralph Ellison might put it) of early American culture. Women's writing exposes the inconsistencies of a
language it transforms. These novels dialogize the language of
republican virtue by setting into play its invariably multivalent
meanings. It renders new meanings to old words. The result is to
collapse linguistic and political boundaries instead of reifying
them. Women succeeded in redefining patriotism where men (as
in Belknap's portrait of Winthrop in 1798, or Henry Ware's eulogy of John Adams in 1826) had failed. Women's historical
romance thus reconstituted gender through creative rhetorical
strategies of synthesis and exchange.

Virtuous Marriage

The endings of these books, it would seem, disappoint just about
everyone. There is no better evidence, so the argument goes, for
the "conventional" nature of women's historical romances than
the literary convention of the marriage plot itself. Not only do
traditional critics make this complaint, but so do those critics

who are in the business of refurbishing the reputations of women writers.[85] They lament, for example, that Hobomok disappears in the end (and with him the possibilities of a new, radical American marriage), or that Hope's rebellious nature seems to be defused by her marriage to Everell. Context again provides a more precise barometer for the politics of the historical novel. The presumably fairy-tale marriages concluding *Hope Leslie* and *Hobomok* actually compose a progressive model of conjugal relations in early republican culture. Where this model comes from, however, is today a matter of some debate.

The debate is characteristic of studies of early America because it involves the issue of the relative importance of republicanism and liberalism. Jan Lewis has argued that during the post-Revolutionary era republican ideology lent marital relations new – and antipatriarchal – signification. Because early nationals saw conjugal and political relations as part of the same continuum, marriage "became infused with political meaning": "The dynamic [of marriage] was republican and anti-patriarchal: it juxtaposed the virtuous, independent child and the oppressive, corrupting parent, and it found in the union of two virtuous individuals the true end of society and the fit paradigm of political life."[86] Republican marriage allowed free choice of one's mate and was founded upon the importance of affectional relations. This "doctrine of symmetrical marriage" idealized a companionate friendship of mutual respect and reciprocal confidence that effectively socialized one into benevolence, regulated one's passions, and thereby fitted one for republican citizenship.

Linda Kerber recently has contested this outlook by reexamining the landmark case of *Martin v. Massachusetts* (1805)[87] as an example of how, in the hands of Federalist conservatives, the corporate and hierarchical strains within republican thinking actually militated *against* the idea of women as freethinking, morally autonomous members of the republic.[88] Only "the logic of liberalism," which placed so much emphasis on the integrity of individual rights, genuinely worked to expose and even challenge the ethical discrepancy (in, for example, coverture laws) between Revolutionary principles and post-Revolutionary realities.[89] Liberalism, moreover, promoted in early national culture the idea of marriage as a volitional union of "independent moral actors."[90] The conflicting views of Kerber and Lewis may result from their consulting different sorts of primary texts as well as essential problems in defining "republicanism." Whereas Lewis cites materials that understand "republican" behavior in antipatriarchal terms, Kerber focuses on a milieu of conservative Federalists for whom hierarchical "dependence" in the family ensured social and political stability in the republic. If Kerber's revision narrowly contextualizes "republicanism" within a High Federalist milieu (Thomas Paine and Theodore Sedgwick, after all, could invoke very different models of conjugal relations to secure a "virtuous republic"), it nonetheless highlights the importance of liberalism in modernizing the cultural canons of American marriage and promoting the ethos of voluntarism.

This contemporary historiographic debate over the complex relations among ideology, marital relations, and women's citizenship is significant to the literary politics of women's historical romance. But one point of agreement here is crucial to reading the politics of marriage in historical romance. Despite their very different views of the nature of republicanism, Lewis and Kerber each show how early nationals interpreted the relationship between marital and political relations as part of a continuum.[91] Indeed, even in an era in which public and private spheres (theoretically) were becoming more distinctive, and in which coverture highlighted the hypocrisy of American democracy, early nationals still generally upheld the *political* importance of marriage in a republic. The discussion of *Hope Leslie* in the *North American Review,* for example, actually took up this issue by arguing for the importance of female intellect to an ideal of companionate marriage. The educated woman warranted her husband's "respect" as she became "the real companion of his life": "How much more estimable, useful, enlightened, he is like to be with an accomplished fellow creature, than with a brainless idol in his house and in his bosom."[92] Sarah Hale urged American men to recognize that better educational resources "can only qualify woman to become a rational companion, an instructive as well as an agreeable friend."[93] Similarly, Samuel Knapp's introduction to his progressive-minded *Female Biography* (1834) assumed that domestic and political life resided on a continuum: "It is unquestionably true, that where men are in thralldom, women share the evil; and that when tyranny is the basis of government, that it will find its way into domestic life."[94]

This context allows for a rereading of the marriage plots of *Hope Leslie* and *Hobomok.* Like the seduction novel before it, historical romance continued to dramatize political relations in terms of familial relations. The idealized marriages concluding these romances seriously model the terms of modern republicanism. They do so by staging a free, natural exchange of affections and respect between men and women, one that significantly implies an egalitarian politics of gender. Writers such as Sedgwick and Child, in other words, idealized a political norm of marriage that crucially modernized republicanism itself. Such a norm synthesizes liberal and republican ideologies because it construes women as freethinking, morally independent individuals and the republic as a phenomenon contingent on ethics.

In *Hope Leslie* the relationship between Hope and Everell is saturated with a rhetoric of reciprocal affection. Conjugal feeling democratizes political relations only so far as it is premised on a free, independent exchange. Sedgwick's convoluted marriage plot, which situates Everell in the middle of a triangle consisting of Hope, Esther, and Magawisca, revolves around this political principle. When Everell awkwardly realizes that "he could not say what he did not feel" (233) to Esther, this not only facilitates Esther's final freedom in the end as an unmarried woman (like Sedgwick herself) but also suggests the absurdity of any cultural system of marriage violating free will. The narrator's claim that "there was [between Everell and Esther] to use the modern German term, no elective affinity" (278) lends liberalism egalitarian meanings by punning on Calvinist rhetoric. Ironically, Esther is the first to sense the "reciprocal emotion" between Everell and Hope (265), an ideal that Magawisca later confirms: " 'Nelema told me your souls were mated – she said your affections mingled like streams from the same fountain' " (330).

Hobomok's subversion of Roger Conant's authority similarly relies on a symmetrical model of marriage. Mary's gradual awakening to her feelings for Charles begins to disrupt her loyalty to her father: "When at length she found a being who understood her feelings, and who loved, as she had imagined love, her whole soul was rivetted. The harshness of her father tended to increase this, by rendering the stream of affection more undivided in its source" (47). Mary's shifting loyalties are heavily politicized insofar as her sequence of lovers disrupts the authority of the patriarchal communitarianism that Roger Conant symbolizes. By moving Mary from hierarchical to egalitarian relations, Child implicitly redefines the republic itself, divorcing it from an older, premodern understanding of subordination. This in turn disrupts the political and cultural association of the Puritan commonwealth with a modern republic, distending historical time for contemporary readers.

These novels manage the marriage plot in such a way as to pursue the logic of domestic virtue to its most empowering ends.

The reconstructed republican men – Charles Brown and Everell Fletcher – have to learn that even conjugal love is secondary to domestic love, a fact that leaves women free to pursue virtue outside the context of a husband's authority. When confronted with Charles's hints that they flee to England, for example, Mary Conant's response establishes this kind of autonomy: " 'Never while my mother lives, Charles, I would not leave her even for you' " (48). Later, when she confesses her "wicked thought" that her mother's death would set her free, Charles praises her ability to overcome it and reaffirm her selfless devotion to Mrs. Conant: " 'Be ever thus, my own dear girl . . . I could not love you if you were otherwise' " (82). So what appears to be a companionate marriage actually enacts – through male abdication in the name of a higher (feminized) principle – a subtle shift in gendered power relations.

Hope Leslie's resolution to its convoluted marriage plot also legitimates the limitations of male power. At one point Magawisca tries to convince Hope that she should accept Mary's and Oneco's marriage. " 'Ask your own heart . . . ,' " she urges Hope, " 'if any charm could win your affections from Everell Fletcher' " (331). Hope summons "all her courage" and answers with a tolerably firm voice, " '. . . yes – yes, Magawisca, if virtue, if duty to others required it, I trust in heaven I could command and direct my affections' " (331). Everell's reaction virtually repeats Brown's:

> We hope Everell may be forgiven, for the joy that gushed through his heart when Hope expressed a confidence in her own strength, which at least implied a consciousness that she needed it. Nature will rejoice in reciprocated love, under whatever adversities it comes. (331)

Note the syntax here. Sedgwick manipulates it just as effectively as she does republican diction to suggest the primacy of domestic love. Until we reach the first sentence's secondary clause, we gather that Everell's "joy" results from Hope's independence rather than from her implicitly stated love for him. This moment, which really determines the remainder of the novel's love plot, translates "reciprocated love" into something contingent on female "strength" that is aligned curiously with the power of selflessness.

This cultural context for marriage informs as well the most controversial subject of these novels: miscegenation. Most critics want to see *Hope Leslie*'s political posture toward interracial relations in a relatively progressive light. Richard Slotkin, for example, has argued that in *Hope Leslie* "Miss Sedgwick ... aligns herself with the more radical environmentalists in asserting that Mary's proper place is now with her Indian husband and in seeing this acculturation in a positive light, rather than as a sort of degeneracy."[95] But during the pivotal scene where Hope eventually meets her sister, Mary, the novel's progressive stance vis-à-vis acculturation is complicated by its ethos of domestic love that tends to dissolve racial difference in the name of Christian feeling. Moreover, this scene also demonstrates the tortuous problems the text has in defining "nature" itself. Hope's first sight of her sister "in her savage attire, fondly leaning on Oneco's shoulder" horrifies her, and "a sickening feeling came over her, an unthought of revolting of nature; and instead of obeying the first impulse, and springing forward to clasp her in her arms, she retreated to the cliff" (227). When the two are seated, "Hope knew not how to address one so near to her by nature, so far removed by habit and education" (228). Almost immediately, however, "the energies of nature aw[a]ke" within Hope as she embraces her sister. One would think Hope's affective response would subordinate race to gender in the context of "nature," but Hope soon admits that Mary "might look more natural to her" in English garb (228). As Mary's interpreter, Magawisca tells Hope that Faith's childhood memories, her last link to Anglo culture, are as insubstantial as "the vanishing vapour on the far-off mountain" (229).

The next moment is crucial. In a consummate act of domestic love, Hope prays for Mary, eliciting a response that would seem to suggest such love supersedes all other cultural and racial forces: "Mary understood her action, and feeling that their separation was for ever, nature for a moment asserted her rights; she returned Hope's embrace, and wept on her bosom" (231). So this series of oscillations, which culminate only in the *momentary* triumph of domestic virtue, would seem to reveal profound (and potentially destructive) thematic fissures in the text. What is "nature" – a matter of race? or culture? or feeling? This raises a corollary problem: Can the streams of affection penetrate the borders of difference?

The oscillations in this scene do reveal uncertainties within Sedgwick herself over the legitimacy of miscegenation. Much of *Hope Leslie* suggests sexual tensions between Everell and Magawisca that it cannot fully acknowledge. These are resolvable, it would appear, only by Magawisca's death or physical removal, each of which would eliminate the potential danger she poses to the love between Hope and Everell. A crucial feature of authorial ambivalence lies in an inconsistent characterization of Magawisca. In some ways Sedgwick fears her Indian angel. For instance she has Magawisca give a curious speech about "the law of vengeance . . . written on our hearts" (330). Parading rather flimsily as cultural relativism, these words manage only to invoke an essentialist theory of race that the text has tried to overcome in its presentation of spiritual kindredness between Anglo and Native American women. Magawisca's words, moreover, awkwardly displace the ethos of Christian beneficence that the text, for example, had legitimated in her confrontation with Gardiner in prison. Magawisca really does nothing more in this instance than parrot the masculine discourse of her father, a discourse *Hope Leslie* already has flayed to pieces. But the speech explains, if only inadequately, Magawisca's departure. It frees Hope and Everell to marry.

One might go so far as to say that, for all its antipatriarchal ramifications, the miscegenation plot in *Hope Leslie* nearly subverts the thematics of female virtue. Here again issues of race and acculturation lie in complicated relations to those of gender. Significantly, Magawisca's reply to Hope that the "virtue and duty" of marriage bind Mary and Oneco would seem to reverse the hierarchy between domestic love and conjugal loyalty that the text has already established. What Magawisca is really arguing here is that the sentimental bonds of womanhood, in this case between Hope and Mary, are of secondary importance to those of marriage. How can this be? Even if one were to make the case that in the 1820s a woman writer (supposedly in contrast to Cooper) sanctions miscegenation, the very issue is mediated through fundamentally gendered – rather than racial – considerations. Mary's loyalty to Oneco encodes the liberal terms of affectional marriage that the text promotes ("She and my brother," Magawisca claims, "are as if one life-chord bound them together" [191]). But there's a problem here. Since conjugal love outweighs domestic love in this instance, the rationale for miscegenation undermines the primacy of universal, selfless love later culminating in Esther Downing's (and Catharine Sedgwick's own) decision never to marry. The "disinterested devotion" of domestic love need not " '[g]ive to a party what was meant for mankind' " (350). Race would seem to disrupt, if only temporarily, the gendered ideological design of *Hope Leslie*. Hence Mary and Oneco are removed to the West – to the "deep voiceless obscurity of those unknown regions" (339).[96] And so, oddly enough, such a removal is as much a function of gender as of race.

This is true for *Hobomok* as well.[97] Critics of Child's treatment of miscegenation tend to cast her as an ambivalent radical, arguing that she allows Mary to have what we now might call an alternative lifestyle subverting a patriarchal order.[98] We might, however, turn this view around and ask what Child was *promoting* rather than assailing in this instance. The answer to that question involves the importance of female reason.

Child manipulates the subject of miscegenation by deploying the importance of female reason, a tenet that theoretically lay at the foundation of republican womanhood. Right before her departure with Hobomok, Mary Conant's breakdown demonstrates a precarious balance in female faculty psychology, which, in this case, patriarchal authority unsettles. After news of Brown's supposed death, Roger Conant's coldness to Mary, who "craved one look of tenderness, one expression of love" (122), precipitates an emotional crisis that disables Mary's reason. This in turn problematizes the issue of her volition. The first aftershocks of the news send Mary into a state approximating "insanity," an insensible "chaos" that "almost hurled reason from his throne" (120–1). Contemporary reviewers of *Hobomok* picked up on this. One called Mary's decision for removal "a fit of insane despondency";[99] another noted the "temporary alienation of mind" and a "superstitious feeling" that occasioned Mary's union with Hobomok.[100] As Mary wavers over what to do, Child tellingly calls her momentary hesitancy an "effort of dawning reason and gentler feeling" (122); she soon gives way, however, to "the unreasonableness of grief and anger" (122). Even Hobomok suspects that she has lost her mind as she wavers between incoherent babble and "prompt and rational" replies. Like the rhythms of uncertainty plaguing Sedgwick's novel over this subject, Mary's oscillations signal Child's fundamental ambivalence. Would a reasonable woman run off with an Indian?

To this end, *Hobomok* stages in Mary's exodus the social and political consequences of the superstitious woman. "In the unreasonableness of grief and anger," Mary exchanged ". . . the social band, stern and dark as it was, for the company of savages" (122). The novel at once inscribes and extends its era's norms of republican womanhood. Benjamin Rush, we might recall, theorized that a healthy dose of the sciences could prevent republican girls from growing into dangerously imaginative women. In this context, the language Child uses to describe Mary significantly derives from the Revolutionary-era opposition between lassitude and vigor. At the moment of her fall she is "pale and motionless,"

(123), "dull and cold" (124), "listless and unmoved" (125). In the new circle of the Wampanoag community, Mary continued in "the same stupefied state" until "she gradually awoke to a sense of her situation" (135). And now her reason returns. "Kind as Hobomok was," she discovers, "and rich as she found his uncultivated mind in native imagination, still the contrast between him and her departed lover, would often be remembered with sufficient bitterness" (135). Later, begging for Charles's forgiveness, she admits that " 'my reason was obscured' " (148).

In *Hobomok* miscegenation reformulates the norms of republican womanhood. It does so in a way that distributes contemporary readers into interpretive communities that varyingly uphold either the fragility or the necessity of female reason. Are *all* women, the text asks, so superstitious? Or is it just wicked fathers who debilitate their "natural" capacity for reason? Yet both dubious and optimistic readers during the 1820s are led to similar conclusions when reading Mary's "fate": The female mind is necessary to social and political order. Lose it, and the stable boundaries of a pure republic will collapse. To read this scene in terms of gender ultimately makes Hobomok the one in "captivity." His acculturation, rather than Mary's, takes place (a fact that, as we shall see, Cooper realized when writing *The Wept of Wish-ton-Wish*). Child decontextualizes much of Mary's new existence, but when Sally Oldham finally visits, the scene resembles more the morning rites of bourgeois New England than that of a Wampanoag village. Hobomok kisses his boy and goes off to work to bring home the bacon – or, rather, deer – as Mary shouts affectionately " 'Take care of yourself' " (137). The power of female virtue significantly prepares Hobomok for his final act of selfless love. Even as marriage moves from "idolatry" to genuine affection, however, Hobomok never will fulfill the role of intellectual companion. Mary loves him only as a " 'kind, noble-hearted creature' " (137).

The literary convention of the marriage plot in *Hobomok* and *Hope Leslie* is thus laden with immediately social and political messages. In light of such books as *Means and Ends* or *The Mother's Book* (and many others they wrote), we can say that the conventions of romance afforded Child and Sedgwick greater discursive freedom than did the genre of the domestic manual to engage gendered polemics. The difficulty, for example, with which Child incrementally advanced the importance of the female mind in *The Mother's Book* is replaced by an acutely effective dramatization of the inextricable relationship between female chastity and the female mind. The marriages concluding these novels unite reconstituted versions of republican manhood and womanhood. Just as much as their male counterparts, we should recognize, Mary Conant and Hope Leslie are socialized through marriage, Mary forgiven for her sins, and Hope's self-indulgence finally contained. This new unity of reciprocal affections, which updated the republican belief in the socializing virtues of marriage to emergently liberal beliefs in free choice and moral autonomy, modeled a new order in which affective benevolence became the unifying adhesive of the republic. The marriage plot, then, not only signals the republic's future promise but also redefines the meaning of a republic itself.

Let us recall again Sedgwick's description of the aged war veteran in her letter to her brother, for it suggests, as I claimed at the outset of Chapter 2, the rhetorical strategies informing *Hobomok* and *Hope Leslie*. The gendered meanings of virtue are subject to prescient manipulation in order to produce new, modern meanings of a republic in these novels. Their "utterances" inscribe cultural tensions arising out of an era in which classical republicanism became increasingly obsolete. In their dialogue with nationalist histories, both texts register that obsolescence by recodifying new meanings of "virtue." If, as Shirley Samuels has argued, sentimentality embodies in nineteenth-century domestic narrative a paradox of the body itself, "a double logic of power and powerlessness,"[101] these texts both dramatize and enact female power through the disembodying ethos of female virtue. But if domestic virtue theoretically made women the invisible stewards of male morality, both texts go one step further in making their heroines' bodies, as well as their minds, the literary and political subjects of republicanism. It is as much the physical activities as the abstract principles of these protagonists that divest Puritanism of its cultural and metaphoric status in early republican America.

We finally can see the ideological intersections between theology and gender. For these two famous literary apostates from Orthodox Calvinism, fictionalizing Puritan history afforded the revision of the doctrine of innate depravity that, we should recognize, contained particularly gender-political implications. Post-Revolutionary conservatives who drew upon traditional Whig thinking did so in a way that pronounced the postlapsarian assumptions underlying a vision for the necessity of good order in society.[102] The politically conservative association of the Puritan commonwealth with the American republic was premised on such a Calvinist world-view. In another letter to Charles in 1812, Sedgwick implied that male authority depended upon this assumption: that "all the misanthropic sayings of all the old bachelors and cynics that have ever lived can not [sic] counteract . . . the mass of flattery you have so elegantly served up in your letter."[103] Finally, then, we can see the politics of *Hope Leslie*'s theology, its affinities with liberal, Arminian ideas. The novel launches a decidedly feminized assault upon a hierarchical, patriarchal politics contingent on Calvinist theology. Its objections to orthodox Calvinism and classical republicanism were simultaneous and reciprocal. As a literary convention, then, marriage becomes the site of the historical translation from republican/cyclical time into progressive time, a change signaling the escape from the necessity of a patriarchal brand of republicanism.

Indeed, these novels' aesthetic features, their sense of characterization and plot as well as their narrative texture, finally reveal their immediate concerns with the contemporary republic rather than the Puritan commonwealth. The criticisms of *Hobomok* and *Hope Leslie* by older Hawthorne scholars, as well as the praise heaped on them by recent revisionists, *both* result from these texts' contemporary historicity. In this highly unstable historical moment, their treatments of language make women's historical romance another form of linguistic (and hence political) interpretation. No less than Noah Webster himself, Lydia Child and Catharine Sedgwick attempted to codify the highly protean language of the early republic. Such an act of "fixing" language paradoxically meant dismantling, in effect, the Puritan Ebenezer. Like these women writers, Fenimore Cooper entered the lists of Puritan history in context of an established field of language and ideology. Cooper's novel about frontier Puritanism engaged not only a generation of New England history-writing but also, as we shall see, women writers such as Child and Sedgwick. Like those that had preceded him, Cooper took up the subject of Puritanism with its immediate, "republican" implications in mind.

4

THE "HIVE OF AMERICA":

JAMES FENIMORE COOPER'S THE WEPT OF WISH-TON-WISH AND THE HISTORY OF KING PHILIP'S WAR

Then, New England has long since anticipated her revenge, glorifying herself and underrating her neighbors in a way that, in our opinion, fully justifies those who possess a little Dutch blood in expressing their sentiments on the subject. Those who give so freely should know how to take a little in return.

– Cooper, Preface to *The Chainbearer* (1845)

The common faults of American language are an ambition of effect, a want of simplicity, and a turgid abuse of terms. To these may be added ambiguity of expression.

– Cooper, *The American Democrat* (1838)

As just about everybody knows, James Fenimore Cooper disliked New Englanders.[1] He appears to have held Yankees accountable for most of the ills plaguing nineteenth-century American society: material acquisitiveness, the restless movements to the west, and the erosion of hierarchical privilege. One critic of Cooper has called his disease "New Anglophobia,"[2] and if it was pathological, it certainly worsened during the 1830s and 1840s, after his return from a seven-year stay in Europe. During this period Cooper faced waning popularity, bitterly launched numerous libel suits against a Whig press that lampooned him, and witnessed what he believed was social anarchy during New York's Anti-Rent turmoil, which led to his writing the Littlepage series, a trilogy of novels (*Satanstoe* [1845], *The Chainbearer* [1845], and *The Redskins* [1846]). These novels largely held the enterprising Yankee accountable for the social problems besetting the republic.

Cooper's critics have noted as well the historical premises of his social criticism. On the face of it, Cooper blamed Puritanism as the primum mobile of American rapacity, which has led critics to place his writing about New Englanders in a psychohistorical context. Indeed, their interpretations of *The Wept of Wish-ton-Wish* (1829), Cooper's first and only novel of Puritan New England, set in the Connecticut frontier during the time of King Philip's War, parallels more recent critical readings, encountered in Chapters 2 and 3, of Catharine Sedgwick's and Lydia Child's disdain for New England's Fathers.[3] In both cases, the Puritans are located as the source of a contemporary problem, whether it be Yankee acquisitiveness or patriarchical control. As early as the 1930s, for example, the renowned Americanist Robert Spiller noted "Cooper's life-long antipathy for all things of New England," arguing that it arose from his belief "that the middle class ideal had been brought to America by the Pilgrim and Puritan fathers."[4] Most significantly, this outlook on Cooper has been influenced increasingly by Max Weber's famous theories about Protestant culture and the spirit of capitalism. Much of the critical discourse about *The Wept* during the 1960s and 1970s has been shaped by it. For instance, Kay Seymour House concluded that in *The Wept* "Cooper sets forth most of the latent forces of Puritanism bequeathed to the Yankee."[5] The Weberian argument is even more pronounced when Allan Axelrad claims that in "*The Wept of Wish-ton-Wish* [Cooper] delves into the ethos of seventeenth-century New England Calvinism."[6] As "pragmatic rationalizers of culture," Cooper's Puritans sublimate iconoclastic impulses that only later surfaced among modern Yankees: "Cooper intuitively grasps the fundamental drift of the Weber thesis in his astute observations of the practical consequences of Puritan piety."[7]

With all its emphasis on latent behavior and sublimation, Weberian psychohistoricism would seem to resist Jane Tompkins's warning to stop looking for complex psychology in Cooper's work because it is nowhere to be found.[8] In her influential *Sensational Designs: The Cultural Work of American Fiction, 1790–1860* (1986), Tompkins persuasively takes Cooper's critics to task for trying to explain away traditional aesthetics (including psychological complexity) in Cooper's fiction. As an alternative approach, she reads the second of the Leatherstocking Tales, *The Last of the Mohicans* (1826), as an example of Cooperian melodrama. Like virtually all of Cooper's work, *Mohicans* is "social criticism written in the allegorical mode."[9] The novel allegorizes the tragic conflict of racial and cultural types in America, asking "the question of how and whether men can dwell together in unity,"[10] ultimately demonstrating that they cannot. Although Tompkins persuasively situates Cooper's treatment of racial "kinds" in context of American culture during the middle 1820s, she still underestimates Cooper's ability to create convincing psychological characterization and themes. Even the most dubious reader of Cooper (and I am certainly *not* one of these) recognizes, for example, the profound, unspoken intimacy between Uncas and Cora Munro in *Mohicans*, or Elizabeth Temple's simultaneous horror of and fascination with the violence of the American wilderness in *The Pioneers* (1823). But more important, the implication of Tompkins's argument is that we never seriously can talk about psychological depth in Cooper, only about what she calls "surface." In other words, she suggests that social allegory and psychology are in this case mutually exclusive categories of literary study.

This is an unnecessary opposition. In this chapter I aim to synthesize these alternative approaches to Cooper that look for psychological depth and social allegory, in order to reconceptualize the relationship between psychology and history in *The Wept of Wish-ton-Wish*. In context of the larger cultural discourses about Puritanism in early republican America, *The Wept*'s inquiry into the psychology of Puritanism has immediate social and political implications. My argument is this: Cooper's novel is much less a critique of Puritanism per se than of the liberal mythology underlying its representation during his own day. Just like Sedgwick's choice of the Pequot War, Cooper's choice of King Philip's War is no accident at all. He picked the single most powerful event in Puritan history (and early national historiography) that implicitly championed liberal, individualist values. And these were values that he believed were ruining America.

This view of *The Wept* again involves some reconsideration of it as a "history." Traditional readings of the novel, as I have suggested, make Cooper out to be a proto-Weberian figure, just as other critics have done for Melville and Jung, and Hawthorne and Freud. By attributing to Cooper such prolific prescience, his critics aim in this instance to raise his canonical stock (the problem that Tompkins sees in Cooper scholarship as a whole). In this schema, *The Wept* serves as a case study in the historical evolution from Puritan piety to Yankee materialism, a process that had its seedbed of acquisitiveness in the very founding of New England. Moreover, such a historical model reveals the influence among Cooperians of Georg Lukacs's influential study *The Historical Novel* (1924). Lukacs admired Sir Walter Scott for pioneering a literary form whose nuanced psychological portraits derived from a larger sense of historical process. "Scott," he argued, "endeavors to portray the struggles and antagonisms of history by means of characters who, in their psychology and destiny, always represent social trends and historical forces."[11] As an obvious heir to Walter Scott, Cooper has been viewed in light of the Waverly model, which, in the case of *The Wept*, presumably delineates the historical transition from a feudal to a bourgeois society.[12]

Cooper's critics are quite right to suggest that his critique of Puritanism involves the issue of acquisitiveness. But they have overlooked the immediacy of such a critique. Readings of *The Wept* that insist upon Cooper's debunking of Puritanism lose sight of its essentially contemporary ideological project, specifically as an embittered commentary on the nature of liberalism in the early republic. In this chapter I rehistoricize *The Wept* by showing how the novel implicitly engages in dialogue with contemporary New England historiography. What I have called the early national Ebenezer, after all, managed to promote liberal principles by carefully negotiating them in the context of both traditional ideas and language. *The Wept* exposes the true agenda of New England filiopiety, pointing out its inconsistencies, disentangling the meanings of its language where others actually thrived on its convenient ambiguities.

Any reader of *The Pioneers* (1823) and *The Prairie* (1827), two of the Leatherstocking Tales, recognizes the fears with which Cooper viewed liberal acquisitiveness and unbridled individualism. These were exactly the values underwriting early national discourse about King Philip's War. Cooper's revisionary history divests New England historiography of those rhetorical and ideological inconsistencies residing within the historical trope of Puritanism. Like *Hope Leslie* and *Hobomok*, *The Wept* may also be considered a novel *about* republican language. Cooper interrogates the discourses of Puritan "virtue" to critique what he saw as the debasement of such traditional republican words as "industry" and "vigor." This social critique involved a gendered one as well. The latter part of this chapter looks at Cooper's treatment of race and miscegenation as a rebuttal, of sorts, to the formulas of androgynous masculinity and sentimental republicanism that texts like *Hobomok* and *Hope Leslie* had offered earlier in the 1820s. *The Wept*, then, is part of a cultural dialogue taking place during this decade about the nature of "virtue" in early republican America.

Notions of New England

One might better understand *The Wept*'s skepticism about New England as a reliable standard for republican values by comparing the novel to its immediate predecessor, *Notions of the Americans picked up by a Travelling Bachelor* (1828). Not unlike Jefferson's *Notes on the State of Virginia* (1785), which refuted European Enlightenment theories about degeneracy in the New World, *Notions* was intended as both an imitation and an inversion of European travel memoirs that tended to denigrate American life.[13] Indeed, through the persona of John Cadwallader, the English bachelor's traveling companion and instructor, Cooper showed an uncharacteristically effusive optimism about American progress. Hence *Notions* has been read as an "exaggerated, decidedly utopian impression of the moral and intellectual character of the American people," a "classic statement of " 'the American dream,' " "propaganda," and an avowal of "democratic faith."[14] Recent reevaluations of the text, however, rightly have noted those tremors of uncertainty about the republic lurking beneath its confident surface.[15] To help assuage these anxieties, I would argue, Cooper invoked New England as a premodern antidote to liberal America. And this, as we have seen, is exactly what New England history-writers had been doing for years.

These anxieties contaminate many of the numerous paeans to American prosperity and progress. As a surveyor of the nation's material and moral landscape, *Notions'* Travelling Bachelor soon imbibes the liberal faith in progressive history. Yet early on in *Notions,* one of the most ostensibly optimistic affirmations of American success contains within it rhetorical tensions revealing uncertainty about the state of union:

> The secret of all enterprise and energy exists in the principles of individuality. Wealth does not more infallibly beget wealth, than the right to exercise of our faculties, begets the desire to use them. The slave is every where indolent, vicious, and abject; the freeman active, moral, and bold. It would seem that this is the best and safest, and consequently the wisest Government, which is content rather to protect than direct the National prosperity, since the latter system never fails to impede the efforts of that individuality which makes men industrious and enterprising.[16]

What initially appears to be an equation between liberal acquisitiveness and natural law (the "exercise" of greed is equated with that of the body) is nonetheless cast in terms of republican moral oppositions. Revolutionary culture's contrasts between freedom and slavery, vigor and indolence, and Europe and America, all

manage to defuse the danger in declaring the virtues of liberalism. This tension appears and reappears as a leitmotif in *Notions*.
It crystallizes an ongoing dialogue between liberal and classical
impulses in the text (and in Cooper himself), one that informs
crucial symbolic moments as when, for example, the return of the
great hero of the Revolution – the Marquis de Lafayette – arrives
in New York harbor amid "the bustle and activity of the American
world."[17]

In *Notions*, New England exemplifies a premodern ideal that at
once controls and validates modern America. One way of gauging
this rhetorical maneuver is to recognize how the region is linked
to cyclical, rather than progressive, history. Like the contrast
between colonial Virginia and Puritan New England in contemporary histories, the one between contemporary New York and
New England here dialogizes the meanings of a "republic." "New
England may justly glory in its villages!" the narrator exclaims, for
they afford "space, freshness . . . neatness and comfort," as opposed to a "crowded, commercial, or manufacturing population."[18] Its pastoral simplicity, its rich swales of land divided by
fences signaling human cultivation, reaffirm a sense of organic
order. *Notions* in this regard vocalizes late-eighteenth-century beliefs, espoused, as we have seen, by Benjamin Rush, in the inextricable relations among physical, moral, and political health. Agrarian simplicity is accompanied by the people's "disinterested
kindness": "In the midst of this picture must man be placed,
quiet, orderly, and industrious."[19] Like New England history-
writers, Cooper (or rather his ambiguously optimistic persona)
praised New Englanders' preeminent concerns with education,
which ensured the region's communitarian character and social
stability.[20] According to the Travelling Bachelor, New Englanders
"are, even to this hour, distinguished among their own active and
quick witted countrymen, for their enterprise, frugality, order,
and intelligence."[21]

New York offers a very different model of a republic. Letter
VIII, addressed to the Baron van Kemperfelt, opens by portraying
New York City as a model of commercial activity: "In dwelling on
its [the city's] admirable position, its growing prosperity, and its
probable grandeur, I wish to excite neither your hopes nor your
regrets."[22] Cooper, of course, wants to instill the former in his
audience; the motif of American progress, after all, was the reason the book was panned so mercilessly by the English literary
press.[23] This theme coalesces in the predominant image of New

York City, the "Commercial Emporium of this nation."[24] Its "natural advantages" have enabled it to surpass "auxiliaries" like Boston, Philadelphia, and Baltimore.[25] A rhetoric of "prosperity," "supremacy," and "power" saturates the description of a commercial center, whose continued growth guarantees that the United States is "to be foremost among the nations of the earth."[26] Its contrast with New England, then, represents two competing versions of the public good during the early republic. Yet Cooper repeatedly returns in *Notions* to New England's "active and healthy virtues," noting time and again its central role in the Revolutionary war effort, as an antidote to the uncertainties of modernity. New England stabilizes *Notions,* grounds the text in what I have called a discourse of Puritan order legitimating American progress. In this historical logic Puritanism functions as the source of American stability: "Still he who would seek the great moving principles which give no small part of its particular tone to the American character," he maintains, "must study the people of New-England deeply."[27] No less than, for example, Timothy Dwight's "Greenfield Hill," *Notions* oddly partakes in regional imperialism. If the text parodies the excesses of New England discourse (to which its author, as a member of New York City's Bread and Cheese Club, must have been attuned), it also perpetuates them. Evidently, New England was a powerful medium for premodern ideas.

Why, then, did Cooper immediately subvert it in his very next work, *The Wept of Wish-ton-Wish*? One answer lies in the issue of audience. While Cooper was working on the novel in March 1828, he wrote his publishers, the Careys of Philadelphia, "At my return [from a planned trip to Germany which never occurred] there will be a book for America. This will be the first of a series written especially for my own Countrymen. I shall be stationary in the winter at Paris, and finish a tale which is already on the Anvil."[28] His rhetoric here not only signals his lifelong obsession with America's civic morality but also distinguishes *The Wept* in this case from its predecessor intended for European skeptics of American republicanism. If *Notions* dramatizes a dialogue about the nature of republicanism, *The Wept* extends and complicates it, interrogating both the very premises of American "progress" and the practice of New England historiography itself.[29] *The Wept* critiques the canons of liberalism as they were written into the period's historiography of King Philip's War. So this is where we begin.

"The Progress of the Settlements"

King Philip's War lasted little more than a year, but it was by far the greatest single calamity in seventeenth-century Puritan New England. Between June 1675 and August 1676, about half the towns in colonial New England were destroyed, the region's economy all but ruined. Much of its local population, which was scattered about in small towns and farms, was killed, including roughly a tenth of its men available for military service.[30] The immediate causes of the war lay in intercolonial competition (principally between tiny Plymouth and Rhode Island, both of which held dubious charters) for Wampanoag lands under the control of its sachem, Metacom, or "Philip," as he was known to colonials. Beginning in the middle 1660s, Plymouth's governor, Josiah Winslow, aggressively began pressing the Wampanoags to accept virtual protectorate status under Plymouth. A series of diplomatic maneuvers and hostile accusations during the 1660s and early 1670s led to increased tensions between colonials and Wampanoags. Philip eventually resisted colonial pressure. By 1675, New England's political leaders had accused him of plotting conspiracies and of murdering a Native American, one John Sassamon, who was friendly with the English.[31] Open warfare began in June of that year with a Wampanoag attack on the newly established town of Swansea, Massachusetts. Other tribes, such as the Narragansetts, joined forces with Philip, and by the winter of 1675–6, it appeared as though the colonials might be driven to the sea.

Looking back on the events of 1675–6, early national New Englanders recognized the severity of the crisis. They certainly understood the war in terms of the future destiny of New England and, by extension, of America itself. As one writer put it, "[The war] was a contest of no ordinary character, not a history of sieges and battles, not a war merely against the physical force of our fathers, but against all they held dear to them."[32] It was, as Emma Willard claimed, a moment of potential "extinction" and "total extirpation" for the Puritans.[33] Early national histories were shaped by a number of ideologies coloring an episode that might otherwise have appeared to be a matter of Puritan hunger for land. A combination of various historiographic theories – Puritan ideas about the guiding hand of Providence, the post-Enlightenment faith in the (westward) progress of "reason" and "civilization," and an emergent ideology of Manifest Destiny positing the disappearance of Native Americans – together, conflated

Nature and Divinity as the source of moral and historical order. They lent credibility to colonial expansion.

My purpose here is not to offer yet another revisionist history of Puritan expansionism but to articulate how and why early nationals rhetorically justified the spatial and historical movements of colonial New England. To rationalize New England's gradual domination, and to euphemize the war's long-term causes, early national history-writers drew upon these ideologies. Crucial here is the capacity of republican language to defuse – indeed, even to sanctify – Puritan expansion. An uncanny rhetorical logic deflected ancestral guilt by mediating frontier acquisitiveness through the republican discourse of "industry" and "enterprise." These words, as we have seen, retained premodern connotations even as they increasingly encoded new, liberal meanings. The cultural contexts for this kind of language helped exculpate Puritan New England – and nineteenth-century America – of material greed. Recall Salma Hale's praise for the Fathers, which I noted in Chapter 1, for it ethically frames the causes of war:

> The habits of industry and economy, which had been formed in less happy times, continued to prevail, and gave a competency to those who had nothing, and wealth to those who had a competency. The wilderness receded before adventurous and hardy labourers, and its savage inhabitants found their game dispersed and their favorite haunts invaded.[34]

The very language of "industry and economy" subtly defuses the passage's overall endorsement of a modern, competitive social arena premised on the natural logic of "competency." If the passage hints at a Native American perspective on an Anglo invasion, its passive construction significantly skirts the ethical issue of colonial intentions. The frontier simply "receded."[35]

This process of "civilization" combines the legacies of Enlightenment theory and providential history in ways that prefigure the antebellum rhetoric of Manifest Destiny. Premised on natural law, the *translatio studii,* which assumes the westward course of "civilization," dates back at least to George Berkeley's "Verses on the Prospect of Planting Arts and Learning in America" (1726). The wide currency of the idea of the westward progress is apparent, for example, in the premises of Hale's claim that the war "was the natural consequence of the sales of land, which were at all times readily made to the whites."[36] In this same vein, one of the most renowned antiquarians in New England, Samuel Drake, who helped reprint numerous narratives of the war during the nineteenth century, could praise King Philip and still call him "the implacable enemy of civilization."[37] The controlling ethical opposition that structures the war's narrativity was the distinction between "the arts of civilized men" and "the simple savage," or "the restraints of law and civilization" and "the freedom of the savage life."[38] By today's standards of objective historical study, Jeremy Belknap offered perhaps the most presciently objective account of the war, acknowledging "the irregular lives of many of the eastern settlers . . . [and] their want of due subordination," but he nonetheless maintained that "providence had smiled upon [the settlers'] undertakings, their settlements were extended, and their churches multiplied."[39] For Belknap, the dissemination of both technology (or "arts") and religion signaled "a civilized way of living."[40] Providential blessing was thus aligned with Enlightenment theory.

The moral leverage afforded by these dual legacies was further enhanced by Anglo-American views about the relationship between property and civilization. For early nationals considering colonials' and Native Americans' respective rights to the land, the virtue of Puritan "industry" helped define the terms of "civilization" itself and thereby justify the war. In this sense, Emma Willard's conclusion that the hunting grounds of "savage nations" were displaced by "the hum of civilization"[41] is telling, for it suggests the virtue of the industrious bee. Not only did early nationals praise the virtuously industrious behavior that produced the "arts of agriculture" and "establishment of mills," but they juxtaposed it directly with with the presumed "indolence and sloth" and "effeminacy of debasing habits" of the Wampanoags. This could lead to the absurd claim that the "national character" of Philip and his people was infected with the "vices of Europe."[42] Hence the war helped to codify liberal standards of property ownership via a sanctifying discourse of American virtue that polarized race according to one's relationship to property.

That the real issue of King Philip's War, however, was the nation's economic potential is apparent in these histories' rhetoric of empire. Either by design or default, early nationals recognized the net result of this horrific episode in just these terms. For instance the epigraph to the first Samuel Drake edition of *The History of Philip's War* included a snippet of verse (from the Renaissance poet Camoens) that read: "What wars they wag'd, what seas, what dangers past, / What glorious empire crown'd

their toils at last." Indeed, the conflation of republican and liberal impulses that, as we have seen, shaped the entire historical
discourse of New England at this time, easily found expression in
an episode synthesizing both the heroics of war and economic
expansion. Even a stodgy conservative like Benjamin Trumbull
concluded that the "war terminated in [the Native Americans']
entire conquest, and almost total extinction. At the same time, it
opened a wide door to extensive settlement and population."[43]

Perhaps the most transparent instance of this liberal agenda
was occasioned by, of all things, the subject of historical fiction.
When Rufus Choate demanded in 1833 an original historical
romance of New England based on the model of Sir Walter
Scott's *Waverly*, he claimed (rather duplicitously) that King Philip's War simply popped into his head as a possible subject for
such an oeuvre. This seems highly unlikely, however, in context
of the war's representation at this time. For Choate's choice of
subject implies a desire to link together literary nationalism and
national destiny. Scott, Choate claims, would "spread out before
you the external aspects and scenery of that New England, and
contrast them with those which our eyes are permitted to see, but
which our fathers died without beholding. And what a contrast!"[44] Choate goes on to exalt the "ripened fruits of two hundred years of labor and industry" which produce "populous
towns" and a "refined and affluent society."[45] The purely literary
possibilities of the war eventually become subsumed within a
larger narrative of American progress cloaked in a discourse of
classical republican manliness: "the germs of this day's exceeding
glory, beauty and strength" are to be found in Puritan "labor"
and "general industry."[46]

One cannot attribute this phenomenon merely to Puritan legacy. Whether or not New England's ruling magistrates and ministers embarked on a self-conscious mission of expansionism, Puritan historians often took the exact opposite approach to their
early national heirs, arguing that the dispersal of New Englanders
was *the very reason* for God's judgmental wrath. This is the argument of the standard history of the war, Increase Mather's *A Brief
History of the War with the Indians in New-England* (1676).[47] Written
during the war itself, Mather's jeremian history relentlessly reproaches second-generation backsliders for "the sinful *Degenerate
Estate* of the *present Generation in New-England*."[48] Mather begins
by establishing the moral rights of the colonists to the land of
New England, which "the Lord God of our Fathers hath given to
us for a rightfull Possession."[49] But he then goes on to argue with

merciless consistency that the Lord chastens (in this case through the agency of Native Americans) whom He loves, even though they may be a wayward people. Time and again, Mather relocates the problem of frontier restlessness as the root cause of New England's problems, citing, for example, the case of one "old Wakely" who has gone off to live in Casco Bay far away from any established church. Unlike early nationals, Mather wryly debunks the enterprising individualist as a man of superficial piety who "would sometimes say with tears, that he believed God was angry with him, because although he came to *New-England* for the Gospels sake, yet he had left another place in this Country, where there was a Church of Christ . . . and had lived many years in a Plantation where there was no *Church, nor Instituted Worship.*"[50] Wakely is killed by Indians, his violent death a sign of a larger moral and metaphysical crisis.

Yet this was not always the case with colonial histories of the war. One of the most popular ones, Benjamin Church's *Entertaining Passages of King Philip's War* (1716), was reprinted numerous times during the 1820s and 1830s and consulted by Cooper in writing *The Wept*.[51] Much of its appeal surely lay in its tales of high adventure, since Church himself had been a leading participant and had led the group of Rangers who successfully hunted down Philip himself in August 1676. The real significance of the aggressive reprinting of Church's narrative in early national letters is that it modeled an autobiographical subject whose uncanny synthesis of martial virtue and material gain expressed tensions in contemporary civic culture.[52] The introductory epistle, "To the Reader," immediately establishes this persona of an enterprising individualist who sets aside personal gain for civic duty, a persona that, in light of the text's recirculation in the 1820s and 1830s, evidently captivated early national audiences:

For in the year 1675, that unhappy and bloody Indian war broke out in Plymouth colony, where I was then building, and beginning a plantation at a place called by the Indians, Sogkonate, and since, by the English, Little Compton. I was the first Englishman that built upon that neck, which was full of Indians. My head and hands were full about settling a new plantation, where nothing was brought to; no preparation of dwelling house, or outhouses, or fencing made; horses and cattle were to be provided, ground to be cleared and broken up; and the utmost caution to be used, to keep myself free from offending my Indian neighbors all round me.[53]

Church himself in this short passage not only recounts but enacts the causes of war. Cultivating newfound space, he dramatizes a historical process of displacement – where both Native American lands and language are imperialized and reconstructed – that is legitimated through his insistence on his own virtuous industry. Church "had wholly laid aside his private business and concerns, ever since the war broke out."[54] The popularity of his narrative during the Jacksonian era suggests the extent to which this auto-biographical subject was made to codify an ethos of frontier individualism that encompassed martial duty as well, an ethos Jackson himself cultivated to launch his political career. A carpenter's son from Duxbury, Benjamin Church through his restless individualism was perpetually on the move to Plymouth, Bristol, and various other places. Mill owner and constable, pioneer entrepreneur and town magistrate, his representativeness embodied both unmistakably liberal energies as well as the martial and civic contexts with which to validate them.[55]

Early national New Englanders's ability to rewrite the history of King Philip's War depended in part on the elasticity of republican language. Cast in a potently ambiguous lexicon of republicanism, the kind of enterprising individualism exemplified by Benjamin Church took on the most pristine, noble qualities. The war resulted unfortunately, even inevitably, from the virtue of Puritan industry. The ability of metaphorical Puritanism to "transfer" ("metaphor," after all, means to "ferry across") republicanism to modern liberalism is precisely the subject of *The Wept of Wish-ton-Wish*. This is more than mere regional animosity on Cooper's part. Surely, the subject of the war was part of cultural rivalries between New England and New York over their respective roles in defining that elusive construct of "national identity" with which early nationals were obsessed.[56] For example, John Gorham Palfrey's review of *Yamoyden* (1820), an epic-length poem by James Eastburn and Robert Sands, took to task these regional outsiders for siding with King Philip and thus "throw[ing] a gauntlet to New England."[57] But Cooper's revisionary history was much less an account of colonial injustice and more an exposure of contemporary New England's tendency to mythologize its ancestors in ways that spoke to their own immediate needs. The key issue is this: Cooper's exposure of the ambiguities within Puritan piety simultaneously involved a surgical analysis of the unstable language of republicanism, a language that early national New Englanders manipulated to justify both the war and liberal America.

Industry and Providence

"This work is a failure," began one early reviewer of *The Wept of Wish-ton-Wish*. His severity, however, arose largely from a sense that Cooper was "fighting his battles o'er again," rehashing the same materials and themes he had developed earlier in the 1820s in *The Pioneers, Last of the Mohicans,* and *The Prairie*. This particular observation, I think, is more significant than the reviewer's complaints about Cooper's sometimes flattened characterizations and contrived plot constructions, for it begins to suggest the intertextual thematics of *The Wept,* its concern, in other words, with the frontier as the locus for examining American civic culture (one thinks, for example, of the many scenes of waste and excess in *The Pioneers*). The frontier is not exclusively the place of mythic energies (the forces of order and disorder that Natty sees in Glenn's Falls in *Last of the Mohicans*), but also, and especially in context of America during the late 1820s, the place of social and political developments that, as we have seen, paradoxically kindled in New England conservatives an anxious fascination with progress. The 1833 edition of *The Wept,* we should remember, is entitled *The Borderers,* which, if less romantic, more succinctly captures the immediate social and political topoi of the text.

This is not to say, however, that *The Wept* merely contains a recycling of themes woven in earlier Leatherstocking Tales. Its specific dialogue with New England history is apparent even in the Preface to the 1829 edition, where Cooper begins to reveal his awareness that the war was appropriated as a historical rationale for an emergently liberal republic. "At this distant period," he begins, "when Indian traditions are listened to with the interest that we lend to the events of a dark age, it is not easy to convey a vivid image of the dangers and privations that our ancestors encountered, in preparing the land we enjoy for its present state of security and abundance."[58] Even as this suggests Cooper's quirky, sometimes cantankerous optimism for America, its apparent parody of New England filiopiety is sustained as the Puritans are said to have converted the land "into the abodes of civilized man."[59] Cooper significantly avoids Puritan "industry," opting instead for the much more blunt pronouncement of the "growing power of the whites."[60] The ironic effect is even more brutal in light of his deadpan praise for that "venerable historian of Connecticut" who is, of course, Benjamin Trumbull.

This crucial substitution of power for virtue marks Cooper's dialogue with contemporary New England history. It begins to suggest his reevaluation of the viability of Puritan history to stand as a model of civic behavior. The immediate cultural context for *The Wept* helps clarify the major claims made about it by modern critics. Much critical discussion, as I noted at the outset of this chapter, makes the novel out to be a proto-Weberian statement about Protestant psychology. Others have argued that in the novel Cooper is ambivalent toward Puritanism, specifically toward Mark Heathcote, the frontier patriarch whose essential nobility is complicated by his religious zeal. Heathcote, it would seem, embodies all of Cooper's complicated responses to patriarchal authority in general and his own father, the frontier aristocrat William Cooper, in particular.[61] Another line of argument emphasizes the novel's generational theme, where Cooper depicts what Perry Miller once called "declension in a Bible Commonwealth."[62] Heathcote, despite his excesses, is the real hero in the novel. As John P. McWilliams claims, "a heroic age of apostolic faith gives way to a secular age of material well-being and clerical despotism."[63]

In light of the general New England–centrism in early republican historiography, and especially its effusive glorification of the first-generation Founders, one cannot but wonder whether Cooper so readily would follow suit. For it would place him in line with a long tradition of New England filiopietists from Cotton Mather to Jedidiah Morse. Rather, I would argue that Cooper's dubious view of this tradition makes Mark Heathcote in *The Wept* a case study in Puritan acquisitiveness. Moreover, the novel's ambivalence to Puritanism actually results from Cooper's relation to immediate cultural discourses about Puritanism in the early republic. *The Wept* is Cooper's (qualified) revision of the Ebenezer.

From the outset of the novel, Cooper probes the terms of "virtue" upon which this cultural trope was founded. New England's origins, as its chroniclers reminded everyone, were essentially pristine. "Their motives were various," the historian Joseph Felt acknowledged, catching himself in the next breath: "Still the prime movers for settling the colony purposed, as already signified, to prepare it as an asylum for those on whom the hand of prelacy was too heavily laid."[64] But this kind of praise was ironic (if not downright hypocritical) in light of the obvious fascination with New England's commercial growth that Felt and others were experiencing. For this reason, Cooper immediately problematizes these conventional assumptions about New England's other-worldly origins. Plymouth Plantation's self-devoted and pious refugees, who fled from religious persecution, had landed on the rock of Plymouth less than half a century before the time at which the narrative commences, and they, and their descendents, had already transformed a broad waste of wilderness into smiling fields and cheerful villages.[65]

In Cooper the Fathers tellingly "transferred their fortunes and their families" (2) to New England. This not only deflates early national history-writing's claim that these English immigrants had given up everything, but it also complicates the narrative's distinction between New England's "religionists" and those "reckless and gay" adventurers "in the more southern provinces" (2), a distinction, we should recall, on which early national New Englanders insisted. Such a precise deflation of commemorative mythology continues as Cooper summarizes the progress of successive generations. This is a strategy of parody, one sustained throughout much of the novel, attesting to Cooper's sense of the power of early republican language to euphemize greed:

> But enterprise and a desire to search for still more fertile domains, together with the temptation offered by the vast and unknown regions that lay along their western and northern borders, soon induced bolder adventurers to penetrate more deeply into the forests, abandoning as it were all their ties and hopes of communication with what it was their practice to call the old world. (1)

In this instance Cooper teases out the ungovernable energies – desire, temptation, abandonment, penetration – that are imbedded within the liberal virtue of "enterprise." Exposed for what it truly is, the virtue of New England's "self-devoted" fathers takes on less benign implications. For Cooper, the history of King Philip's War would seem to engender a war of *words* subject to infinite revision.

Just what *is* "the march of civilisation" (2)? The novel begins by asking this typically Cooperian question, and it does so specifically by interrogating the liberal mythology of Puritanism and exposing its rapacious implications. Cooper wryly reminds the reader that the original grant for Connecticut "extends from the shores of the Atlantic to those of the South Sea" (2). After ironically commiserating with the first settlers' "apparent hopelessness of ever subduing" the continent, he claims that during the mid-1630s this "Herculean labour" nonetheless began, and, from that period to [the present], the little community [of Connecticut] which then had birth has been steadily, calmly, and prosperously advancing in its career, a model of order and reason, and the hive from which swarms of industrious, hardy, and enlightened yeomen have since spread themselves over a surface so vast, as to create an impression that they still aspire to the possession of the immense regions included in their original grant. (2)

Here are exposed those very fissures between republicanism and liberalism that were gradually becoming synthesized in early national culture. The modern advance of American prosperity is sanctified by its literal and symbolic passage through the premodern ideal of Puritanism ("a model of order and reason" with its "industrious, hardy, and enlightened yeoman"). Yet the image of the Puritans' descendants swarming upon the South Sea islands manages to burlesque the supposed virtue of Puritan industry. The hyperbolic trope of the industrious bee cultivating a limitless frontier exposes the absurd logic of a cultural metaphor.

These acquisitive contexts for Puritan "industry" shape the characterization of Mark Heathcote, who, we are told, employs "the implements of industry peculiar to the advancement of a newly-established country" (3). Nowhere is Cooper's use of Benjamin Church's *Entertaining Passages* more apparent than in the creation of Heathcote, for Church's obvious worldliness ironically colors his insistent humility in the face of divine providence. The relationship between divine causation and purely secular "means" was, of course, reconcilable within Puritan theology. Yet its fictive portrayal here presents tensions between sacred and secular impulses that ultimately point up Cooper's satiric view of the reinvention of Puritanism during his own era. Heathcote's "delusive piety" (4) is actually more a historiographic subject than a theological one; it establishes the novel's demystifying project. From the outset Cooper deflates the "subtleties of sectarian doctrines" (4) consuming Heathcote's sensibility: "When the world was a little uppermost in his thoughts, as will sometimes happen with the most humble spirits, he had even been heard to speak of a Sir Mark of his family, who had ridden a knight in the train of one of the more warlike kings of his native land" (4). Likewise, Heathcote's clear visions of Heaven "were seen through a tolerably long vista of quiet and comfortable enjoyment in this [world]" (4). Cooper satirizes an old soldier whose "peculiarity of doctrine" (which is not "particularly original") ironically "rendered it advisable for him to retire still further from the haunts of men" (8).

Heathcote is a living metaphor for what I have called the double-voiced discourse about Puritanism, the embodiment of liberal energies wrapped up in the signifiers – the language, dress, gesture, and so forth – of Puritan piety. By thematizing Puritan piety in this fashion, Cooper actually meditates on the nature of liberalism itself. *The Wept of Wish-ton-Wish* queries the ramifications of "industry." Unlike Irving's *History of New York* (1809), *The Wept* is not merely a broadside against Puritan religious hypocrisy. Even New Englanders, after all, sometimes lambasted the "delusive piety" of Puritanism to point up its religious excesses. Cooper's frequent focus, however, upon Mark Heathcote's motivations consistently suggests significant ruptures between language and action that effectively dramatize the uncontrollably acquisitive nature of the Puritan Everyman and thereby expose the inconsistencies in contemporary New Englanders' portrait of him. Heathcote's "self-denying and subdued habits" (the basis for justifying King Philip's War in post-Revolutionary discourse) are problematized by "the species of negative prosperity" he enjoys on the margins of Hartford (9). His "keen degree of worldly prudence," which, of course, has contributed to the Wish-ton-Wish's "prosperity and peace" (17), begins to qualify his supposed refusal to submit to "the temptations of the world." During the novel's first battle scene, this tension between liberal reality and commemorative ideal becomes particularly clear. When Reuben Ring and a comrade by chance peer into Heathcote's spiritual retreat, they find it stocked with carnal delights – the best dairy products, a cavalier's buff jerkin, " 'a good store of cheer.' " Reuben can't help but acknowledge that the " 'captain looketh well to the body' " (178). While the two quickly rationalize Heathcote's behavior, the narrator urges "some further inferences" (179).

The fact that Puritan acquisitiveness describes both father and son complicates the view of the novel's portrayal of generational decline. No less than his father, Content Heathcote embodies unacknowledged impulses for the world. The first scene of them together (amid the valley's "fine and fruitful season") suggests how Content's piety confuses the object of love:

The toil went on none the less cheerily for the accompaniment [of prayer], and Content himself, by a certain glimmering of superstition, which appears to be the usual con-

comitant of excited religious zeal, was fain to think that the
sun shone more brightly on their labours, and that the earth
gave forth more of its fruits, while these holy sentiments
were flowing from the lips of a father whom he piously
loved, and so deeply reverenced. (13)

Providence blesses the "labours" – or industry – that converts the
wilderness into the American version of the biblical garden. As
Mark tells the regicide figure (named Submission in the novel),
the Lord "knows so well how to change the wilds into the haunts
of men" (22). Yet during the first battle, Content's despair over
the loss of his land suggests his real desires. Trapped inside the
burning blockhouse, he utters uncontrollably, " 'The in-gathering
of a blessed season is about to melt into ashes before the brand
of these accur –' " (155). A fellow combatant suddenly interrupts
him, chastising him to juxtapose the "wealth" of granaries with
spiritual wealth.

Of course, one can find these tensions in Puritan texts themselves. Much of Bradstreet's poetry ("Some Verses upon the Burning of Our House"), the secular matters of Samuel Sewall's *Diary*,
Cotton Mather's biography of Sir William Phips, all belie secular
concerns in Puritan writing. *The Wept*'s extended critique of the
entire Puritan community, however, reveals its specifically contemporary objections to a liberal set of values underlying narratives of the war in the early republic. The narrator's comment,
for example, on Mark Heathcote's failure to convert Conanchet
suggests the inadequacy of Yankee values of ingenuity and utilitarianism: "The agents they [the Puritans] saw fit to employ, in order
to aid the more hidden purposes of Providence, were in common
useful and rational" (90). The Heathcotes' early morning dili-
gence exemplifies only a more extreme version of the convolu-
tions between New Englanders' sacred and secular impulses. "Ere
the glow of the sun had gilded the sky over the eastern woods,
this [the Heathcotes'] example of industry and providence was
followed by the inmates of every house in the village, or on the
surrounding hills" (220). By associating industry with divinity,
and yet simultaneously complicating the association itself, Cooper parodies contemporary discourse about the causes of King
Philip's War.

The purpose of such a parody is to query the relationship
between progress and civilization. As we have seen, such a yoking
together of "industry" and "providence" in early national historiography was premised on progressive theory that *The Wept*'s treat-

ment of the frontier vigilantly dismantles. In *Changes in the Land: Indians, Colonists and the Ecology of New England* (1983), William Cronon has analyzed the dynamics of colonial deforestation, showing the effects of European agricultural and economic practices on the ecology of colonial New England. Clearing land for farming, resources for fuel, and shipbuilding materials was driven increasingly by a modern market mentality: "The colonists themselves understood what they were doing almost wholly in positive terms, not as 'deforestation,' but as 'the progress of cultivation.' "[66] The imagery surrounding this historical reality pervades Cooper's novel. As the novel's first panoramic sweep of the valley notes the debris and disorder that "civilization" entails, it begins to reappraise Puritan industriousness and, by implication, the causes for King Philip's War:

> The fertile flats, that extended on each of [the Connecticut River's] banks for more than a mile, had been stripped of their burthen of forests, and they now lay in placid meadows, or in fields from which the grain of the season had lately disappeared, and over which the plough had already left the marks of recent tillage. . . . Rails, in which lightness and economy of wood had been but little consulted, like the approaches which the besieger makes in his cautious advance to the hostile fortress, were piled on each other. . . . In one spot, a large square vacancy had been cut into the forest; and though numberless stumps of trees darkened its surface, as indeed they did many of the fields on the flats themselves, bright green grain was sprouting luxuriantly from the rich and virgin soil. . . . High against the side of an adjacent hill . . . a similar invasion had been made on the dominion of the trees: but caprice or convenience had induced an abandonment of the clearing. . . . In this spot, straggling, girdled, and consequently dead trees, piles of logs, and black and charred stubbs, were seen deforming the beauty of a field, that would otherwise have been striking from its deep setting in the woods. (13–14)

What begins as a kind of Crevecoeurian organicism subtly changes to serve the purposes of revisionary history. Putting nature to moral-allegorical use, like the Hudson River school painters, Cooper suggests evidence (as in the practice of girdling trees) of reckless waste "deforming" the landscape. Cultivation is troublingly associated with "caprice or convenience." In the context of the Cooper canon of the 1820s, then, Heathcote and Company are associated with egregious violations of land committed by the Ishmael Bushes and those irresponsible citizens of Templeton.

The image of waste suggests the very causes of King Philip's War. Cooper's landscapes are so often read mythically that one forgets their immediate contexts.[67] In the longer passage just quoted, cultivation is narratively converted into aggression: The Puritan fences look like "the approach which the besieger makes in his cautious advance to the hostile fortress." Symbolism, in other words, starts to take on historiographic meaning. The equation between the landscape's signifiers of hostility and the "besieger" later informs the novel's battle scenes, as the "waste" associated with cultivation – "the thousand objects that may exist in a clearing, to startle the imagination" (48) – symbolically suggests that the war's causes lay in liberal waste. Ruth and Content Heathcote, Eben Dudley, and Reuben Ring are all involved in an epistemological struggle, ironically of their own making, to interpret the wilderness correctly. At night each girdled stump and discarded log of the clearing may in fact be an approaching Native American. Indeed, the landscape's "waste" uncannily assumes life during the first battle scene: "Then the cries of the two adventurers were answered by a burst of yells from a wide circle that nearly environed the hill. At the same moment, every dark object in the fields appeared to give up a human form" (137). Hence Puritan industry – the debris of the cultivated fields – actually symbolizes the causes of war that ironically describe "civilization" itself.

The problematics of historicism involves the novel's reader as well. In parallel scenes staging debates between Native Americans and Puritans over the causes of war, Cooper wrestles over the terms of civilization and situates his reader as a historian, of sorts, negotiating alternative interpretations of colonial history. In these scenes he subjects his own era's discourses of Puritan virtue and providential design to intense scrutiny. This is apparent during the first battle scene when Ruth Heathcote explains the causes of the war to her daughter: " 'He that hath made the earth, hath given it to us for our uses; and reason would seem to teach that if portions of its surface are vacant, he that needeth truly may occupy' " (149). But in this scene mother and child subtly reverse roles, as the elder apparently loses confidence in her argument, and the younger steps in to mimic her father, Content, that the virtue of "toil" has converted the "tangled forest" into a fruitful field. Later, however, when Content and Metacom take up these same issues, Cooper reevaluates this formula. When Content tries to mythologize the self-sacrifice of the Puritan errand, Metacom (or Philip) will have none of it: " 'If the country they have left is pleasant . . . if our trees are but bushes, leave them to the red man' " (298). Throughout, Content clings to sacred history in order to justify the Puritan presence. Only " 'the secret designs of his sacred purpose,' " he claims, will fully explain Puritan rights to the land (297). By first claiming that the Lord " 'hath led his servants hither that the incense of praise may arise from the wilderness,' " Content can in the next breath confidently rebuff Philip in secular terms, stating, " 'and what is now seen of abundance in the valley, hath been wrought by much labour' " (298–9). Philip's retort directly assails this providential argument. Why, he taunts, did the Puritans prosper again so easily after their earlier chastisement by the white man's God? Content can answer only "meekly" (a wonderfully ironic epithet because it is enterprising New Englanders who inherit the earth) that " 'God ceased to be angry' " (300). The Puritans, as the text shows it, are the "cunning" ones (300, 302, 304).

In these debates *The Wept* exposes the acquisitive energies of contemporary liberalism. This is not so much a commentary on Puritan hypocrisy as it is a reevaluation of contemporary New Englanders' capacities to pawn off liberal optimism as sacred history, a historiographic maneuver in which Puritan industry was configured as divinely blessed. Now we can begin to fathom fully the extent of Cooper's parody of the "march of civilization" (2); such early national cant eventually becomes the "march to power" (248). To this end, Cooper uses the novel's most egregiously self-promoting figure, the minister Meek Wolfe, to expose further the cheap rationales for uncontrolled individualism. The sermon he gives justifying Puritan rights to the land "strangely blended" the "hidden purposes of Providence" and "the more intelligible wants and passions of man" (322).

Yet *The Wept*'s critique of unbridled individualism is complicated by its understanding of historical process. Even though the novel insistently exposes the excesses of Puritan industry, at key moments it affirms the forward sweep of American history in which colonial Americans perform the "necessary improvements" (53) upon a "state of nature" (48). This tension derives from an apparent uncertainty about the viable relations between the land and labor and between America itself and progressive history. Those moments in *The Wept* where Cooper does manage to espouse progress do not argue merely for its inevitability (as Natty does, for example, by using the metaphor of the tide in the beginning of *Last of the Mohicans*), but rather fantasize it in ways that deny the logic of liberalism. This occurs at just about the middle of the novel. Contemplating the Puritan origins of America, Cooper's narrative tone suddenly changes. So do the contexts for civic discourse. Colonial Connecticut at this moment exhibits "a portion of that enterprise which has since made her active little community so remarkable" (199). Like early national histories of the war, *The Wept* cheerfully surveys "those improvements which have converted a wilderness into the abodes of abundance and security, with a rapidity that wears the appearance of magic" (199). Puritan America's "impetus for improvement," Cooper notes, "was actively in existence" (201) as a result of the labors of "the American husbandman" (204).

What happens at this crucial moment, which resembles the beginning of *The Pioneers,* is that at least for a short period, American history is divested of the tragedy of cyclical republican time. The earlier, parodic sense of "swarms" of immigrants overrunning the colonial frontier "to distant scenes of industry" now uncannily becomes benign. This significantly shows how, in Cooper, Puritanism can perform the same cultural role as it does in other New England histories, which again recalls its role in *Notions of the Americans* and testifies to the power of colonial New England as a stable metaphor for republican civic ethics. For Cooper uses the Puritans at this moment to model a hierarchical and communitarian ideal, a well-ordered community of egalitarian propertyholders (the "surprising air of equality" of its buildings) under the moral stewardship of patriarchy and church. Like his New England counterparts, once Cooper acknowledges the legitimacy of agrarianism, he then can embrace the modern republic. "It is scarcely necessary to say, that in a country where the laws favour all commendable enterprise, where unnecessary artificial restrictions are unknown, and where the hand of man has not yet exhausted its efforts, the adventurer is allowed the greatest freedom of choice in selecting the field of his enterprise" (199). Hence *The Wept* participates in a larger cultural discourse of Puritanism wherein modern liberalism dialogizes the language of republican virtue. History signifies progress, and progress the virtue of industry and enterprise; the novel's chaotic welter of "waste" now transforms into neatly piled logs and felled trees. George Dekker attributes these historical transformations to the influence of eighteenth-century stadialist theory (derived, in Cooper's case, largely from Sir Walter Scott), which posited progressive stages of history that every civilization undergoes. As Dekker sees it, the novel operates as a case study in a historical transition from a primitive to protobourgeois condition.[68] But even though the midway point of the novel dramatizes this historical movement, *The Wept* as a whole wavers over the very nature of historical "progress." It negotiates with uncertainty the relations among land, work, and waste.

What, in other words, is the relationship between "improvement" and "waste"? The uncertainty surrounding this issue – apparent in Cooper's contrasting visions of Puritan "virtue" – register those in American legal theory during this same era. Early-nineteenth-century jurisprudence, as Morton J. Horwitz has argued, was characterized by an increasingly rapid movement away from "the antidevelopmental consequences of the common law."[69] American jurists came to challenge traditional theories of the common law, rooted in eighteenth-century jurisprudence, that saw it as natural, immutable, and just. They increasingly embraced an instrumentalism that, during an era of commercial and industrial modernization, effectively allowed them to promote economic development. As Horwitz notes, the English common law was clear about waste: Any change a tenant brought about on the land was considered waste for which the tenant was liable. Changes in the jurisprudence of "improvements," however, still produced legal ambiguities: "[T]here remained deep disagreements in the first quarter of the nineteenth century over how far a tenant could go in transforming land for purposes of economic development."[70] Although *The Wept* concerns private, rather than rented, property, the legal and cultural uncertainty surrounding "waste" is germane to the text's treatment of property rights. Noting Cooper's conservative sensibility, some critics rightly have noted his high regard for the stability and order that the common law provided.[71] Yet *The Wept* complicates this view of Cooper. The novel tensely negotiates the meaning of "waste" as both the reckless changes envisioned by the common law and the unproductive (or "inefficient") lands by nineteenth-century instrumentalism. Hence *The Wept* raises crucial legal issues that pervaded the courts of America during this era: How does one determine a "reasonable use" of property? What is the "efficiency" of such use? And to these questions it provides no stable answers.

"Men of Vigilance"

The context that I have been delineating for *The Wept* locates the immediate civic and political issues embedded within its psychologizing of Puritanism. Its ambivalence toward Puritanism, which ostensibly occurs on levels of both psychology and theology, derives from its immediate need to define the nature of republicanism. The nuanced subtleties between Puritan piety and worldliness actually contain a commentary on contemporary liberal discourse. Cooper's strategies of mimicry, parody, and hyperbole expose the way dangerously acquisitive meanings inhabit pristine cultural epithets of Puritan "industry" and "the march of civilisation." In the context of contemporary narratives about King Philip's War, they testify to his objections to New England–based historiography. The novel is Cooper's dialogue with contemporary New Englanders, with himself, and, as we shall see, with contemporary women writers of the day.

Gender compounds the tensions within *The Wept*'s versions of republicanism. The issue is particularly significant because it helps to reconceive of the relationship between Cooper and contemporary New Englanders. In crucial ways, the apparent regional rivalry still shares a similar understanding about the nature of masculine citizenship, which becomes most readily apparent in *The Wept*'s two lengthy battle scenes that work to romanticize Revolutionary republicanism. As we have seen with the Pequot War, King Philip's War historically exemplified an atavistic yet culturally resonant ideal of republican *virtu*. To early nationals, Philip presumably had plotted a widespread Native American conspiracy against the colonials, and so the war represented a conflict of extremely high stakes where the winner would control the destiny of New England.[72] Moreover, in the context of Revolutionary republicanism, the war demanded a colonial response that simulated the *rage militaire* of 1775.[73] "Bold, hardy, and enterprising," one historian proclaimed, "though little versed in regular warfare, the [English] troops were well qualified for military service in the woods."[74] So self-conscious were early nationals of a political–military typology, in which 1675 provided a type for 1775, that someone like Samuel Drake could claim without embarrassment that Benjamin Church's tactical crossing of Bristol Bay to surprise the enemy prefigured Washington's crossing of the Delaware by "but a few days more than one hundred years."[75] As in the rhetoric of the Pequot War, Puritans admirably demonstrated a mode of masculine virtue presumably requisite to republican life. "Nothing but a vigorous effort could save [the colonists]."[76] Even a virtual massacre of a Narragansett fort at Pettyquomscott in December 1675 (a political blunder that brought this tribe fully into the war) was said to be "conducted with spirit, and . . . the most obstinate valor on the part of the English."[77] Revisionist historians today doubt the claim that New England easily raised volunteers, but early nationals thrived on it, for it sustained a republican mythology of yeomen freeholders who put down their plows and armed themselves to save the republic.[78]

Early on in *The Wept,* Cooper would appear to debunk this kind of self-congratulatory political typology. Puritan *virtu* is subjected to his characteristic irony. By juxtaposing Heathcote's love for firearms with his desire to convert Conanchet to Christianity, Cooper highlights the contradictions in Puritanism between Old Testament and New Testament values. The virtue of citizenship, moreover, is made indistinguishable from sheer militarism when the narrator suggests that Heathcote is a kindred spirit (and "boon companion") to Oliver Cromwell and takes delight in listening to "the murderous conflicts of the civil wars" (10). Such excesses find their counterpart in Puritan shortcomings. A minor character, Eben Dudley, initially serves as a kind of stock figure for Brother Jonathan, Cooper's parody in this case of the stout-hearted yeoman's "manly courage," when Eben's beloved, Faith Ring, finds him sleeping at his post. The " 'famousest sleep-walker in the Connecticut Colony' " (126), she says.

But this satire suddenly collapses during the first Native American attack. In this scene Cooper enacts the masculine fantasy of Revolutionary republicanism that, as we have seen, Sedgwick in *Hope Leslie* critiqued as just another form of savagery. The novel's Puritans demonstrate those traditional capacities ensuring the survival of the republic. Time and again, he shows himself to participate in a regional mythology that he otherwise debunks. Even its rhetoric – "the sturdy yeoman," "the vigilance of the defendants," their "vigorous" and "manly" response to impending danger[79] – is at these moments indistinguishable from that of contemporary New Englanders who praised their ancestors as "men of vigilance and spirit."[80] Eben Dudley never becomes a mental giant, but Faith Ring's recognition that " 'there is real manhood in the brawler Dudley' " signals an important thematic rotation that gradually occurs as *The Wept* reconstructs (or recovers) the meaning of masculine republicanism.

Yet the novel reveals thematic inconsistencies in this regard. The subject of masculine republicanism, as we have seen, problematized Sedgwick's treatment of race and gender in her revisionary history of the Pequot War. Cooper's inconsistency derives from similar ideological sources but for different reasons. Like

Hope Leslie's fourth chapter, *The Wept* is structured around two extended battle scenes. Although Cooper only narrates, rather than dramatizes, the Puritan massacre of the Narragansett fort in the winter of 1675, he nonetheless points out its injustice. "It is said that a village of six hundred cabins was burnt," *The Wept*'s narrator states, "and that hundreds of dead and wounded were consumed in the conflagration" (250). The "conscientious religionists" were forced to reconsider "the lawfulness of their cause" (250). These parallel scenes of massacre suggest the kind of equivalence that Sedgwick fully pronounces in *Hope Leslie*. But such an equivalence effectively is eclipsed by the narrative's insistence that Puritan virtue prefigures the American Revolution. The Preface to the 1829 edition of *The Wept* creates this historical synchronicity. "The first blow was struck in June, 1675, rather more than half a century after the English first landed in New-England, and just a century before blood was drawn in the contest which separated the colonies from the mother country."[81] The novel's humanist affinities and historical ironies, in other words, are compromised by its larger design of codifying masculine republicanism.

This again attests to the power of Puritanism as a cultural metaphor. Nowhere are *The Wept*'s tendencies to promote masculine patriotism more apparent than in its representation of the regicide figure Submission. The three English regicides of Charles I, who fled to New England after the Restoration in 1660 (and were sheltered by loyal Puritans there) symbolized to early nationals the struggle of liberty against monarchical traditions associated with Europe. Early nationals learned about the legend of the Angel of Hadley (where one of the regicides, William Goffe, magically appeared to save the town from destruction during a Native American attack) from eighteenth-century histories written by Thomas Hutchinson, who served as governor of Massachusetts Bay before the Revolution, and Ezra Stiles, president of Yale University (whom, as we have seen, Delia Bacon used as a historical source to rewrite history in the image of Puritan women). "Placing himself at their head," one account during the 1820s said of the supposed Angel of Hadley, William Goffe, "and animating them by his address and evidently superior knowledge in military tactics, he enabled them to make a successful resistance, and so compelled the savages to withdraw."[82] David Ramsay praised "the valour and good conduct of an aged, venerable man."[83] In the following chapter, I explore the problematics for early nationals of associating the regicide with republican patriotism (and one that informs, as we shall see, Cooper's ultimate decision to exile Submission from Puritan society), but for now we might recognize the ways in which Cooper's treatment of Submission recycles this legend of Puritan-republican mythology.

Critics have noted Cooper's anxieties over the excesses of Revolutionary patriotism in his early romances of the Revolution, *The Spy* (1821) and *Lionel Lincoln* (1825).[84] In the chaotic "neutral ground" of warfare and disorder, the cant of "liberty" could be perverted so that patriotic vigilance blurs ambiguously with the naked violence of mercenaries and mobs. However, despite Cooper's fears of the patriotic zealotry exemplified by the regicide, the bottom line in *The Wept* is that Submission's call to arms saves the community. Even as the hypocritical minister Meek Wolfe's sermon calls attention to the amorphous sources of Puritan piety, it reenacts the heroic valor necessary to the *res publica*. " 'Lift your eyes upward my brethren – ,' " Wolfe pompously exhorts his congregation, when Submission appears. " 'Rather turn them to the earth!' interrupted a voice from the body of the church; 'there is present need of all your faculties to save life, and even to guard the tabernacle of the Lord' " (271). Cooper's intended irony – the entanglement between the Puritans' self-conscious piety and the stimulating "interests of life" – is compromised severely by the spectral presence of the Minutemen on Lexington Green. The real ghost of this scene is not located in the Puritan imagination (as Hawthorne would suggest in "The Grey Champion") but in an early national one fantasizing the sine qua non of Jacksonian virtue: " 'Now, bold Englishmen,' " Submission commands, " 'strong of hand and stout of heart, you have training in your duty, and you shall not be wanting in example! . . . . Here is an opening for your skill: scourge the cannibals with the hand of death! On, on! to the onset and to victory!' " (279).

What critics see as *The Wept*'s ambiguities are comprehensible in cultural context. Cooper's simultaneous debunking of Puritan "industry" and verification of New England's martial valor show how the novel engages cultural discourses of Puritan order and enterprise. Metaphorical Puritanism helps demystify the novel's ambiguities without reducing either text or context to one another. Most significantly, *The Wept* reveals the impossibility of polarizing republicanism and liberalism. This becomes most obvious during the climactic moment of the first battle scene when the settlers retreat to the blockhouse. The text focuses on it specifically as the central symbol of republican valor and yet, as we have seen, Heathcote's possessions undermine this presentation. Or do they? During the Puritan retreat, the blockhouse would seem to synthesize competing classical and liberal understandings of republicanism that the text continuously navigates. Cooper's attempt to keep them separate fails at the very moment the settlers tellingly muster all their Yankee shrewdness to save themselves in battle. Their escape into the well (pushing the willing suspension of disbelief well past readers more tolerant than Mark Twain) exemplifies the "wonderful aptitude of expedient, and readiness of execution, which distinguish the American borderer" (181). Republican *virtu* and Yankee ingenuity are inevitably conflated. With its Spartan facade enshrouding an acquisitive interior, the blockhouse symbolizes civic ethics in the early republic.

Cooper insists, however, on dichotomizing republican values. For the loss of a communitarian ideal bears significantly on future events. The narrator at one point offers a homily that really explains the vulnerability of the Heathcote home during the second battle scene: "Still, as man has never been the subject of a system here, and as each individual has always had the liberty of consulting his own temper, bolder spirits early began to break through a practice, by which quite as much was lost in convenience as was gained in security" (204). When Submission successfully repels the second attack, and the Puritan saints retreat through their gates to safety, the scene fractures into two symbolic spheres where the protected "circle" of community (as opposed to Lydia Child's recurrent image of imprisonment in *Hobomok*) provides a place of refuge. Outside this circle of community stands the Heathcote mansion ("a considerable dwelling on the opposite side of the valley . . . not wanting in the more substantial comforts of a spacious and commodious frontier residence" [220]). As a symbol of first-generation Puritanism, it is subject to invasion because of the materialist qualities which early nationals either denied or euphemized. To recap: If the frontier provided Cooper a proven, marketable commodity of adventure and violence, a place of historical transition, and perhaps even a symbolic place of timeless, mythic tensions between order and chaos, it offered as well a fictive place from which to critique the ancestral pieties of contemporary New Englanders. The frontier in *The Wept* locates a nexus between Cooper's characteristic anxieties and his sense of the hollow solutions of commemorative New England historiography. Like Sedgwick, he wrote about war as a way of waging a campaign for a reimagined republic.

Cooper and the Violence of Androgyny

The thematic relations between gender and republicanism in *The Wept* naturally raise questions about its relationship to women's historical writing during the 1820s. Recent discussions of the politics of Cooper's work have emphasized the need to place each text as part of a larger dialogue with other texts. Geoffrey Rans, for example, unfolds the paradoxes of the Leatherstocking novels by reading the allusive details in each novel in context of the others so that they vibrate intertextually in a large web of meaning.[85] Nina Baym extends this kind of interpretive strategy to writings by Cooper's contemporaries – specifically, women writers – in order to articulate the gendered differences of the " 'Indian story' " during the 1820s. Numerous writers "revised each other from gendered perspectives": *Yamoyden* prompted Child's writing of *Hobomok*, which in turn elicited Cooper's response in *The Last of the Mohicans,* a novel that Catharine Sedgwick had in mind as she wrote *Hope Leslie.*[86] I would widen this web of intertextuality even further. By considering texts outside the Leatherstocking canon and, even more importantly, outside the boundaries of literary discourse, we might gain a more comprehensive sense of the cultural politics of race and miscegenation during this era. The notion that *The Wept* has specific literary antecedents during the 1820s is suggested by the comments of one reviewer who faulted *The Wept* for virtually plagiarizing *Hope Leslie*'s treatment of miscegenation; Cooper, he claimed, simply substituted a tragic ending to the Faith/Oneco plot.[87] Perhaps of greater consequence is a conceptual premise underlying this entire study. All of these historical novels and plays negotiated issues such as race within the context of a larger range of historical writing. History and historical fiction conversed across familiar, permeable boundaries. The pattern of literary responses and revisions during the 1820s, which Baym has noted, was part of a widespread struggle over the gendered meanings of republican virtue.

The re-creation of King Philip during the early national era derived from cultural changes in the meaning of republican manhood. Even more dramatically than the Pequot, Philip was made into a model of masculine virtue, a consummate patriot who, despite his inevitably "savage" qualities, embodied ideals circulated in Revolutionary America. This owed virtually nothing to Puritan historiography. William Hubbard may have begrudgingly admitted that Philip's peer, the Narragansett sachem Conan-

chet, died valiantly, "as if . . . some old Roman Ghost had possessed the body of this Western Pagan,"[88] but generally Puritan
chroniclers of the war spared their readers the republican parallels, opting instead, as the poet Benjamin Tompson did in "New
England's Crisis" (1676), simply to villify Native Americans, calling Philip a "greasy lout" and "vaporing scab" who seduced his
people to violence through promises for plunder.[89] Early nationals, however, re-created Philip largely in the image of republican
heroism and through a republican discourse of rights, liberty,
and property; as with the Pequots, they juggled his conspiratorial
guilt and valorous leadership to impugn and mythologize him
simultaneously. This recognition of his patriotic virtue informs
Samuel Knapp's claim that Philip's attempt to consolidate various
tribes against the English "was one worthy of the most sagacious
statesmen of any age."[90] He was "a deep politician, with a heart
glowing with the love of his country, and burning with indigna-
tion against the prosperous strangers, who were extending themselves over the inheritance of his fathers."[91] A mighty prince
among men, Metacom's association with Caesar or Alexander
combined romantic heroism with the ideal of classical *virtu*. And
this encomium usually extended to all of the Wampanoags who
"viewed themselves as a free and independent people."[92]

If this characterization of Philip implicitly questioned the issue
of property rights on which the "march of civilisation" was premised, it was was further complicated by the general instability of
the meaning of "virtue" itself. Philip's historical characterization
tellingly inscribed as well the eminently modern – and masculine – qualities of affective benevolence and sentimental devotion. In fact, the early republic's representation of King Philip is
so crucial because of its gendered – rather than racial – ramifications. It exemplifies a syncretic ideal of republican manhood
during this transitional era, what I would call a logic of androgyny. Women writers such as Sedgwick and Child, as we have seen,
exploited the complex legacy of eighteenth-century affectionalism and nurturance to re-create selectively, indeed, to androgyn-
ize, the norms of republican manhood. As a complex icon of
republican culture, Philip provides a context for gauging those
efforts by women writers to revise classical republicanism.

One might consider Washington Irving's portrait of Philip in
The Sketch Book (1820) to fathom the gendered tensions inhering
in modern republicanism. Geoffrey Crayon's sentimental encomium in "Philip of Pokanoket" concludes by wavering between
the sachem's masculine and feminized virtues. Philip combines

the noble qualities of a consummate "patriot" and "soldier" with those softer feelings which, one should recognize, characterize Crayon himself. The Whiggish legacy of Irving's eulogium is obvious enough: "Proud of heart, and with an untameable love of natural liberty, he preferred to enjoy it among the beasts of the forests, or in the dismal and famished recesses of swamps and morasses, rather than bow his haught spirit to submission and live dependent and despised in the ease and luxury of the settlements."[93] Yet this context for Philip's humanity is complicated by a newer understanding of humanity itself, as Philip is "alive to the softer feelings of connubial love and paternal tenderness, and to the generous sentiment of friendship."[94]

Antebellum historical melodrama depended heavily on modern virtues of affect and benevolence to elicit sentimental responses from its audience. Indeed, the early American theater made use of Metacom to facilitate heroic drama. Perhaps the preeminent (or simply most bombastic) actor in nineteenth-century theater, Edwin Forrest, found his greatest role in Philip by announcing a prize contest (of five hundred dollars) for the best play whose hero was a Native American. Not unlike Americans today (including myself) who flock to the Disney production of "Pocahontas," early nationals craved romantic stories of Native American history. An aspiring actor and playwright, John Augustus Stone, heeded Forrest's call, and late in 1829 *Metamora; or the Last of the Wampanoags* opened at the Park Theatre in New York City, with Forrest in the lead role of King Philip.[95] Critics of the play have emphasized a number of thematic and ideological tensions pervading it. About forty years ago, Roy Harvey Pearce presciently took up the subject of race in the play, and concluded that its ambiguous characterization of Philip "furnishes us the richest evidence of the imbalance between the convention of the noble savage and the idea of savagism."[96] More recently, Bruce A. McConachie has considered the play as an important example of "Jacksonian yeoman theatre" which "provided an arena of conflict for highlighting and partly resolving the ideological differences between [republicanism and liberalism] so that the culture of liberal capitalism . . . could emerge as fully hegemonic in the mid 1850s."[97] Both these interpretations hinge upon the importance of melodrama. For Pearce, sentimental melodrama enables the displacement of the savage stereotype with the noble savage ideal; for McConachie "yeoman melodramatic culture" makes the theatre the place where audiences' political anxieties and ambiguous self-images are worked out emotionally.

The fact that melodrama relies on sentiment helps to explain the premium *Metamora* places on Philip's capacity for feeling. This complicates McConachie's thesis that the play inscribes the emergent ideologies of American masculinity. In *Metamora* the "noble savage" is highly androgynized. The play, via Metamora (yet another name for Metacom or Philip), registers the period's highly fragile protean meanings of republican manhood. The hero embodies both justice and mercy, violence and tears. As a context for Conanchet in *The Wept,* the latter qualities actually get him killed. Like Cooper's novel, Stone's play is an ongoing meditation on the nature of masculinity and political authority in the early republic. Throughout the drama Metamora wavers between republican vigilance ("Death! Death, or my nation's freedom!"[98] he paraphrases Patrick Henry) and New Testament altruism. What is crucial here is that the qualities heightening the sentimental pitch of the play – the softer feelings fulfilling Metamora's humanity – actually undermine the Wampanoag sachem's political effectiveness against the English. Christian virtue produces the Aristotelian tragic fall. Metamora dislikes the English yet discourses on religious toleration, is cast as the consummate warrior and yet sympathetically refrains from taking others' lives during battle. He also spares the life of an adversary whom he must know surely will betray him to the English.[99]

Metamora's soft heart, the play suggests, results from the very same female influence that Hobomok undergoes at the Conant home. In parallel scenes, the Puritan woman, Oceana, and his own wife, Nahmeokee, successfully appeal to his benevolent capacities for Christian love, codifying for contemporary audiences an emergently Victorian role for women to refine the classical austerities of republican manhood. However, Metamora's submission to his wife's charitable nature (he spares, in a moment of *hamartia,* a political enemy against his better judgment) signals a political downfall that even Nahmeokee cannot ignore. "Come not near me," Metamora sternly admonishes her. "Or thou wilt make my heart soft, when I would have it hard like the iron and gifted with many lives."[100] But it is too late. In this instance verbal irony arises from an avowal of *virtu* filled with sound and fury, yet signifying nothing. Like Irving's Philip and James Eastburn's Yamoyden (which inspired Child's novel), who sacrifices his life for his unforgiving father-in-law, Metamora embodies those qualities which at once humanize and doom him, producing sentimental regret in audiences and at the same time validating the inevitable expansion of America.

This strategy thus produces sentiment for both melodramatic and political effect. Cooper's novel at once exploits the logic of androgyny, which facilitates this artistic maneuver, and metacritically analyzes it. As all students of King Philip's War have recognized, Conanchet's formal entrance into the war during the winter of 1675–6 made him the most powerful sachem (because of Philip's losses by this point) now fighting the English.[101] Cooper's substitution of Conanchet for Philip in *The Wept* (although the latter does appear) replaces one Native American "republican" for another.[102] In *The Wept*, Conanchet's fate dramatizes the untenable formula for manhood that Cooper sees in the fictions of Child and Sedgwick. Historical romance of the 1820s, in other words, constitutes a large intertext of republican masculinity mediated through race.

This is significant, I think, because critics of *The Wept* tend to elide the issue of gender as they examine race and captivity in the novel. During the 1960s George Dekker took Leslie Fiedler to task for painting Cooper, in *Love and Death in the American Novel* (1960), as a racist of sorts who viewed miscegenation with horror.[103] More than thirty years later, a loyal Cooperian like James Wallace in effect carries on Dekker's project by articulating cogently Cooper's anti-essentialist and relatively progressive views of race.[104] But even Wallace's analysis hinges on the key statement that the "essential interpretive problem in *The Wept of Wishton-Wish* is how to understand the captivity of young Ruth Heathcote."[105] Scholarship on the novel has focused almost so unilaterally on the captivity of whites that it has overlooked the fundamental importance of Conanchet's captivity; if Cooperians acknowledge that Conanchet is a wavering figure in the tradition of Sir Walter Scott, they do not recognize this to be a function of gender as much as race.[106] I would like in what follows to resituate the importance of Conanchet's captivity in the novel, for it demonstrates how Cooper's well-known resistance to feminization (noted by D. H. Lawrence, Fiedler, and others)[107] informs his treatment of both Puritanism and republican manhood. The cultural trope of Puritanism offered Cooper a model of republican masculinity against which he could further interrogate the gendered cultural solutions of contemporary women writers.

Conanchet's fate is remarkably like Hobomok's. By situating Conanchet in the Heathcote home, Cooper tests the political consequences of domestic "influence." Ruth Heathcote experiences much greater success than her husband, Mark, had in converting Conanchet, although the terms of conversion are different. The descendant of the unjustly executed Miantonomo, Conanchet shows an inability to execute what *must* be a politics of retribution. This is his missing of the mark, his tragedy. Conanchet's political shortcomings result from his earlier exposure to the domestic ethos of Christian love. The Narragansett sachem internalizes a feminized ideology that continually vies with his masculine understanding of *communitas*. Conanchet's internalization of early national cultural tensions is made visible (and foreshadows his ultimate fate) during the first battle scene when his "gentle expression" pierces his "dark visage." Ruth knows this, for she trusts her children's lives to him. Not unlike Magawisca, Conanchet struggles with gendered ideologies entangled with the two sides of Indian "nature":

> The flashing of his eye as it lighted on this sad object [a human bone], was wild and exulting, like that of the savage when he first feels the fierce joy of glutted vengeance; but gentler recollections came with the gaze and kinder feelings evidently usurped the place of the hatred he had been taught to bear a race who were so fast sweeping his people from the earth. The relic fell from his hand, and had the gentle Ruth been there to witness the melancholy and relenting shade that clouded his swarthy features, she might have found pleasure in the certainty that all her kindness had not been wasted. (187)

As Conanchet is transformed from a vessel of vengeance to one of love, the rhetoric of Indian-ness travels awkwardly over the issue of nature itself: "savage" behavior ambiguously is "taught," or acculturated. Yet what Cooper apparently views as domestic imperialism producing "kinder feelings" (a parallel to the masculine work of axes and plows) divests Conanchet of any real, viable power. Moreover, his conjugal bliss with Ruth/Narra-mattah produces the same kind of civilized refinement. When he looks sternly upon his wife, her returning gaze dramatizes a female influence that presumably traverses the borders of race: "The firmness [of Conanchet's look] had passed away, and in its place was left the winning softness of affection, which, as it belongs to nature, is seen at times in the expression of the Indian's eye, as strongly as it is ever known to sweeten the intercourse of a more polished condition of life" (315).

Conanchet's physique itself symbolizes the cultural logic of androgyny. For decades Cooper's critics have noted its importance. Conanchet's body serves as a text with which to read and, in light of women's writing of the 1820s, to reread the political ramifications of sentimental masculinity. This moment in *The Wept* drives a rift into the gendered syntheses of women's republicanism (apparent, for example, in Hope Leslie's vigorous benevolence, Charles Brown's benevolent vigor), and argues that in a male world of military politics Revolutionary and Christian virtues are ultimately irreconcilable:

> In form and features, this young warrior might be deemed a model of the excellence of Indian manhood. The limbs were full, round, faultlessly straight, and distinguished by an appearance of extreme activity, without however being equally remarkable for muscle. In the latter particular, in the upright attitude, and in the distant and noble gaze, which so often elevated his front, there was a close affinity to the statue of the Pythian Apollo; while in the full, though slightly effeminate chest, there was an equal resemblance to the look of animal indulgence, which is to be traced in the severe representations of Bacchus. (293–4)

Both Fiedler and Dekker have misread this crucial passage in the novel. Whereas Fiedler faults Cooper for presenting here "the hint of something revolting to a higher race," Dekker takes Fiedler to task for not citing the rest of the passage, in which the narrator claims that Conanchet's "austerity" is tempered by "the charities of humanity."[108] But Dekker's apologia loses sight of Cooper's irony in its cultural context. The juxtaposition between Apollonian masculinity and Dionysian femininity (his "slightly effeminate chest") symbolizes Conanchet's hopelessly conflicted nature, a fact that ultimately dooms him. What Cooper soon calls Conanchet's "peculiar fulness of chest" symbolizes the feminization – and hence invalidation – of male political leadership.

Conanchet's remorse after the first battle foreshadows his tragic decision during the second to spare the Heathcotes' lives. Conanchet argues absurdly that his Narragansett warriors are tired of taking scalps. " 'Why does Metacom look so hard?' " Conanchet asks an angry, impatient Philip (309). His attempt to rationalize his own tenderness is especially ridiculous, since it was the Puritan massacre at Pettyquomscott, as well as the failed negotiations with Roger Williams in Providence, Rhode Island, that finally brought the Narragansetts into the war. (The Narragansetts themselves are shocked at "his intention to abandon a conquest that seemed more than half achieved" [320]). In the face of this politically untenable argument, Metacom scorns Conanchet, taunting him that Narragansett women will have to supply food for their men. By sparing their lives, Conanchet in effect destroys himself, since later it is Content who prosecutes his capture and sanctions his execution. Conanchet's feminization reaches even further. When he relinquishes his right to keep his wife, Narra-mattah (the younger Ruth whom he took away after the first battle), Conanchet acknowledges – just as Everell Fletcher and Charles Brown do – the superiority of domestic love to conjugal love: " 'The Manitou of your race is strong,' " he tells his wife cradled in Ruth's arms. "He telleth a mother to know her child' " (319). Then he cries.

What Cooper views as the political impracticality of androgyny culminates with Conanchet's self-sacrifice for his newly adopted father, Submission. On its surface, this looks to be a Cooperian fantasy of male bonding between consummate warriors on opposite sides; but it actually dramatizes a reciprocal exchange of male sentiment (what Submission calls " 'many acts of kindness, each in our several fashions' ") that traverses race and heightens the pathos of both Conanchet's death and Submission's exile. Christian love collapses race, re-creates identity: Submission avows that " 'my heart is Indian.' " Conanchet, he claims, is a good Christian: " 'and come of what race, or worship in what manner thou may'st, there is One to remember it' " (368). In the end, Conanchet willingly uses himself as a decoy in order to save Submission. Such selflessness, the text suggests, is the logical conclusion of affective, Christian virtue, and it leads only to a great sachem's political demise.

In context of gender and republican culture, then, Conanchet's is the most significant captivity in the novel. What happens to him parallels the fate, as one critic has argued, of Uncas in *The Last of the Mohicans*, who is transformed by "the power of mother."[109] Moreover, the scene of Conanchet's death ironically rewrites the Puritan record, as it is described in William Hubbard's *A Narrative of the Trouble with the Indians* (1677), in order to critique the contemporary norms of manhood as others – and particularly women – were codifying them in the 1820s. In the face of death, according to Hubbard, Conanchet presumably acted like the model Indian chieftan: "And when he was told his Sentence was to dye, he said, he liked it well, that he should dye before his heart was soft, or had spoken any thing unworthy of himself."[110] No greater moment of verbal irony reverberates in *The Wept* than its inversion of this sentimental scene. Poised "like a chief seated in council," the dying Conanchet whispers to Uncas, " 'Mohican, I die before my heart is soft' " (389). Yet the Narragansett sachem dies *because* his heart is soft. Like Hobomok (or Charles Brown, Everell Fletcher, Delia Bacon's William Goffe), Conanchet embodies the conflation of gendered forms of virtue. Other writers, such as Eastburn and Sands, as well as Irving, who sought the appropriate historical materials to fulfill a protoromantic aesthetic of melancholy, borrowed from Hubbard.[111] *The Wept* exploits this moment from Hubbard, at once secreting feeling and calling attention to the political limitations of such sentiment. As in Sedgwick's performance of the Pequot War, the racial other in *The Wept* becomes the site of a gendered dialogue over the nature of the modern republic.

Oddly enough, then, Cooper's revisionary history of King Philip's War makes him a fit parallel for Increase Mather. How Cooper would shudder at the comparison! For the Puritan divine and the American novelist, both of whom were acting as historians of sorts, the war occasioned a jeremiad to an immediate, backsliding generation. The sins of modernity that *The Wept* addresses involved two things simultaneously: the emergence of a liberal republic viewed anxiously by Cooper, and the contemporary rhetoric of New England history that euphemized the forces of unbridled individualism. Throughout the book I have argued that all of these historical romances are *about* language itself in the early republic. This returns us to one of the epigraphs for this chapter. Ten years after *The Wept*, in *The American Democrat* (1838), Cooper complained that, "The common faults of American language are an ambition of effect, a want of simplicity, and a turgid abuse of terms. To these may be added ambiguity of expression."[112] He then proceeds to discuss the languages of servants, laborers, ladies and gentleman, articulating throughout the abuses of a changing language that suggest his deeper anxieties about a changing America. Language is about class, about social stability, about political order. As Thomas Gustafson has shown, political and linguistic projects were inextricably related in early national America. In this context, *The Wept*'s interrogation of such politically charged words as "industry," "property," "cultivation," "waste," and "progress" reveals Cooper's dialogue with historiography as much as with history, his attempt, in other words, to combat the chaotic tendencies of the elasticity of republican language and to restore (or imagine) its fixed, original meanings. Such a rhetorical project in effect critiques the naked, entropic acquisitiveness of modern liberalism, which finds later expression in such rapacious characters as Jason Newcome, Stead-fast Dodge, and Aristabulus Bragg.[113] In this sense, then, *The Wept* is like *Hobomok* and *Hope Leslie*. All three are at once secular histories and cultural critiques, fables of marriage and fantasies of racial encounter. And all three, no less than Noah Webster's *American Dictionary* of 1828, are lexical reconstructions of repub-lican language.

Such a concern with republican language shaped Cooper's novel *Lionel Lincoln* (1825), about Revolutionary New England, the first of an intended (but later aborted) series of thirteen romances dramatizing each of the thirteen colonies' role in the American Revolution. Like so many others, Cooper attributed New England's radical brand of patriotism to the libertarian spirit of its Puritan founders. Like *The Spy*, however, *Lionel Lincoln* is rather anxious about popular discourses of "liberty," "freedom," and "rights." The premier spokesman for the Revolutionary cause, for example, is an escapee from an English asylum. Indeed, *Lionel Lincoln's* encounter with Revolutionary republicanism in New England politically symbolizes a psychological struggle within himself, in which the forces of madness and stability vie for his soul. Both *The Wept* and *Lionel Lincoln* suggest the dangers of a radical libertarian spirit. What was the status of Revolutionary "zealotry" in a post-Revolutionary world? Early nationals, of course, used this word to describe the witchcraft trials held in Salem in 1692. In contemplating Puritan witch-hunting, as we shall see, they were actually reconsidering the American Revolu-tion itself.

5

WITCH-HUNTING AND THE
POLITICS OF REASON

In such [democratic] states therefore it is a thing inevitable, that the people should be beset by unworthy flatterers and be intoxicated with their philtres. Sudden, blind and violent in all their impulses, they cannot heap power enough on their favourites, nor make their vengeance as prompt and terrible as their wrath against those, whom genius and virtue have qualified to be their friends and unfitted to be their flatterers. . . . When therefore a demagogue invites the ignorant multitude to dwell on the contemplation of their sovereignty, to consider princes as their equals . . . is it to be supposed that aristocratic good sense will be permitted to disturb their feast or to dishonour their triumph?

    – "Political Thoughts," *The Monthly Anthology and Boston Review*
    (1805)

Ratcliffe was exasperated at Carrington's habit of drawing discussion to this point. He felt the remark as a personal insult, and he knew it to be intended. "Public men," he broke out, "cannot be dressing themselves today in Washington's cold clothes. If Washington were President now, he would have to learn our ways or lose the next election. Only fools or theorists imagine that our society can be handled with gloves or long poles. One must make one's self a part of it. If virtue won't answer our purpose, we must use vice, or our opponents will put us out of office, and this was as true in Washington's day as it is now, and always will be."

    – Henry Adams, *Democracy* (1880)

Episodes such as the Pequot War and King Philip's War in early republican historical literature remade the Puritans into a model of patriotism. If we think back to a crucial moment in *The Wept of Wish-ton-Wish,* where the stouthearted Connecticut settlers are suddenly besieged by Native Americans, we can begin to reconsider this historical trope for Revolutionary republicanism. In this instance Cooper praises what he distinctly calls Puritan "zeal." Even though, as we have seen, he treats, with characteristic irony, Puritan piety as a sort of "delusion," the scene as a whole nevertheless dramatizes the "pressing necessity" of selfless patriotism.[1] Puritan zeal in *The Wept*, however, is not always so admirable. It sometimes decidedly means "the strong colouring of fanaticism which tinged the characters of the religionists of those days,"[2] a foible suggesting as much social and political disorder as it does radical sectarian religion.

Indeed, Puritan zealotry is significantly associated in *The Wept* with witch-hunting. "Had the genuine benevolence of [Mark Heathcote's] character been less tried, or had mingled in active life at a later period, it might possibly have been his fate to share in the persecutions which his countrymen heaped on those who were believed to deal with influences it is thought impious to exercise."[3] The novel even links Heathcote to Cotton Mather himself (that "grave and respectable authority" on witchcraft) during a scene in which the settlers discuss Eben Dudley's encounters with the "wonderful" sounds of the invisible world. Here Heathcote serves the ends of satire by acting as a Matherian mouthpiece on "the prince of the powers of darkness." Through the invisible presence of Mather the scene suggests the violence of the Salem witchcraft trials. An anachronism, to be sure, and an important one. For such a historical context cannot help but render negative connotations to the substance of Puritan zealotry – an epithet used as much as any to describe colonial New Englanders. As opposed to the two battle scenes, where Puritan zeal momentarily models a virtuous republicanism, the allusions to witch-hunting distance early national readers from their ancestral past. The narrator, after all, calls Dudley's experience a "delusion."[4]

I emphasize these moments in *The Wept* in order to locate another, crucial arena for the multivalence of early republican language and the political anxieties from which it arises. Cooper's difficulty in *The Wept* is that he, like so many others during this era, cannot fix stable meanings to Puritan "zeal." The boundaries between virtuous patriotism and political fanaticism would seem to be unalterably permeable. Puritan deficiencies in reason, in other words, raise decidedly *political* fears. The novel exemplifies a larger problem in early republican culture concerning the nature of patriotism itself. Anxieties about the people's "passions" were particularly acute for conservatives, who were witnessing the gradual rise of democratic, popular political parties between the 1790s and 1830s. The purpose of this chapter is to show how and why these anxieties were inscribed upon the record of Puritan witch-hunting, particularly the famous (or infamous) episode at Salem in 1692, where the people's zealous passions destroyed social and political order. I situate the Salem witchcraft trials as a historical trope displaying the supposed danger of an emergently popular politics in America.

For a number of reasons, I think, we read Arthur Miller's famous play about the Salem witchcraft trials, *The Crucible* (1953), as a political allegory of Cold War America, but fail to allow for a similar kind of political reading for early national discourse about Puritan witch-hunting. Perhaps one reason is our own historical proximity to McCarthyism. Another factor that has affected literary criticism on witchcraft fiction involves formalist concerns that tend to isolate literary works from their political contexts. In the early part of the twentieth century, the first real critical survey of witchcraft fiction argued that this episode of Puritan history provided a "colorful" subject for fledgling historical romancers. Plagued by their often peripheral position in the international literary scene, these writers were seeking fresh materials to fulfill the call for a truly American historical romance that W. H. Gardiner had given in his famous review in 1822 of Cooper's *The Spy*.[5] In other words, scholars have focused for an entire generation on issues of literary aesthetics and literary nationalism, citing the romantic potential of Puritan witchcraft, "as that instance from the regional past that resonated most strongly with supernaturalism of traditional Gothic, and as proof that New England culture was not so humdrum as early national critics had feared."[6]

The central importance of Hawthorne to the American canon in general and to historical romance in particular also has contributed to the elision of earlier literary works about witchcraft. As I noted at the outset of this study, influential studies by Michael Davitt Bell, Michael P. Colacurcio, and George Dekker invaluably have served students of Hawthorne and antebellum literary history, but their cogent discussions of Hawthorne's psychological and historical themes have taken place at the direct expense of earlier writers.[7] Someone like Bell, for example, rightly noted more than twenty years ago that "[w]hat interests these writers about the witchcraft crisis is not the process of its development and eruption, but its general meaning for the nineteenth-century present. And by and large the witch trials are seen as yet another instance . . . of the Puritan persecution of innocent victims."[8] Yet in the next breath Bell claims that Hawthorne is the "main exception" to this rule, asserting his superiority before even considering the immediate political and cultural contexts for "persecution." Whereas Bell psychologizes a tale like "Alice Doane's Appeal" (1835), which likely was composed during the late 1820s, Colacurcio does so by historicizing it in the context of the Puritan epistemological crisis over spectral evidence at Salem, with the ultimate aim of demonstrating Hawthorne's acute historical sensibility.[9] Finally, another factor contributing to the elision of the politics of fanaticism during the 1820s is a long-standing religiocentrism in early republican literary studies. Buell, for example, has shown how witchcraft further contributed to the "proxy war" between liberal and orthodox camps in nineteenth-century New England.[10]

Although this approach illuminates the period's discourses about witch-hunting, I shall explore the subject's political ramifications to show how in fundamental ways these groups often spoke the same conservative language. I reconsider the politics of witchcraft fiction by recasting the cultural context for it. My argument is this: The legacy of classical republicanism (and specifically its fears about "factions") that accompanied the actual rise of American political parties between the 1790s and 1830s, significantly shaped the historical literature about Puritan witchhunting. The fact that both Federalists and Republicans, and later Whigs and Democrats, appropriated – and refashioned – republican ideology to serve political ends again testifies to its enduring cultural currency. Even more dramatically than the Puritan persecution of Quakers, the subject of witch-hunting was mediated by republican assumptions about factions where demagogic leaders, as so many lamented, manipulated the passions of the people. For political conservatives,[11] Puritan witch-hunting functioned as a historical metaphor for the onset of popular politics in America.[12]

This context allows for the excavation of the political meanings of words that, as any reader of witchcraft literature can attest, simply saturate the genre – words like "delusion," "infatuation," "fanaticism," "superstition," "bigotry," and "zeal." Such a context, however, also allows for important distinctions in the treatment of witch-hunting between historical romance and historiography. By reading historical fiction in context of a broad range of history-writing, we may gauge with some precision the genre's alternatively republican *and* romantic impulses. The texts I discuss here – John Neal's *Rachel Dyer* (1829), John Greenleaf Whittier's *Legends of New England* (1831), the aptly named drama

Superstition (1824) by James Nelson Barker, as well as numerous others – appeared at a time characterized by both Jacksonian politics and emergent ideologies of romanticism. It is no surprise that writers who inherited conservative political beliefs and yet wanted to see themselves as romantic "artists," approached the era's politics of reason with difficulties. I spend sufficient time in this chapter first locating the ideological background to conservative discourse about political parties, and only then proceeding to analyze its inscription in historical literature. Puritan history mediated contemporary anxieties about political change. Early nationals were forced to grapple with the problem of the nature of Revolutionary patriotism in a post-Revolutionary world.

The "Middle Path in Government"

Republicanism traditionally resisted the kind of interest group politics that we know today. Because classical theory conceived of the *res publica* in strictly corporate and consensual terms, interest groups were dubbed "factions" and were considered the bane of republican life. Interests themselves signified the evils of vice, luxury, and corruption that eventually beset all republics and signaled their inevitable decline. Perhaps the most prolific writer on the evils of faction in early-eighteenth-century England was the Opposition leader Henry St. John, Lord Bolingbroke. Between the 1720s and 1740s, Bolingbroke and others excoriated the corruption of the administration of Sir Robert Walpole. They juxtaposed the people at large, dubbed the "Country," with the host of self-seeking stockjobbers, financiers, and placemen who made up the "Court." "Faction is to party," Bolingbroke began the analogy, "what the superlative is to the positive: party is a political evil, and faction is the worst of all parties."[13]

Even though he was later scorned by many American conservatives for his deist beliefs, Bolingbroke helped influence Revolutionary America's conspiratorial view of politics. Factions were believed to embody the "basest passions" where "men were unwilling to sacrifice their immediate desires for the corporate good."[14] As one New York orator put it later in the 1790s, factions thrived upon *"that spirit which renders either the governor or governed more concerned for the private interests, passions, and prejudices, than for the national interests, in their conduct respecting the government."*[15] One immediately sees that this discourse politicized faculty psychology by juxtaposing the passions with reason as the source of human motivations. Its theoretical roots lay as well in Scottish Common Sense philosophy. As Daniel Walker Howe has shown, conservative adaptations of Scottish affectionalism (the belief that the moral sense lay in the heart, a tenet central to the thought of Francis Hutcheson, for example) increasingly looked to reason as the source of personal morality and political order. Like the state itself, the individual was ideally balanced by a hierarchy of faculties, at the top of which governed reason: "Left to themselves, the lower powers [one's appetitive impulses] would escape control and wreak havoc. An unregulated faculty – whether pride, licentiousness, or some other appetite or emotion – was called a 'passion.' "[16]

The Revolutionary settlement of 1787–8 significantly recast the danger of factions. As so many have noted, the advent of "modern" politics involved reconceptualizing "factions" as something that could be controlled rather than eradicated. This, of course, is the argument of the famous tenth *Federalist* in which James Madison tried to provide a theoretical foundation for a modern republic characterized by an institutional system of checks and balances.[17] "In some degree the Revolution," John Murrin and Rowland Berthoff have argued, "accelerated the transformation from truly communal consensus to the explicitly majoritarian democracy of the nineteenth century in which political parties institutionalized and even promoted conflict by appealing to the self-interest or prejudice of the individual voter."[18]

Historians of American politics, however, have demonstrated that the legacy of Whig theory shaped the rise of the first two party systems in early republican America. One of the most prolific students of the rise of American political parties, Ronald P. Formisano, argues that a kind of cultural schizophrenia characterized the transition from premodern to modern politics: "The period from the 1780s to the 1820s possessed almost a split personality: intensely passionate in partisan conviction but inhibited by antipartisan assumptions about the nature of politics and society."[19] Others who have analyzed the rise of a second American party system, which occurred between 1824 and 1840, tend to agree. During this formative era, Whigs and Democrats culled selectively from republican traditions to gain the upper hand on the opposition. Whigs drew on the antimonarchical discourse of the Revolution to label Jackson "King Andrew." Democrats accused Whig financial programs (particularly the National Bank) of being a guise for noxious "moneyed interests." Whigs actually tried to turn their apparent lack of party organization into a virtue. Democrats fashioned themselves the Bolingbrokean Country – "the tribune or sentinel of the people in defense of the republic," which was a deft maneuver, considering they were the party in power until 1840.[20] In this "watershed decade" of the 1820s, then, which was characterized by a "fluid character" and a capacity for "blending" premodern and modern styles,[21] republican ideology was co-opted, refigured, disfigured, and redeployed to fulfill partisan ends. Nevertheless, republican discourse about factions endured.

The convergence of this discourse with the subject of Puritan witch-hunting involved conservative fears about democracy itself. Republican ideology depicted a process where artful demagogues manipulated the people's passions, so that eventually the tyranny of many would be followed by a tyranny of one. In this schema reason guaranteed the republic's protracted existence. Benjamin Rush, we should recall, considered reason to be "the only just sovereign of the mind."[22] His Preface to "A Plan for the Education of Public Schools" (1786) avowed that its prescribed regimen for schoolchildren would "assist in removing prejudice, superstition, and enthusiasm"; in this context, Rush's allowance of a pittance of scientific knowledge for American girls aimed chiefly "to prevent superstition."[23] Moreover, this cultural fear of uncontrolled passions extended to American leaders as well as to the masses. Ambition was a devilishly prickly thing. Only "the control of reason" and the "checks of conscience," as Mercy Otis Warren explained, could prevent the "noble principle" of ambition from turning into "tyranny, and the wanton exercise of arbitrary sway."[24] In this context, then, significant subtleties of language describe George Washington's famous "Farewell Address" (1796), which was printed upon his departure from office. Admitting that the "spirit [of party] is inseparable from our nature, having its root in the strongest passions of the human mind," Washington still urged Americans to remain neutral from entangling foreign alliances. Factions, he explained, were engineered by "ambitious, corrupted, or deluded citizens" who masqueraded as zealous patriots.[25] I italicize the distinction Washington makes here, for it reflects the general view that factions combined the excesses of both the designing and the deluded. And the distinction, as we shall see, informs this era's treatment of the episode at Salem.

From the 1790s to the 1820s the spectre of Jeffersonian and later Jacksonian democracy haunted Federalists, moderate National Republicans, and proto-Whigs, who desperately clung to a fantasy of hierarchical order. In this political discourse "reason" and "passions" were used as code words for deference and democracy. "National passions," John Adams argued in *Discourses on Davila* (1805), inevitably bred demagoguery: "This national at-

tachment to an elective first magistrate, where there is no competition, is very great; but where there is a competition, the passions
of his party, are inflamed by it, into a more ardent enthusiasm."[26]
Appalled by Jeffersonian political principles, as well as the anar-
chic implications of deism, conservative New England divines
similarly warned against "the propensities and passions peculiar
to human nature ... [and the] destructive courses of error
and delusion"; the masses' "strong delusions" gave voice to "the
boasted experiment of liberty and revolutions," a democratic
cant that proved only "the madness in the heart of the sons of
men."[27]

Such insanity presumably was confirmed by recent history. During the early phases of the French Revolution, the Jacobin Reign
of Terror horrified many Americans, making them even more
acutely aware of the violent anarchy that the masses, under the
bewitching spell of artful demagogues, would create. In the cant
of conservative Whiggery, High Federalists like Timothy Dwight
and Noah Webster declaimed the Terror as a "dance of Jacobin
phrenzy" and "a whirlwind, a tornado of passions."[28] In "The
Revolution in France" (1794), Webster elaborated on the theories
of David Hume to distinguish carefully between "superstition"
(the mind's susceptibility to "unaccountable terrors") and "enthusiasm" (the mind's "unaccountable elevation"), concluding that if
they were not the same thing, they nonetheless produced the
same terrible effects. What struck Webster as the most darkly
ironic feature of the Jacobin terror was that, as deists, the Jacobins
had turned the ideal of reason itself into yet another form of
superstition. "But I will meet your philosophy upon your own
ground," he challenged the Jacobins (and particularly their Jeffersonian supporters at home), "and demonstrate, by the very
decrees which demolish the ancient superstition, that you your-
selves are the most bigotted men in existence."[29] What he called
"the mad rancor of party and faction"[30] described the inevitable
fate of radical egalitarian democracy. Americans, he warned,
would do best to keep to "the middle path in government, religion and morals, which has ever been found practicable and
safe."[31]

In light of a number of factors in the 1790s – the erosion of
consensual politics, the proliferation of Democratic Clubs, and
many Jeffersonian Republicans' support for the political changes
in France – conservative fears of egalitarian politics were particularly strong. More important than the sense of urgency informing
Webster's diatribe, however, is its ability to gloss the political

meanings of an early national language of irrationality. The signifiers of Jacobin excess that Webster and others used – "superstition," "delusion," "enthusiasm" and "bigotry" – today suggest what
many see as the supposed backwardness of religious fundamental-
ism with which bourgeois urban Americans often distance themselves from the Bible Belt. In the early republic these words were
not only socially but politically inflected as well.

So far as this discourse was shaped by class-driven fears, it
conflated not only society and politics but also politics and religion. Chronic laments about the loss of reason arose partly from
the spate of evangelical revivals that turn-of-century America witnessed during the Second Great Awakening. As Nathan O. Hatch
has shown, the democratization of American Christianity threatened established religion and its status quo hierarchies of authority by sanctioning the legitimacy of irrational states of mind.
Populist revivals "empowered ordinary people by taking their
deepest spiritual impulses at face value, rather than subjecting
them to the scrutiny of orthodox doctrine and the frowns of
respectable clergymen."[32] Baptists, Methodists, Adventists, the
Christian Connection: The acceptance by these groups of
dreams, trances, visions, moments of ecstatic joy and horror, lay
at the essence of a culture of revivalism that was as much politically antiauthoritarian as it was religiously evangelical. Perhaps it
is no surprise that the rise of democratic Christianity "opened the
door to religious demagogues."[33] On the other end of America's
religious spectrum stood deists who also posed a challenge to
established religion. Henry F. May has shown that the "Didactic
Enlightenment" in early-nineteenth-century America was a defense of reason and moderation against deistic skepticism associated with the French Revolution for the sake of preserving social
and political order.[34] Elite conservatives, then, feared evangelical
culture on one side and rational deism on the other, two polarized forms of religious dissent that nonetheless similarly challenged established religious and political authorities. The episode at Salem thus conflated religion and politics.

For conservative New Englanders the rise of Jacksonian politics
only confirmed those fears that the French Revolution had enkin-
dled. The rhetorical politics of faculty psychology sounded well
into the antebellum era. Self-appointed moral stewards of the
republic, such as Emma Willard, the founder of the Troy Female
Seminary, included Washington's "Farewell Address" (along with
the Declaration of Independence and the Constitution) in the
appendix to her *History of the United States* (1831). Willard praised
Washington's "paternal anxiety" about "those maxims of virtue

and prudence, from which [America's] prosperous condition had arisen. . . . Americans should learn [them] in youth, and practice [them] in later life."[35] Likewise, in *The Duties of an American Citizen* (1825) Francis Wayland, the pastor of Boston's First Baptist Church, warned his readers about the danger of factions. Americans, he maintained, must shun "those feelings of party animosity to which a free people, in the present imperfect condition of human nature, must always be liable."[36] Note the Whiggish urgency of Wayland's rhetoric: If the people's "decisions become the dictates of passion and venality, rather than of reason and of right, that moment are our liberties at an end; and glad to escape the despotism of millions, we shall flee to the despotism of one."[37]

The crucial dilemma implied in all of these exhortations concerns the problematic nature of patriotism itself. As Pauline Maier has argued, many Revolutionary political theorists (Jefferson, for one) posited the ultimately positive effects of mass gatherings, whose unpleasantly violent activities nonetheless prevented the habitual abuses of governments to last for very long. Crowd action thereby ensured the preservation of liberty in republican governments.[38] But was such "patriotism" tenable in a post-Revolutionary world? What were the implications of the "passions" now? As J. G. A. Pocock has shown, ever since *Cato's Letters* appeared in the *London Journal* during the early 1720s, Whig theorists had struggled over the fact that "passions are called good when they serve the public and bad when they do not."[39] If this prickly distinction dates back to Aristotelian theory, it describes as well the political difficulties in post-Revolutionary America as people persisted in acting "out of doors" during the 1780s. Patriotism, John Adams declared, was essentially a passion, and "even in . . . esteemed, beloved . . . characters, the passion, although refined by the purest moral sentiments, and intended to be governed by the best principle is a passion still."[40] As Jeremy Belknap considered the political situation in France, he asked, ". . . have we not reason to fear that the cause of liberty may be injured by the intemperate zeal of its friends, as much as by the systematic opposition of its enemies?" What is telling here is Belknap's use of a qualifying adjective, as though "zeal" under other conditions might be utterly benign. He goes on to offer a definition of rational patriotism where "wisdom, harmony, and fortitude" joined "on the side of liberty," thereby avoiding the "anarchy and distress" besieging France.[41] Similarly, in the thirty-seventh *Federalist*, where Madison makes the crucial transition from the Confederation's defects to the Constitution's virtues, he tempers patriotic virtue with a healthy dose of restraint: "But the truth is that these papers. . . . solicit the attention of those only who add to a sincere zeal for the happiness of their country, a temper favorable to a just estimate of the means of promoting it."[42] Like Webster's location of the "middle path," Madison's persona is crafted out of what he calls a "spirit of moderation."

Post-Revolutionary redefinitions of patriotism involved a larger recodification of republican language. Webster's *American Dictionary* (1828), for example, even more systematically inscribes the politics of reason than did his diatribe on the French Revolution. He defines "superstition" as a religious phenomenon ("False religion; false worship"), but his consistent emphasis on "excess" in each definition begins to resonate politically. "Bigotry" similarly denotes an "[o]bstinate or blind attachment to a particular creed . . . *party*, sect, or opinion" (italics added). Webster quotes the conservative Federalist Fisher Ames to illustrate the meaning of "enthusiasm": " 'Faction and *enthusiasm* are the instruments by which popular governments are destroyed.' " Yet Webster's entry for "zeal" demonstrates the difficulty of disentangling "true" patriotism from "party spirit." Zeal means "[p]assionate ardor in the pursuit of any thing," and could be "manifested . . . in a good or bad cause." Just as George Washington distinguished between the "upright zeal" of a "truly enlightened and independent patriot" and the zealotry of "deluded minds," and Madison in the *Federalist* clings to a "sincere zeal," Webster defines "bigotry" as only an "unreasonable zeal." This implies its benign possibilities. The explication for "enthusiasm" hedges in the same way: "Hence the same heat of imagination, chastised by reason or experience, becomes a noble passion . . . an ardent zeal that forms sublime ideas, and prompts to the ardent pursuit of laudable objects. . . . Such is the *enthusiasm* of the patriot, the hero and the christian."[43]

In context, then, the difficulties that *The Wept of Wish-ton-Wish* has in defining zealotry is much less a Cooperian than a cultural problem. The political typology connecting colonial and Revolutionary patriotism was sufficiently problematized in the aftermath of the war as to confound the distinction between patriotism and anarchy. Such ideological instability inhered within the rubric of "zealotry" – the key word for Puritan witch-hunting – which signifies simultaneously "true" and "false" patriotism. The intersection of the discourses of witch-hunting and party politics mark an uneasy cultural transition from premodern to modern politics. If the virtue of reason theoretically defined the border between

them, we can still see the fragile logic beneath this cultural solution. Did the "zeal" of true patriotism contain any less "passionate
ardor" than that of false patriotism? After all, passion, as Webster
unconsciously admitted, could be enlisted "for a good or bad
cause." And how could passion ever be "reasonable"? Puritan
history inscribes these rhetorical and political dilemmas.

The Fury of 1692

To history-writers of the early republic the Puritan witch-hunt was
a decidedly political event. As the most celebrated of all Puritan
witchcraft episodes, Salem instanced an absolute upheaval of society. It was a "tornado," a "fury," a "furious volcano," or a "delusion" where the "pillars of civil government were shaken."[44] Certainly, Puritan sources, principally Cotton Mather's *The Wonders of
the Invisible World* (1692) and its counterpart, Robert Calef's *More
Wonders of the Invisible World* (1700), offered sufficient evidence
of social and political disorder. From the strange fits of Abigail
Williams and Elizabeth Parris, which precipitated the events, to
the severe proceedings of the Court of Oyer and Terminer, the
entire episode dramatized what Mather called "a Troubled
House."[45] Early national history-writers thematized this problem
and made it the central lesson from which contemporary readers
hopefully would benefit. In doing so, they were following the
didactic logic of nationalist history whose aim, among other
things, was to show "the blessings of political union, and the
miseries of faction; the dangers of unbridled liberty, and the
mischiefs of despotic power."[46]

These historians forced a political interpretation of the episode on their readers. Abiel Abbot reminded everyone in no
uncertain terms that "[t]his delusion is not confined to religious
subjects." "There seem founded deep in human nature passions,
which often prevail over the understanding, an enthusiasm, a
frenzy which hears not the voice of reason."[47] One of the period's
most involved analyses of the history of witchcraft and superstition was Charles Wentworth Upham's *Lectures on Witchcraft*
(1831). A Unitarian divine carrying a mean grudge against Cotton Mather, Upham concluded his work with a passage cited at
the outset of this study, which chastised its immediate audience
for missing the point of history. Upham declared that "whenever
a community gives way to its passions . . . and casts off the restraints of reason, there is a delusion. . . . It would be wiser to
direct our ridicule and reproaches to the delusions of our own

times, rather than to those of a previous age, and it becomes us to treat with charity and mercy the failings of our predecessors, at least until we have ceased to imitate and repeat them."[48]

Nearly everyone called Salem a "delusion,"[49] an epithet whose implications of class politics are perhaps not immediately audible to modern ears. Hence liberals like Hannah Adams remarked that Salem had demanded "coolness and caution,"[50] while Alden Bradford claimed that the tragedy furnished "melancholy proof of the weakness and credulity *of the human mind.* . . . When reason and philosophy are disregarded, credulity and prejudice can effect every thing but miracles."[51] In these righteous assessments reside post-Enlightenment concerns over the progress of reason in America. Had the republic historically escaped Puritan "gloom"? Hence early nationals often resorted to rhetorical hedging, as is apparent in the qualifying frame for the following remark: "If the phantom [belief in witchcraft] still exists, it is only in the dark recesses of ignorance, where men shut their eyes to the light of philosophy, and are not ashamed to be considered ridiculous."[52]

As the politics of Upham's invocation of reason shows, Harvard-centered liberals, who took potshots at their Orthodox counterparts via the Salem episode, nonetheless expressed political fears transcending sectarian animosity. Clearly, more than theology, or even race and gender, the issue of class shaped early national historical discourse about Salem. Again, the similarities between sectarian antagonists like Jedidiah Morse and Hannah Adams belie class-driven fears of popular democracy. Morse lamented that "a terror of the public mind . . . was driving the people to the most desperate conduct," while Adams observed that the "strength of prejudice" and "the force of imagination" produced a "gloom and horror" that "in some respects appeared more replete with calamity, than even the devastations of war."[53] The virtues of reason and moderation supported apparently fragile social divisions that, Adams believed, the episode at Salem dreadfully inverted. For both, the real "tragedy" of Salem occurred when "profligate characters" began to accuse those "of superior rank and character" – the "most respectable families." Even Governor Phips's beloved wife![54]

Yet race and gender also play a significant role in the period's historical accounts of Puritan witch-hunting. The danger posed by the inversion of hierarchy, for example, was presumably no different than an invasion by Native Americans.[55] Some historians today, as David D. Hall has noted, see Puritan witch-hunting as a means to punish social deviancy, where status quo groups further shored up their power by assailing the social margins.[56] Early nationals, however, viewed the episode in exactly the opposite way. They placed the blame for "the tempest of passion" on the politically disenfranchised – Caribbean blacks, white women, and young children – who temporarily assumed a political voice. Jedidiah Morse was not alone in offering an obfuscating theory of racial influence to explain the roots of Puritan "gloom": It was the fireside lore of Indian legends and superstitions that "laid the basis of much superstition, and furnished fuel for approaching terrors."[57] Tituba, the slave of the Salem village minister Samuel Parris, also was made out to be a culprit, since the superstitions of people of color, the argument went, unfortunately infected the community at large:

> [Since] they were supposed to be adepts in the science of witchcraft. . . . [t]he attention of the publick mind was immediately roused. . . . Children of not more than twelve years of age were permitted to give their testimony; [West] Indians were called to tell their stories of wonder, and women their nocturnal frights. For a time the counsels of age were unheard; wisdom was confounded, and religion silenced.[58]

The syntax here is crucial for understanding the implied historical argument. Its passive constructions make absent the subject of the magistracy, ministers and church elders; by displacing their culpability in this fashion, the passage places blame on marginal groups. Political tumult, then, presumably results not only from alien superstition but from those emotionally wrought Puritan goodwives and children who made hysterical accusations (or sometimes feigned afflictions). To complete this theory of the social margins, historians lamented as well the baneful effects of Native American superstitions that only worsened Puritan "gloom."[59] Hence elite conservatives of a later era blamed the Puritan magistracy only so far as it had succumbed to these influences. This historical formula reflected the anxieties of those who faced a democratizing political world in which deference had all but eroded. Here, then, was a neat political formula on the part of elite conservatives to blame the Puritan rulers of "credulity" while still affirming their right to rule.[60]

With the rise of democratic politics in the late 1820s and 1830s, these anxieties only got worse and managed to subsume Salem in what we might now call a presentist discourse. Consider, for example, Abiel Abbot's summation of the importance of Salem to contemporary times and that of Charles Goodrich:

> Have not many been seen in a frenzy on politics, assembled and full of tumult, like the Ephesians, crying out, great is their cause? but they know not why, or wherefore; they will drag this man to death, and that they will raise on their shoulders, but they know not why they kill the one, and extol the other. It is the same spirit that pervades the quack in all professions, and by which his deceptions are so successful.[61]

And Goodrich:

> Now, whenever we see a community divided into parties, and agitated by some general excitement – when we feel ourselves borne along on one side or the other, by the popular tide, let us inquire whether we are not acting under the influence of a delusion, which a few years, perhaps a few months, or days, may dispel and expose. – Nor, at such a time, let us regard our sincerity . . . or the seeming clearness and certainty of our reasonings, as furnishing an absolute assurance that, after all, we do not mistake, and that our opponents are not right.[62]

Like Noah Webster discussing French politics, both Abbot and Goodrich inculcate a politics of the "middle path," promoting what Ronald Formisano has called the "[c]entrism and antipartyism" that dominated American political discourse between the 1780s and 1820s.[63] By its very nature, popular sovereignty would seem to entail violent rhythms of instability – the sanguinary change of power, or "some general excitement." Faced with a political dynamic consisting of political "quacks" and the "popular tide," the republic seems subject to an endlessly whimsical cycle of deluded majorities that are manipulated skillfully by demagogues. In both passages politics are generic; there are no specific issues. In context of the 1820s, however, the danger of a single-issue politics precipitating the people's passions, whether it was tariff nullification, internal improvements, the admission of Missouri into the Union, undoubtedly underlies each exhortation. For this was the very trait that, as one historian has argued, was central to the growth of the second American party system.[64]

The issue of demagoguery raises the question of the role of Cotton Mather in the Salem proceedings. Ever since Calef's acrid treatment of him, Mather has been alternately vilified and defended in histories of Salem.[65] Although his *Wonders of the Invisible World* cautions readers about the dangers of spectral evidence, he stuck by the proceedings of the Court of Oyer and Terminer and defended the policies of Governor William Phips, Increase Mather's handpicked selection when the Bay colony received a new charter in 1691. In the many critiques of Mather's political leadership (or lack of it) during this crisis, there has emerged a kind of bifocal image of him that endures unto this day. On the one hand, there is simply the image among historians of the "credulous and pompous fool"[66] whose steadfast belief in demonology has amused contemporary readers no less than late-eighteenth-century ones like Jeremy Belknap and Ebenezer Hazard, who, if we recall, wrote each other recounting humorous moments in Mather's writings. Yet there is another Mather as well in the popular mind, one who descends from Robert Calef and passes through such historians as Upham, George Bancroft, and Perry Miller himself. In *More Wonders,* Calef certainly blamed Mather for credulity and theological distortions, but he chiefly took him to task for conspiring to fabricate a crisis in order to promote his personal authority and reaffirm the New England Way.[67] This cultural doubling of Cotton Mather, I would argue, derives from early national political culture. To recall the language of George Washington's "Farewell Address," its duality derives from the political theory that factions arose from the "ambitious . . . *or* [the] deluded."

In fact, most early national writers, if they focused on Mather at all, resisted conspiratorial arguments and only mocked Mather's superstitious foibles. Rather than interpreting Mather through the lens of Calef (whose *More Wonders,* we should remember, was reprinted in 1823), they cast Mather and Calef as respectively backward and enlightened sensibilities against whom contemporary readers could measure their own capacities for reason. Calef's rationalism – what David Ramsay called his "plain common sense" – was preferable to the "too credulous" Mather.[68] Many narratives reveal as well a certain nationalistic touchiness about the entire episode at Salem. Some, like Morse (especially because of his Orthodox position), even tried to capitalize on Anglo-American rivalries in order to let Mather and the Puritans off the hook by blaming their superstitions on prevailing English beliefs in witchcraft, or by citing such famous English minds as Mathew Hale and Joseph Glanvil (who both believed in devils) to exonerate the Puritans of unique superstitions.[69] Even these rationales fell short, however. Most early national historians readily acknowledged Mather's crucial role in failing to control popular passions of the moment. Long ago, Perry Miller argued that Robert Calef actually did tie the tin can to the proper tail of Cotton Mather in holding him responsible for conspiring in the "killings" at Salem.[70] But most post-Revolutionary writers tied a distinctly different one to Mather than Calef had, one that sounded contemporary assumptions about the danger of superstition.

When these historians portrayed Mather as Grand Conspirator, however, they did so within the conspiratorial framework of republican ideology. Whiggish fears of conspiracy shaped the Unitarian assault on Mather's reputation. No better instance of this exists than Upham's *Lectures on Witchcraft* (1831). Upham cast Mather as a skillful demagogue, arguing that he showed "an inordinate love of temporal power and distinction." At George Burroughs's hanging, Mather issued an "artful declamation" that "had the intended effect upon the fanatical multitude"; Burroughs's dead body was "trampled by the mob."[71] Echoing Calef, Upham believed that Mather and the leading ministers were "ambitious of spiritual influence and domination," a political maneuver that could be carried out only "by carrying the people to the greatest extreme of credulity, fanaticism, and superstition." Like any "ambitious and grasping" leader, Mather "was anxious to have the support of all parties at the same time."[72] In an age of Jacksonian politics, one can begin to see Upham's urgent exhortation to read Salem as a political trope for the American republic. In this way, he hoped, as he declared in the Preface, to "control public sentiment" and "check the prevalence of fanaticism."[73]

Puritan "zealotry," however, was a tricky subject during this era. Indeed, it reflects the same nuances about the relations between patriotism and passions as does Washington's "Farewell Address" and Webster's *American Dictionary*. The Puritans' founding of New England, their role in the Pequot and King Philip's Wars, their resistance to Sir Edmund Andros and the Stuarts in 1688–9: All of these episodes in early national historiography show the Puritans' exemplifying a "commendable zeal." Yet the zealotry of witch-hunting was not benign at all; it signified unruly, violent mobs who were often manipulated by artful demagogues. Such factious violence was prefigured in Puritan treatment of Quakers in the 1650s, but in witch-hunting it reached its nadir.[74] In the face of these historical facts, some New Englanders tortuously negotiated Puritan zealotry as they strove for a viable solution for the right kind of republican patriotism. Rufus Choate, for example, proclaimed that the "love of liberty there was; but a government founded in liberty there was not one besides. Some things other than the love of freedom are needful to form a great and free nation. Let us go farther then, and observe the *wisdom and prudence* by which, after a long and painful process, our fathers were prepared, in mind and heart, for the *tempered* enjoyment, and *true* use of that freedom, the love of which was rooted in their souls."[75] Puritan or Revolutionary patriotism needed to be tempered by reason. Paradoxically, the republic might crumble from either the excess or the absence of Revolutionary vigilance: Too much of it spawned populist demagogues; too little of it left a nation vulnerable to conspiracies. As they debunked Puritan superstition, in other words, early nationals voiced classical republican ones of their own.

Fictionalizing the Art of Demagoguery

This legacy of conservative republican ideology allows for the discussion of literary politics with some precision. It reveals the significance of witchcraft fiction's generic conventions (conspiring villains, scenes of mass hysteria, demagogic injustice) as well as its language (words like "delusion" and "superstition"). That witchcraft fiction participated in the larger cultural project of promoting reason in the early republic should be no surprise. William Charvat and Terence Martin both have shown that early American fiction arose amid a critical atmosphere influenced by Scottish philosophy and dominated by a concern for the novel's cultivation of the moral sense, which was itself increasingly associated with reason during this era.[76] But early American witchcraft literature politicizes the issue of faculty psychology by dramatizing scenes that specifically show the vulnerability of the common people. It is a decidedly antidemocratic genre. Yet, as we shall see, the rise of romanticism, accompanied by the gradual professionalization of belles lettres, lent very different meanings to Puritan "gloom" and "imagination" in literary texts. These words began to encode the emergent romantic ideologies of imaginative autonomy and artistic power. So the genre negotiated, sometimes tenuously, the political and cultural imperatives of republicanism and romanticism.

Virtually all of these fictions of the 1820s dramatize the breakdown of social and political hierarchies. An early work during this era, the anonymously published *Salem Witchcraft* (1820), imparts a serious political message, despite its generally comic ef-

fects derived from New England regionalism (parodies of court-
ing rituals and learned quacks), slapstick, and eighteenth-century
comic theater (the allegorical characters such as the constable,
Lemuel Lockup, Ichabod Shuffle, and Patience Peabody).[77] What
propels the plot of *Salem Witchcraft* is the frustrated courtship
between Deliverance Hobbes's daughter, Beautiful (a "Gorgon,"
as the narrator notes), and Faithful Handy. Out of spite, another
jilted member of the Hobbes household, Remarkable Short,
helps to bring on chaos in the community by convincing Deliverance that Beautiful's hysterics are the result of diabolism. She
accuses Faithful, Beautiful's reluctant suitor, of being "the black
man." There the witch-hunt begins.

In spite of its plastic characters, awkward plot movements, and
distorted use of historical characters, *Salem Witchcraft* significantly
locates the causes of "delusion" on the social margins. As in
the histories by Jedidiah Morse, Charles Goodrich, and others,
deluded women manage to engulf the community in a general
hysteria culminating a convocation of the "mob." During the trial
scene this "ranting, roaring, and screaming" group overruns the
constables and causes chaos in the courtroom.[78] The "violent
convulsions" of Beautiful Hobbes and Abigail Williams thus only
symbolize a larger social crisis where "all the mob mingled in
their groans and dolorous wailings, as if Pandemonium had broken loose in good earnest, and Satan had come upon earth like a
roaring lion."[79] The "devil" that the text portrays is the specter of
mob politics, which in this case is left unchecked by rulers who
are more credulous than designing. One of the chief magistrates,
for example, Philip Smith, allows his dream world to infect the
real one. The townspeople assume that he's "bewitched" – and he
is, in the early republican sense of this word. Meanwhile, Cotton
Mather's pedantic disquisitions on demonology are debunked as
merely silly rather than manipulative. "If we may believe [Math-
er's account of the ordeal attributing it to the work of the devil],"
the narrator sardonically concludes, "the prince of the air and his
. . . host of spectres, phantoms, apparitions, and hobgoblins, were
let loose upon this devoted place, and at the instigation of old
women, potent in witchcraft, were playing their damned pranks,
upon the inhabitants."[80] The text thus defamiliarizes contemporary readers, distending them from their ancestral roots. Cotton
Mather becomes a barometer with which to measure themselves.

The political danger of the social margins also shapes both the
anonymously published *The Witch of New England* (1824) and
Whittier's first full-length book, *Legends of New England* (1831).

Both texts in effect reinscribe Benjamin Rush's fears that superstitious minds would be tyrannized. In *The Witch of New England* the
town "hag" (a word Cotton Mather used for Martha Carrier) plays
upon the "universally prevalent" fears of witchcraft in Puritan
Connecticut. By assuming the public role of a witch, Annie Brown
successfully intimidates Minister Bradley ("the dark, superstitious
but well meaning clergyman"),[81] his daughter Agnes, and eventually the entire community. Above all else, Annie's power derives
from her ability to manipulate language. "Over common minds,"
the narrator concludes, "she invariably obtained an influence and
stern mastery that she seldom relinquished, and often used with
heartless and unrelenting disdain."[82] Seventeenth-century diabolism, in other words, is reconfigured specifically into the art (as in
"artifice") of politics.

The novel's erratic oscillations between sportive and serious
gothicism derive from deeper cultural anxieties. Its uncertain
wavering results from its attempt to mock superstition and its
lingering sense that the people's passions are no laughing matter
at all. As Annie Brown gradually gains control over the people,
she truly becomes demonic. In one crucial scene, she stands high
atop a nearby hill taunting the people during a funeral proces-
sion (for a young child whom Annie, in effect, murdered). Her
perch is symbolic of her newfound political power.

Like the period's histories that allied class and race in attributing the causes of Salem's delusion, *The Witch of New England*
doubles Annie with another villain, the Native American sachem
Samoset. Both conspirators skillfully exploit the people's passions
to promote themselves politically. Like Annie, Samoset possesses
a "sagacity and cunning [that] often induced the ignorant and
superstitious savages to yield to him the deference and obedience, held to be due to the favorite of their gods."[83] Several
parallel scenes in the novel – the Native American war council,
the Puritans' witchcraft trials, and the persecution of Quakers –
dramatize a danger of zealotry that not only crosses racial boundaries but allies Puritan backwardness with presumably childlike,
superstitious "savages." Brought to "a very considerable excitement" during the banishment of a Quaker, the Puritans would
seem to be no different than the Native Americans whom Samoset rouses "to a pitch of enthusiasm bordering upon insanity."[84]
The result of this equivalence is a skein of racial and political
ironies that makes the Puritans in this case distinctly "other."
Such zealotry has no place in a modern world.

John Greenleaf Whittier's "The Haunted House" similarly dramatizes the political consequences of irrationality. As his critics make clear, Whittier, a Whig reformer and antislavery activist, held an absolute disdain for the "Custom-House Tories" of Jackson's party.[85] Whatever sympathy the narrator initially allows for the tale's lower-class protagonist, the "ill-favored" Alice Knight, who suffers "the mortifications of poverty and dependence," he holds her accountable for "the fierce passions of her nature."[86] Like Annie Brown, her marginal place in the community leads to a vengeful quest for political power, which is ultimately contingent on "the credulity and fears of her neighbors." The victim here is one Adam McOrne, a wealthy landowner of Scottish descent, who refuses Knight's son as a suitor for his daughter. McOrne's roots in the Scottish Highlands make him a perfect parallel for the outback Puritans. As Alice fabricates "imaginary demons," McOrne is "shaken by the controlling superstitions of the time."[87] Hence he is "enslaved," in the eighteenth-century sense of an incapacitated will, and thus temporarily divested of political power.

All of the tale's gothic effects – its wonders of the invisible world – are finally explained in the coda. Here Whittier implicitly asks his readers to measure themselves against McOrne, whose laughter at "the superstitions and credulity of his [Puritan] neighbors" ironically attests to his own.[88] Whittier's coda is significant on another count as well. Like *Salem Witchcraft* and *The Witch of New England*, "The Haunted House" tellingly links delusion to conspiracy. We finally learn that Alice cajoled McOrne's servants into participating in the plot, "partly from an innate love of mischief, and partly from a pique against the worthy Scotchman, whose irritable temperament had more than once discovered itself in the unceremonious collision of his cane with the heads and shoulders of his domestics."[89]

So literary convention and political ideology converge as the genre's stock figure of the town hag signals the political hobgoblin of demagogic politics. As opposed to characters like Hope Leslie and Magawisca, Annie Brown's and Alice Knight's androgynous qualities ("uncommonly muscular," a "wild and untameable beast") debase rather than embellish their humanity. This reveals another political convergence: the one between the cultural discourses of misogyny and conspiracy. Annie and Alice are peculiarly *early national* demons. Republican vigilance is needed in a world of conspirators like Alice and Annie. One sees this ambivalence toward zealotry, for example, in *The Witch*'s trial scene of Annie Brown. As the narrative wavers between sympathy and righteousness, it laments the "miscarriage" of Puritan justice (the use of spectral evidence, the obvious histrionics of the witnesses) but ultimately erases from the text the danger of the evil manipulator.

Such fears evidently could infect Jacksonian Democrats as well. Case in point: James Nelson Barker. His play *The Tragedy of Superstition* (1824) was called by the early American dramatist William Dunlap "an honour to the dramatic literature of the country."[90] The drama's antidemocratic themes are particularly ironic in light of Barker's own political life. His premier biographer has emphasized his absolute, lifelong loyalty to the Democratic Party. Veteran of the War of 1812, and later mayor of Philadelphia, Barker was a member of a political group, "The Democratic Young Men," that helped run Jackson's 1828 campaign in Philadelphia. For his loyalty, he was appointed by Jackson – under part of the spoils system, which Whigs hopelessly decried – as Collector of the Port of Philadelphia, and later by Van Buren as well.[91] Barker's tenure as mayor in 1819–20, however, was plagued by a rash of street crime and rioting, which would appear to have made him more dubious about the people's virtue than his critics have realized. Whatever scant criticism *Superstition* has received contextualizes the play by locating the historical sources Barker consulted.[92] But this altogether misses the contemporary significance of its treatment of what readers generally recognize as the subjects of "bigotry" and "prejudice" and "superstition."

When *Superstition* opened at Philadelphia's Chestnut Street Theater in March 1824, it dramatized the danger of mob violence incited by parvenu political leaders. Much of the drama revolves around the aptly named villain, Ravensworth, a Puritan divine who preys upon the people's passions in order to enhance his own position. From the moment the curtain rises, the dual images of Ravensworth's cottage and the Fitzroy mansion (the home of Isabella, a wealthy immigrant from England, and her son, Charles) symbolize the class tensions that set the plot in motion. The upwardly mobile Ravensworth projects his own envy and arrogance onto the charitable and kindhearted Isabella. He hates her "pride," her "haughty mansion," her "earth-born vanity."[93] Like *The Witch* and Whittier's tale, *Superstition* interweaves its domestic and political plots. Ravensworth obviously is motivated as well by a pathological fear of Isabella's son, Charles, the suitor of his daughter, Mary. To eliminate a threat both social and sexual, Ravensworth stirs up a witch-hunt; and in doing so, he plays upon cultural fears of conspiracy.

In this respect *Superstition* dramatizes for a contemporary audience the dark side of republican zealotry. It is precisely the excesses of republican vigilance that serve to persecute Isabella and Charles as "alien sectaries" (117). When Ravensworth's friend, the more enlightened and moderate Walford, laments that "the [community's] ignorant and envious" members make outsiders "[f]ood for their hate" (117), he is, in effect, acknowledging the dangers of such vigilance. Later, Walford's response to Ravensworth's theories of conspiracy elaborates on this crucial political idea:

> Ah, my friend,
> If reason in a mind like yours, so form'd,
> So fortified by knowledge, can bow down
> Before the popular breath, what shall protect
> From the all-with'ring blasts of superstition
> The unthinking crowd, in whom credulity
> Is ever the first born of ignorance? (130)

As the spokesman of moderation, Walford voices the text's antidemocratic fears of popular politics ("the popular breath," "the unthinking crowd"). The ensuing argument between Walford and Ravensworth over witchcraft is significant on several counts. Barker resorts to the patented apologia, which blamed New England's superstition on English influence. Ravensworth defends the existence of "sorcery" on the authority of the most "eminent" minds across the Atlantic. Barker thus deftly attenuates Puritan guilt while simultaneously Europeanizing his villain. During this argument Walford ventriloquizes the early national complaint that Puritan leaders had succumbed to the influence of "childish petulance, e'en idiocy" and the confessions of "wretches in despair" (130). He deplores the fact that "frenzy's flame / Like fire in tow, ran thro' the minds of men, / Fann'd by the breath of those in highest places" (131). In this instance his voice assumes the tenor of modernity, looking back uncannily through the lens of historical objectivity (as Barker and his contemporaries, they believed, were able to do). The normative voice of reason, Walford, in effect, becomes the text's implied reader.

The real "tragedy" of "superstition" lies in Ravensworth's eventual success in bringing Charles Fitzroy to trial for witchcraft. During this scene, the raging storm outside serves as the perfect objective correlative to the political drama taking place inside the courtroom. One contemporary reviewer actually claimed that the longest of Ravensworth's rabble-rousing speeches was evident of the "truth and force" of "the early history of New England."[94] In this speech Ravensworth (the "performer") acts as an artist, an artificer of language. He manipulates various discourses to achieve this: the metaphysical sublime, Whiggish fears of conspiracy, and the Puritan jeremiad. "Shall we forget," he asks, "that worldly pride and irreligious lightness / Are the provoking sins, which our grave synod / Have urg'd us to root out?" (137). Isabella alone realizes that the demagogue's words "excite the passions of his auditors" (137). The people, "[w]hom bigotry has brutaliz'd," are guilty of "prejudice."

All of this is consistent with the cultural politics of witch-hunting that this chapter has been articulating, the only truly surprising element being Barker's Democratic political affiliation. Things, however, get even more complicated when we consider the play's subplot, which concerns King Philip's War. Just like Cooper, John Stone, Delia Bacon, and Hawthorne (in "The Grey Champion"), Barker's appropriation of the Angel of Hadley legend lends the role of the regicide (called the "Unknown" in *Superstition*) a particular set of tensions reflecting the issue of the place of Revolutionary patriotism in a post-Revolutionary political world. In the preceding chapter, I introduced the political ambiguities surrounding the treatment of the regicide, Submission, in Cooper's *The Wept of Wish-ton-Wish*. I now wish to explore them in Barker's play because they are even more pronounced and begin to suggest the problematics of "democratic" ideology in early republican America.

In *Superstition* the inconsistencies between the play's witchcraft and war plots register a larger cultural uncertainty over the nature of republican masculinity. A recent analysis of the role of the regicide in early republican literature argues that Barker merely transcribed the rejection of the regicides' political radicalism that he found in Thomas Hutchinson's *History of the Colony and Province of Massachusetts Bay* (1764).[95] A Loyalist during the Revolutionary struggle (who had his house destroyed during the Stamp Act crisis), Hutchinson unsurprisingly viewed the regicides as dangerous libertarians. In context of the play's own historical emergence, however, the issue is much more complex than this. Initially portrayed as a mournful outcast, the Unknown *is* penitent about his role in the execution of Charles I, but he nonetheless asks a crucial question about the nature of republican virtue:

> Did these wounds, receiv'd
> In thy holy cause, stream with a felon's blood,
> Was it a felon's courage nerved my arm,
> A felon's zeal that burn'd within my heart? (120)

In this case the question is not whether the Unknown is a felon –
he undoubtedly is – but, rather, what the status is of the republican zealotry he exemplifies.

There is little room for verbal irony in this passage, for the
"courage" the Unknown attributes to himself here is unquestionably validated in Act III. When the Puritan community is endangered by a Native American attack, the Unknown (a "patriot," as
Isabella calls him), true to the Angel of Hadley legend, rallies
the Puritan forces and effectively saves the commonwealth. The
political formula here would seem to legitimate his excessive
patriotism. In *Superstition*, then, such zealotry at once endangers
and preserves the community. The drama's political dilemma has
been foreshadowed in the first conversation between Ravensworth and Walford, which metaphorically addresses the status
of a Revolutionary ideal in a politically changing world:

> Walf. True; the times [of the founders]
> Impos'd a virtue, almost superhuman.
> But surely, the necessity is pass'd
> For trampling on our nature.

> Rav.   We have grown
> Luke-warm in zeal, degenerate in spirit; –
> I would root out with an unsparing hand,
> The weeds that choke the soil; – pride and rank luxury
> Spring up around us; – alien sectaries,
> Spite of the whip and axe infest our limits;
> Bold infidelity, dark sorcery – (117)

Like Catharine Sedgwick and Lydia Child, Barker (via Walford)
suggests that true communitarianism – classical or Christian, Revolutionary or Puritan – depends on postlapsarian premises for
its existence. Ravensworth rationalizes a hierarchical politics
through the doctrine of innate depravity. More interesting than
his duplicity here, however, is the hint of Walford's uncertainty.
Have the "times" in which such patriotic vigilance is indispens-
able really "pass'd"? The age of the founders is long gone, but the
events of Act III, or King Philip's War, would appear to impose
the "necessity" of such republican behavior.

Hence *Superstition* has it both ways, its main plot warning about the dangers of political zealotry and its subplot simultaneously compromising that very claim. This inconsistency raises a crucial question. How, the text asks, could a republican ethos of communitarianism (espoused here by Ravensworth) be maintained without the danger of demagogic zeal? What are the limits of vigilant republicanism? The subject of witch-hunting, in other words, exposed the troubling logic of the communitarian ideal in which vigilance and fanaticism troublingly blurred. The "weeds" that Ravensworth would purge with "whip and axe" (ah, the echoes of Federalist attacks upon Jacobinism!) theoretically could describe *any* dissenting voice – be it Federalist or Republican, Whig or Democrat – in an increasingly fragmented, pluralistic society.

Yet in *Superstition* conspiracies abound everywhere and would seem to demand republican vigilance. The agent for the Stuarts in search of the regicides, Sir Reginald (a "devil") and his nephew George (Mary's sexual assailant) are Europeanized aristocrats who conspire to destroy all semblance of order. Only the republican vigilance of the Unknown and George Fitzroy can deter such predatory forces. The indeterminacy over republican zeal that *Superstition* creates comes to a head during Charles's trial. As Arthur Hobson Quinn has argued, what makes the plot truly tragic is the inevitability of the hero's doom, since "every honorable impulse, every brave action of Charles, conspires against him."[96] Like Oedipus's extraordinary traits, Charles's virtue – his empassioned patriotic valor in this case – causes his tragic downfall. Republican enthusiasm is *both* virtuous and self-destructive. So it is no surprise that Barker (like George Washington, Noah Webster, and James Madison before him, and Rufus Choate later on) rewrites patriotism in the image of temperate reason. The virtue of the play's two heroes (in Charles's "well-disciplin'd mind," the Unknown's cool-headed leadership) involves a precarious negotiation of the culture of republican manhood. Yet even this is not enough to assuage political fears. In the end, Barker retreats from his tenuous solutions, killing off Charles (for purposes of pathos as well as politics) and exiling the Unknown (as Cooper does with Submission) from civilized society.

We should recognize the relationship between civic reason and patriarchal politics that all of these texts imply. The fragile state of the people's faculty psychology signifies the need for social and political hierarchies founded theoretically upon eighteenth-century codes of deference. Even though Ravensworth's rapacity makes him an unfit ruler – as opposed to, say, Belknap's John Winthrop or John Davis's George Washington – Walford provides a viable substitute for a recidivist political leadership that recognizes the people's limitations. Yet this political design significantly is inverted in women's historical writing. In *Hobomok,* as we have seen, Child manipulated this discourse of "superstition" to demonstrate that Mary Conant's movement from Puritan to Native American communities resulted from a tragic loss of reason. Child not only suggests that patriarchal struggles (between Charles Brown and Roger Conant) bring on this tragedy, but also argues for the political importance of *female* reason. Mary's superstitious state of mind sufficiently problematizes the issue of her free will in running off with Hobomok. This politicizes female reason, suggesting its importance to the preservation of American women and, in turn, the entire republic itself. Hence it provides the political and ideological leverage to pursue *Hobomok*'s critique of patriarchal privilege.

This political strategy describes *Hope Leslie* as well, though here Sedgwick complicates it considerably. The subject of witchcraft involves Nelema, an old Native American woman, who supposedly uses demonic methods to cure the snake-bitten Craddock. In staging Nelema's "cure" for him, however, Sedgwick constructs a scene in which a multiple hermeneutics is at work to challenge her own reader's capacity for reason. Consider Hope's description of Nelema's magic in a letter written afterward to Everell Fletcher:

> [Nelema] remained for a moment, silent, motionless, and perfectly abstracted. A loud groan from Craddock roused her. She bent over him, and muttered in an incantation in her own tongue. She then, after many efforts, succeeded in making him swallow a strong decoction, and bathed the wound and arm with the same liquor. These applications were repeated in short intervals, during which she brandished her wand, making quick and mysterious motions, as if she were writing hieroglyphics on the invisible air. She writhed her body into the most horrible contortions, and tossed her withered arms wildly about her, and Everell, shall I confess to you, that I trembled lest she should assume the living form of the reptile whose image she bore?[97]

By offering alternative interpretations for the cause of Craddock's physical recovery (is it from Nelema's medicinal applications, or her magical rituals?), Sedgwick tests her reader's capacity for rational induction. Even Hope herself has difficulty differentiating between magic and science, especially since the "decoction" is rhetorically buried between Nelema's incantations and her ritualized gyrations. Our reading, then, of Nelema's hieroglyphic text parallels our reading of the text of *Hope Leslie,* since both constitute exercises in modern, rational interpretation. Moreover, as an act of reading, the scene indicts Puritan patriarchy. Craddock's sudden recovery ironically dooms Nelema, as Jennet (one of the novel's chief conspirators, we later discover) in all her "madness" and "zeal" accuses Nelema of being an "emissary of Satan." Puritan superstition discredits the claims of patriarchal political authority founded, oddly enough, on a gender-specific faculty psychology positing man's "naturally" superior mind.

My discussion of witchcraft fiction risks the danger of reducing literary discourse to a historical register of political ideology rather than an active participant in a fluid cultural exchange. To complicate the politics of this literary genre, then, I would frame them within this era's emergently romantic ideologies. In the context of this emergence, the historical language of Puritanism again demonstrates an elusive multivalence that complicates the conservative republican contexts for Puritan "gloom" and "imagination." Romantic ideology arose concomitantly with the professionalization and sophistication of the literary marketplace. An evolving view of the "artist" as a vessel of genius and inspiration challenged in part the socially didactic responsibilities of the genteel man of letters. This romantic construction of artistic consciousness privileged the imagination (as opposed to "fancy"), which is important because it served to lend increasingly positive meanings to the language of Puritan irrationality. Literature mediated between the older ideology of disembodied public print that Michael Warner has articulated, and a newer, romantic conception of the private, alienated space of individual genius.[98]

As I noted earlier, critics of witchcraft fiction have recognized that the issue of Puritan superstition was bound up in a larger issue of literary nationalism. Soon after the appearance of *Legends of New England,* Whittier, for example, declared that although America lacked Europe's ancient castles and other catalysts for romantic melancholy, it nevertheless did possess "the tale of superstition and the scenes of Witchcraft [sic]" to provide sufficient material for modern romance. Some up-and-coming American writer, he urged, should produce "an amusing and not uninstructing work" fictively illustrating indigenous superstitions.[99] And in the Preface to *Legends,* Whittier himself claimed that "New-England is rich in traditionary lore – a thousand associations of superstition and manly daring and romantic adventure, are connected with her green hills and her pleasant rivers."[100] These would serve as a repository for romantic effect.

Whittier's indebtedness to Puritan lore for such an effect is apparent everywhere in *Legends of New England*. After making fun of McOrne's superstitions, the narrator of "The Haunted House" uncannily assumes an entirely different tone:

> The days of faery are over. The tale of enchantment – the legend of ghostly power – of unearthly warning and super-natural visitation, have lost their hold on the minds of the great multitude. People sleep quietly where they are placed – no matter by what means they have reached the end of their journey – and there is an end to the church-yard rambles of discontented ghosts – [101]

This narrative aside at once debunks and laments the passing of a primitive age. Just as Cooper and Hawthorne later would do, Whittier bemoans the fate of the imaginative artist in a rational, utilitarian society – what he later calls a "matter-of-fact age." Where "the poetry of Time has gone by forever," he declares, ". . . we have only the sober prose left us."[102] To remedy this situation, he repeatedly relies on Cotton Mather's *Magnalia Christi Americana* as a source of romantic superstitions. "The Weird Gathering," for example, is prefaced by regrets about the "fearful delusion" at Salem, and yet Mather's descriptions of secret witch-meetings offer Whittier the means to conjure up his own titillating supernatural effects. "The Spectre Ship" and "The Spectre Warriors" similarly mock *Magnalia*'s irrationality but nonetheless use Puritan lore to enthrall a contemporary audience in phantasmagoric possibilities. In other words, Whittier *needs* the superstitious Cotton Mather he paradoxically satirizes; he needs as well his reader's imaginative sensibility, which he invalidates in "The Powwow" by equating Puritan and Native American irrationality. Puritan superstition thus services both the text of *Legends* and the beginnings of Whittier's literary career.

This tension between romantic and republican epistemologies helps explain *The Witch of New England*'s inconsistent characterization of its hero, Edward Bradley. Virtually every major character suffers from excessive "passions," but none more so than Edward, who exemplifies a melancholic gloom rivaling the likes of the American painter of this era, Washington Allston. "Born amid scenes wild, noble, romantic," Edward wanders alone in the woods, inhabiting "an ideal world" of the mind.[103] What is most startling about Edward, however, is the language surrounding him, for its republican signification is inverted:

> But the witchcraft of courtesy, – the fascination and exquisite polish of refined manner, – the pale but lovely remnant of deceased chivalry, which even yet, as a beautiful spirit, walks the earth, – were to be seen only in the day dreams conjured by the heat and vapours of a romantic mind.[104]

There is virtue in Edward's gloom; it signifies his spiritual depth, his sensitivity to the divinity of nature, his solitary dignity as an ambivalent outcast. The political texture of the novel's rhetoric becomes even more complicated when the author of *The Witch* actually strains to reconcile romantic ideology with the canons of traditional republicanism. Its flirtations with solitary melancholy are mitigated by the imperatives of the utilitarian age that, for example, Whittier ambiguously lamented. Edward's best friend initiates a tenuous synthesis by dubbing him "a republican *and* a poet," while the narrator assures early national readers that Edward is no "idle and useless visionary."[105] This tenuous synthesis results in a hero who is both "a poet in feeling . . . indulging often in the dreams of imagination," yet a practical man "with skill and enterprise."[106]

The Witch's use of the romantic convention of interpolated tales further shows its ambivalence toward conservative, rational epistemology. In an essay review of 1825, entitled "Recent American Novels," Jared Sparks failed to understand how readers were to believe that a Puritan minister (Edward's father) would listen to his son read a dramatic fragment alluding to Shakespeare, Salvatore Rosa, and the Arabian Nights.[107] By obsessing over fiction's fidelity to historical fact, Sparks fell into the same trap that still plagues contemporary criticism of historical fiction. Edward's reading (called "a witching hour") introduces a fictional hero, Antonio, whose romantic excesses metaphorically point up his own. At first the scene would seem to impart only the premise, derived from Scottish moral philosophy, that an exacerbated imagination endangered both individual sanity and social order (Antonio, after all, suffers from a "heated brow" and "madd'ning misrule"). During the symposium afterward, however, as Minister Bradley and others ironically criticize Catholic superstitions, Edward interrupts. He issues an *own* personal tale now – an obvious parallel to, and yet revision of, Antonio's. This story about the discovery of a secret cavern might be seen as a more sensational version of Philip Freneau's "The Indian Burying Ground," an enthusiastic rendition of surreal crypts, subterranean waterways, and elaborate hieroglyphics. But the cave symbolizes a more exalted ideal of the imagination than Freneau was able to give in the 1780s. In its "dazzling splendour and awful venerableness" Edward hears an "empassioned" minister preach the Word to Native Americans. And at this moment, his power as a romantic artist over his audience parallels that of the minister. During the early republic such power was viewed tenuously: it was "the art of ruling the minds of men."[108]

Yet even this momentary fascination with romantic power is compromised by the novel's unfolding plot. As one can see, the characters of Edward Bradley and Annie Brown suggest a thematic tension between republican and romantic attitudes toward the imagination. But Edward's oscillations – indeed, the entire novel's – between republican sobriety and romantic melancholy come to a head in his Indian captivity. Caught in the throes of irrationality symbolized by the racial other, Edward undergoes the conventional cultural psychodrama of purgation-through-immersion. True to the conventions of frontier romance, his status as a suitable mate for the novel's heroine (in this case the regicide's daughter) is ensured through his ultimate rejection of the Native American temptress. Edward's incomplete but marked drift away from Byronic gloom marks both a psychological and political movement toward an early national political ideal.

Finally, these competing ideologies permit a drastic reconsideration of John Neal's novel of the Salem witchcraft trials, *Rachel Dyer* (1828). For those unfamiliar with the rather bizarre life and work of Neal (whom Hawthorne delightfully called that "wild fellow"), he is probably the closest thing early republican New England had to the democratic pieties, vernacular spirit, and primal longings of the better-known Walt Whitman. Whittier himself called his Yankee kinsman and fellow Quaker "a singular, erratic genius."[109] More recently, David S. Reynolds has dubbed Neal the father of the "Subversive Style" in nineteenth-century American letters, a movement that was "a pugnacious, partly political mode that tried to establish a defiant, quirky Americanness whose excessive irrationalism was intended as a direct affront to what was regarded as the effete gentility of foreign literatures."[110] In this vein, critics of *Rachel Dyer* have argued for Neal's identification with the novel's romantic, tragic hero, George Burroughs.[111] Certainly, Cotton Mather's and Robert Calef's accounts of Burroughs's great strength and mysterious background

evidently presented Neal with romantic potential. But this identification between author and protagonist is more inconsistent
than Neal's critics have recognized. And it shows us significant
cultural relations between art and politics at this time.

Rachel Dyer was conceived originally as a short story for *Blackwood's Magazine,* an English journal to which Neal frequently
contributed while living abroad during the middle 1820s. Because of its length it was never published in the journal, and so
when Neal returned home to Portland, Maine, he both revised
and expanded "New-England Witchcraft," consulting Robert Calef's *More Wonders of the Invisible World,* which had been republished in 1823. The first chapter of *Rachel Dyer* gives a rather
lengthy disquisition on the nature of superstition, particularly the
belief in witchcraft, which Neal defends in decidedly romantic
terms. "We . . . forget perhaps that a belief in [witchcraft]," he
gently reminds his reader, "is like a belief in the after appearance
of the dead among the blue waters, the green graves, the still
starry atmosphere and the great shadowy woods of our earth; or
like the beautiful deep instinct of our nature for worship . . . sure
as the steadfast hope of immortality."[112] Taking his cue from the
patented rationale (which, as we have seen, Jedidiah Morse and
others used to soften the guilt for the Puritan elders) that these
"Englishmen" imbibed their superstitions from Europe, Neal pursues this argument to characteristic excess. Maintaining that most
great thinkers have been susceptible to irrationality (e.g., Socra-
tes, Caesar, Samuel Johnson, and even Neal's own patron in
England – the utilitarian Jeremy Bentham!), Neal's apologia
allows him to promote a romantic worldview. In a roundabout
way, the subject of witchcraft facilitates the textual re-creation of
himself as an artist (of the "heart" and the "blood") by dissenting
from the period's prevailing codes of reason and civic order.

But the novel changes its tune when it subsequently dramatizes
the consequences of irrationality in the Puritans' overly zealous
persecution of Quakers. Following the historiographic logic of
early republican New England, Neal collapses the episodes of
witch-hunting, the persecution of Quakers, and the Antinomian
Controversy of 1637 into a political synchronicity suggesting the
zealotry of factions. When an old Quaker woman, Mary Dyer,
is executed, Elizabeth (read: Anne) Hutchinson issues a curse,
prophetically warning that the commonwealth will severely pay
for its present intolerance. After noting that King Philip's War,
epidemics, and natural disasters bear this out, the narrative
abruptly skips to the beginnings of the Salem hysteria in the

household of "Mathew Paris," Neal's version of the infamous minister Samuel Parris of Salem Village (now Danvers) who helped to propel the hysteria. Although critics sometimes humorously note Neal's historical improbabilities and anachronisms, these aesthetic shortcomings make perfect sense in this case, for, as we have seen, early national discourse read these events as a singular problem. *Rachel Dyer* merely compresses them into a metaphoric moment according to a specific political logic.

In the midst of such injustice enters George Burroughs, one of Neal's typically Byronic heroes. During the novel's first courtroom scene at the trial of Sarah Good, Burroughs dramatically appears to defend her. Because of their opposition to the witch-hunt, Burroughs is finally executed and the deformed Quaker woman, Rachel Dyer, dies in prison. There the hysteria ends. What critics of the novel fail to acknowledge is that Neal's identification with Burroughs is specifically as an *artist* and that such an identification is laden with politically volatile implications.

As a defender of the poor and disenfranchised, Burroughs emerges as a champion of the people who "braved the whole power of [the magistrates] that others were so afraid of" (85). Divested of any real access to political power, Burroughs must resort to language. As a former law student himself, Neal initially has fun with Burroughs's newfound profession, burlesquing the very notion of the courtroom as a suitable setting for romance. But then there appears (and quite inexplicably) a legal advisor who gives Burroughs a quick lesson in how to work the crowd. Suddenly the narrative's comic parodies transform into something much more consequential. The scene crucially provides a map for reading *Rachel Dyer* itself: "Do – just keep the court in play," he tells Burroughs, "keep the judges at work. . . . You have the jury with you now – lay it on thick – you understand the play as well as I do now – " (97). Like the novel itself (and so much of Neal's fiction), Burroughs's oratorical performance in court rambles on, flashes brilliantly, debunks its own limitations in moments of romantic irony, and ultimately fails to get to the point. "Talk – talk – talk – " the lawyer tells him, "no matter what you say – don't give them time to breathe – pop a speech into 'em!" (99). In fact, the point is *not* to get to the point. It is, rather, to manipulate one's audience, to keep them "agog."

The George Burroughs of *Rachel Dyer,* in other words, emerges as a demagogue. By appealing to the people's "courage" and "heroic probity," he urges them to "oppose the race of men that are about you and above you" (131). In this context, Neal's explicit claim that Burroughs's qualities in 1692 would have made him a hero of 1792 is more devilishly ambiguous than anyone yet would seem to realize (149). The relationship of 1692 and 1792: This theorizes a historical typology of political virtue which, as we have seen, was pervasive in early national culture. Yet a troubling ambiguity surrounds it. Is Burroughs meant to be a historical type to Revolutionary heroism (in the name of "liberty" and "the people," the kind of cant Cooper deflated in *Lionel Lincoln*), or to the self-interested opportunism associated with the rise of "factions" during the 1790s? Just as in *Superstition,* this issue involves the more complex, elusive question about the nature of masculine patriotism itself. Burroughs is attributed the "extraordinary gift of speech" and "superior genius" (149) that threaten the control of the magistracy in court. Caught up in the frenzy of his own rabble-rousing, Burroughs defiantly claims, *"You have no power to stop me"* (120, italics his). And so in the face of such a gifted political parvenu, the Puritan magistracy retreats to the only thing that it knows will secure its position: *"[t]he – wisdom – of – our – ancestors"* (122, italics his). At this moment in *Rachel Dyer* the Puritan court becomes a symbolic arena for a commemorative tradition that described both third-generation Puritanism and early republican New England. This tradition upholds the principles of reason, order, and hierarchy against which both George Burroughs and John Neal battle.

Rachel Dyer is thus the site of a peculiarly post-Revolutionary intersection of political and literary cultures. Cynthia Jordan has noted the dangerous intimacy between artistic and political power in Hugh Henry Brackenridge's *Modern Chivalry,* as Brackenridge becomes increasingly anxious to distinguish the "deceit" of Captain Farrago's verbal artistry (meant to control Teague O'Regan's "imagination") from the actual evils of "demagoguery" itself.[113] If this problem of the potential debasement of republican language characterizes as well works like John Trumbull's mock epic poem about the Revolution, *M'Fingal* (1782), and Charles Brockden Brown's *Wieland* (1798), it is inverted in a later work like *Rachel Dyer.* For Neal, the discourses of romantic artistry and political demagoguery define one another. This takes place, we should recognize, in the context of a cultural configuration of "art" (whether it be Upham on Mather, or Webster on the Jacobins) that signified the conspiratorial wiles of "artifice." In *Rachel Dyer,* Neal significantly recasts the "art" of oratorical manipulation as the apex of romantic power. He thereby translates republican politics into a romantic aesthetic indubitably colored with political meanings as it describes the hero Burroughs. In other words, during the 1820s this romantic ideal was inseparable from a political grammar spawned by American Revolutionary culture. *Rachel Dyer* reinterprets and codifies a prevailing cultural equation between art/ifice and demagoguery. In this context, Ravensworth becomes a "performer" in court; Burroughs similarly enjoys what Captain Ahab later experiences on the deck of the *Pequod*, as he excites the passions of his crew with the wonders of the white whale.

But such romantic iconoclasm ultimately collapses in the novel. *Rachel Dyer*'s dissent from the republican canons of reason is compromised by its irrepressibly conservative impulses. Neal's nagging uncertainties about democracy itself are apparent in those moments where he declaims superstition as the source of violent disorder. Despite the first chapter's long apologia for the Puritans, the narrative soon starts ventriloquizing the period's conservative clichés for social disorder: Salem occasions a "frightful superstition . . . raging with irresistible power" (34), a "fury about witches and witchcraft [which] took possession of the people" (47), a "fearful infatuation," a period of "superstitious dread" (61). Further, the loss of reason affects plot, even genre itself. It precipitates the "tragedy" of *Rachel Dyer*'s ending in Burroughs's and Rachel Dyer's deaths. Matthew Paris is the chief culprit of the novel. His belief in demonology "was a dreadful superstition, a faith mixed up with a mortal fear" (48). Bereaved, and even deranged, over his wife's recent death, Paris undergoes strange visions that serve to confirm his suspicions about his daughters' fits and later implicate Tituba (as both subject to and subject of superstitions), who in turn brings on the "fury" that consumes the entire community. In Mathew Paris's characterization, then, Puritan "gloom" accrues malignant meanings.

So too does Puritan "zealotry." In characteristic fashion, Neal uncannily turns Burroughs, the Byronic and Jacksonian hero, into a voice of reason who resists the violent madness around him in court. Like a chameleon, Burroughs changes from buffoon, to artful demagogue, and then to the embodiment of reason and moderation. He consistently outwits the magistracy's jurisprudence, showing the absurdity, for example, of the circumstantial evidence of the knife used to implicate Sarah Good (a feat that would have pleased Calef, who included a similar incident in *More Wonders*). Neal writes himself into a characteristically illogical corner by having the romantic artist-demagogue stand as conservative ideal of civic and political equanimity. The Puritan prosecution's "great show of zeal" is juxtaposed with Burroughs's "gravity and moderation that weighed prodigiously with the court" (97–8). The reevaluation of Puritan irrationality, the melancholic gloom and fervent zeal that produces witch-hunts, undermines the romantic ideology that the text generally promotes.

One might be so bold as to say that two John Neals inhabit the pages of *Rachel Dyer*. There is, on the one hand, the avowed champion of romantic iconoclasm (the lover of Poe's "thunder and lightning"), and, on the other, the republican writer who hopes his reader's "excitement" over *Rachel Dyer* is that which involves "a search after *rational* truth."[114] Despite the modern critical mythology surrounding Neal's "spirit of contradiction," the democratic text of *Rachel Dyer* cannot slough off fears about popular politics in the politically changing world shaping its *own* appearance in 1829. Puritan zeal in *Rachel Dyer* ultimately leads to violent anarchy. At Burroughs's trial, the novel's ongoing thematic tension between romantic individualism and civic reason becomes especially strained. The courtroom simultaneously stages Burroughs's "superhuman" strength and the "weight of delusion" that eventuates in mass histrionics. "[T]he powers of the air" invade the courtroom, setting the masses into a frenzy that the magistracy cannot control. These are the very forces that persecute Burroughs and Rachel Dyer.

This meditation on political power involves the larger consideration of republican community and the passionate vigilance requisite to maintaining it. These "Maccabees of the seventeenth century" persecute the disenfranchised margins, persecute "difference" itself: the impoverished Sarah Good, the Quaker Rachel Dyer, and the racially mixed Burroughs. What is the source of Burroughs's reason: his whiteness? his Native blood? If Neal's racial politics are muddled, his class-driven fears create surprising parallels between himself and contemporary conservatives. Consider the similarities, for example, between *Rachel Dyer*'s commentary on Puritanism and Noah Webster's on Jacobinism:

> The persecuted of to-day become the persecutors of to-morrow [sic]. They flourish, not because they are right, but because they are persecuted; and they persecute because they have the power, not because they whom they persecute are wrong. (35)

> The authority of all the commissioners is nearly dictatorial. They arrest, try and condemn, in a most summary manner. Not only difference of opinion, but moderation and espe-

cially the possession of money, are unpardonable crimes, punishable with death, in the view of these delegates of dictatorial power.[115]

In both cases, the evil of fanaticism describes the logical extension of a Revolutionary political ideal in a modern world. These fears in early republican America spanned party, region, and political affiliation. Cooper, for example, claimed in *The Wept* that "a glimmering of [Puritan] superstition . . . appears to be the usual concomitant of excited religious zeal."[116] Rufus Choate tried to recast the relationship between Puritanism and the American Revolution in a way that avoided the pitfalls of the French Revolution: "Hence, I think, the sober, rational and practical views and conduct which distinguished even the first fervid years of the Revolutionary age. . . . No riotous and shouting processions . . . no unloosing of hoarded-up passions of ages from the restraints of law, order, morality and religion, such as shamed and frightened away the new-born liberty of Revolutionary France."[117] Staunch Federalist and Yankee "Wild Man," ambivalent Democrat and idealistic Whig: If the four do not dissolve the meaning of political labels, they still collectively mark the coordinates of political anxiety characterizing early republican America.

No less than Arthur Miller's *The Crucible,* then, the literary renditions of Puritan witch-hunting in the early republic are permeated by political concerns of the day. If, as one critic of the origin of the second American party system has argued, modern politics provided an expanding electorate with an "emotional drama" of feverish campaigns and passionately contested elections, the didactic arena of history-writing dramatized democracy's potentially disastrous possibilities.[118] We can locate the politics of literature with some precision by comparing it to other kinds of historical texts and even to the larger "text" of American politics in which the principles of reason, consensus, and hierarchy were increasingly abandoned as parties scrambled unabashedly for the popular vote.

The historical literature of witch-hunting was shaped by these social and political realities. Its premodern cast in this regard suggests widespread fears of an increasingly atomized, fragmented, acquisitive, and democratic culture, fears that finally confronted the "excess of the passion for liberty" that Benjamin Rush in 1788 had warned was a perpetual plague to otherwise healthy republics. Rush tellingly called this disease "anarchia."[119]

As the subject of Puritan witch-hunting bore this legacy, its status as a political metaphor raised a number of cultural questions that remained unresolved. What was the status of Puritan "superstition" – to the artist? to the member of a social and political elite? How could one distinguish between the zealotry of patriots and factions in a world where organized political parties were simply becoming a fact of life? This returns us to considerations drawn at the outset of this study. In constructing a new version of the Ebenezer, the memorial meant to codify the terms of civic ethics, nationalist historians confronted the dark side of a political typology that read the republic through the values of the Mayflower Compact and Winthrop's speech aboard the *Arbella*. The very subject of witch-hunting reveals the ways in which early nationals groped for a new definition of republican patriotism, one that rode tenuously between admiration and repugnance for the Founders' zeal, and which nearly always encountered the terrible paradox that the stability of the communitarian ideal would seem to engender a concomitant fanaticism. The literature of witch-hunting, then, was constructed on the unstable cultural foundations of a post-Revolutionary republic.

AFTERWORD:
AMERICAN ORIGINS OF
PURITAN SELVES

Few bodies or parties have served the world so well as the Puritans.
– Ralph Waldo Emerson, *Journal* (January 1824)

The virtue of citizenship appears to be in retreat these days. In the wake of the Republican "revolution" of November 1994, the frequencies of American politics are now dominated by the theme of "less government," a euphemism, one suspects, for a decrease in federal income taxes. While Americans still sentimentalize such communitarian dramas as the rescue workers who sifted through the rubble of the Oklahoma City Federal Building, American politicians risk their necks in calling for the people's selfless virtue. The unbridled individualism unleashed by Reagan's presidency was supposed to have found its humane equipoise in George Bush's proclamation of a "kinder, gentler nation" and a "thousand points of light." However, such calls upon citizens to divest themselves of selfish interests tend to fall upon deaf (or even resentful) ears. Look where it got George Bush. Bill Clinton's attempt to reinvoke a sense of civic responsibility by coupling it with the promise of the "New Covenant" for smaller, more efficient government inadequately checked a Republican political discourse that managed to translate citizenship from civic to personal responsibility. Bob Dole is only one of many misinterpreters of Emersonian "self-reliance." If anything, it is the extreme Right that has co-opted the discourse of Revolutionary republicanism, championing the "rights of the people," and the memory of April 19 on Lexington Green, as the ideological foundation for a stand against government. Even if they are

210

unwilling to embrace the militia movements, most Americans appear to want to just be left alone.

One wonders if citizens of the early republic were actually any different. In the aftermath of the American Revolution, however, they did inhabit a culture that considered the ethical contours of citizenship more seriously than we do today. Throughout this book I have positioned the subject of Puritanism within the early republic's cultural politics of citizenship, in which a complex ideological inheritance was continually subjected to the demands of modern life. Between the 1780s and the 1830s, discourses of Puritanism adapted themselves to changes in the meanings of a "republic." Granted, the premises of this study position *me* within an academic discipline increasingly engaged with highly political subjects such as gender, race, and class in literature. But I believe it makes no sense to offer a "political" reading of, say, an aristocratic New England woman's rendition of her ancestors' "massacre" of an Algonquin tribe, or a supposedly loyal Jacksonian Democrat's play about Puritan witch-hunting, without delineating a larger mosaic of cultural beliefs with which to gauge the "politics" of historical literature. If nothing else, such contexts circumvent the tired, flaccid cliché of the cultural conflict between "individualism" and "community" during this era. For the polarities of this opposition were themselves undergoing ideological change.

What are the limits of this book? What a horrible thing even to think about! Certainly, the boundaries of class consign this study to the bourgeois and aristocratic ranks of the early republic, and scholars interested in early-nineteenth-century culture may wish to investigate discourses of Puritanism (in songs, ballads, newspapers, popular gatherings) among urban groups such as artisans and middling tradesmen. One limitation of this study, however, is also its strength. By delimiting a specific historical period, I have repositioned a genre of American literature arising during the 1820s in the context of its intellectual-historical origins rather than of its future significance to the "flowering" of midcentury New England. Such bracketing always falls prey to accusations of "periodization," but sometime during the 1830s the fragile tensions between republicanism and liberalism began to dissolve as the canons of acquisitive individualism, market capitalism, popular democracy, and the commercial pressures behind the course of empire more firmly established themselves. This is apparent, as I have shown, not only in the introductory section of the first

number of the *Democratic Review* but also, to cite another example, in a review of the historical novel, *Merry-Mount* (1849), in
which the author declared that cultural interest in Pilgrim history
arose chiefly because New England's founders "unconsciously laid
the seeds of a mighty empire there."[1] By the end of reconstruction, as the authors of *Old Naumkeag: An Historical Sketch of the
City of Salem* (1877) make clear, modern capitalism reconfigured
Puritan virtue in the same way it did Emersonian philosophy:
"New England was, indeed, a wilderness into which every man
must go with a sturdy self reliance and hew a new path for
himself, if he would have one."[2] A comparison with the passages
from Salma Hale's *History*, with which I began this study, shows
they both in many ways say the same thing. Yet the earlier discourse marks the emergence of a brand of liberalism still in
dialogue with premodern assumptions about a republic.

   The passage of a half century marks important changes in the
historiography about Puritanism that, of course, register larger
cultural transformations. The republication, for example, of Jeremy Belknap's *American Biography* in 1877 demonstrates this. One
reads this edition on three temporal planes: those of the subject
matter of colonial history, the early republican cultural assumptions in Belknap's prose, and the changes in those assumptions
evident in the editor's voluminous notes to Belknap's text. Most
of these notes are purely factual. The editor, for example, offers
strictly prosaic commentary on the English investors' dissatisfac-
tion with the Plymouth colony: "They became anxious, as prudent
men might well be, to escape from their connexion with an
enterprise which had thus far proved a failure."[3] This lacks the
fervor with which post-Revolutionary historiography invested in
first-generation settlement. Its detachment reveals as well traces
of a colder, scientific – one might even say naturalistic – world-
view. This is even more pronounced when the editor comes
around to evaluating the leaders of New England. As we have
seen, Winthrop's stature (as the Washington prototype) went relatively unchallenged in early republican letters, but here in 1877
he loses out to John Endicott, "undoubtedly the finest specimen
to be found among our governors of the genuine Puritan character." And what distinguishes Endicott? Precisely those qualities
(which worried Hawthorne in "Endicott and the Red Cross") that
make up realpolitik: resolution, severity, fearlessness. Endicott
has "the eye keen to discern the first moment for action, . . .
[and] the quick resolve to profit by it."[4] Endicott is the consum-

mate modern politician, the Abraham Lincoln who engineered the preservation of the Union. So the comparison, then, between Belknap's text and the editor's notes constitutes something of a historical rupture. The notes translate republican principle and anxiety into the stark realism of post-Reconstruction America.

One discerns the dissipation of republican ideologies upon which the Ebenezer of the early national period was founded. By the time Vernon L. Parrington's first volume of *Main Currents in American Thought: The Colonial Mind, 1620–1800* appears in 1927, Puritanism has been recast in context of an overarching theory of the progress of democratic institutions and agrarian values. In this schema, the seventeenth-century English Revolution is seen as "a rebellion of the capable middle class . . .": "Puritanism was a frank challenge of the traditional social solidarity of English institutional life by an emergent individualism."[5] Yet the Puritan migration to America was accompanied by an Old Testament theocratic legacy that makes figures such as John Winthrop and John Cotton basically good guys whose severity resulted from their being hopelessly shackled to aristocratic assumptions of hierarchy, deference, and order – the very traits, in other words, for which New England Federalists and Whigs had lauded their ancestors. "To the modern reader of [Winthrop's History] there is something almost childish in Winthrop's insistence on public deference to his official position."[6] Such infantilizing rhetoric is premised on a progressive view of history whose telos is an agrarian democracy that, Parrington believes, America has achieved (and perhaps lost in an industrial age). By now, moreover, the early national period's double-voicedness has given way to the rather bald summation that the Puritan leaders, despite their aristocratic pretensions, were essentially aggressive capitalists "with a sharp eye to the main chance as any London merchant."[7] Because New England congregationalism was such a disruptively democratic force, Parrington argues, colonial leaders were forced to install a theocratic system to ensure "cohesive solidarity." But in light of the Puritans' bourgeois acquisitiveness, what does this really mean? If Parrington's treatment of Puritan materialism lacks the acerbity of Fenimore Cooper's in *The Wept of Wish-ton-Wish*, it nonetheless is "traced" (in the Derridean sense) with the presence of his nineteenth-century forebears. The tension between social order and liberal enterprise loses the dialogic complexity it once had. But we should recognize that Parrington's *premises* about the Puritan origins of American republicanism derive from an earlier period. What Parrington inadvertently does is fold a discourse of Puritan order into one of Puritan enterprise. Colonial communitarianism services the entrepreneurial interests of a ruling elite.

The premises, then, of Parrington's discussion begin to suggest the invisible presence of a cultural mythology of Puritanism. One should not overstate the case. Despite the obvious changes in cultural representations of Puritanism over the course of the next century, the early republic's correlation of Puritanism and "virtue" appears to produce correctives and rebuttals way down the historical road. Less indulgent with Puritanism than Parrington was the poet (and amateur historian, of sorts) William Carlos Williams, whose *In the American Grain* (1925) contains a chapter excoriating the Puritans, their cultural legacy, and the entire commemorative mythology surrounding them. Williams, it might be noted, fails to distinguish between Puritans and Separatists, but this does not slow down his harangue. Like his poetry, Williams's historical writing argues imagistically, and generally claims that from the time of the English Reformation the "seed" of Puritanism was deprived of any true spiritual and cultural "flowering." Colonial New England repeatedly is characterized as "empty," and "small," and consists of a "lowly people" so deluded in their own "dreams" and "fairy tales" of providential mission that they cannot recognize the "earthly pride" impelling their base, mean-spirited existence.[8] Williams's modernist scorn for mass culture is reserved for contemporary Americans who cannot divest themselves of the lore of Thanksgiving Day: "[The Pilgrims'] misfortune has become a malfeasant ghost that dominates us all."[9] Such a conflation of gothic and legal imagery reveals the horror that Puritanism's cultural legacy has bred "an atavism that thwarts and destroys."[10]

More interesting than Williams's elitist longing for eternal values, however, is his particular rhetoric. Like Parrington's assessment of the fallacies of aristocracy, Williams's dismantling of Puritan mythology testifies to the resilience of a narrative that I have explored in the preceding five chapters. Much of "Voyage of the Mayflower" is an attack on Puritanism that is nonetheless premised on the very idea of it as a political trope for contemporary America. Williams sardonically admits that "they were the first American democracy," and yet much of his gripe with Puritanism is in terms of an enforced homogeneity. The text's modernist stripes fully show themselves when taking on that communitarian ethos so highly pronounced in post-Revolutionary America: "Ev-

erything attests to their despoiled condition: the pitiful care for
each other, the talk of the common wealth (common to all alike,
so never the proud possession of any one)."[11] Their emptiness,
moreover, proves that "if they were pure, it was more since they
had nothing in them of fulfillment than because of positive virtues." What kind of commemorative discourse is he responding
to? The same question arises when he skewers their "vigorous
hypocrisy" and the "doggedness of a northern race," as though
the myth of Saxon liberty, which early nationals read onto Puritan
history, doggedly has endured into the 1920s. This is especially
ironic, given Williams's call for a "vigorous revolt" against Puritan
cultural legacies. He cannot write himself out of the masculine
rhetoric of the American Revolution.

The tendency to blame Puritanism for the supposed repressive-
ness of American society is not consigned, of course, to modernist
erudition. What Williams calls "the hard, repressive pioneer soil
of the mind" is a poetic figure instancing yet one more mundane
declaration that our culture's ills descend directly from the
founding of New England. How different is Williams's complaint
from that of a recent writer to *Time* magazine responding to Bob
Dole's attack on Hollywood as the source of the nation's cultural
degradation?: "The notion that music and cinema are responsible
for the meltdown of U.S. society is utter nonsense. . . . America is
ailing and in denial. Chief among the many ills exacerbating
our sick spirit is bogus puritanism. Ill-minded men wed to this
pernicious folly inhibit us from ordaining reasonable policies
regarding sex, drugs, violent crime, taxes, the military and foreign policy."[12] This outstrips even Williams. Not only controversial social issues but also taxes and military spending are rooted
in a cultural genealogy of Puritanism. Usually, the complaint
narrows itself to sexual and psychological repression, the subtext
being that Americans could actually enjoy themselves and live
healthier lives if it were not for the bane of their New England
heritage. Our history supposedly marks our cultural shame, our
inability to fulfill a Continental European freedom about which
we fantasize most vocally over drinks at cocktail parties when the
subject turns mellifluously to what's wrong with America today.
And we "solve" these problems by unconsciously theorizing ourselves into the awkward position of all-too-knowing Daisy Millers.

So Emerson's commentary in his *Journal* on the Puritans, cited
in the epigraph at the start of this Afterword, is doubly ironic. It
situates him in a more conventional cultural position vis-à-vis his
Puritan ancestors than the one to which readers of the beginning

of *Nature* are accustomed. Read in the context of Americans' chronic propensity to totalize Puritanism, however, Emerson's perhaps jejune sentiments of the 1820s may be inverted entirely to signify that Puritanism can be made into virtually *any* kind of cultural problem plaguing American culture. Throughout this book I have sought to cut the cable, so to speak, between Puritanism and contemporary America, opting instead to articulate its cultural legacy within the terms of an identifiable historical moment. And I reckon that the wages aren't the same at all. For the "spirit of Puritanism" noted by the authors of *Old Naumkeag* in 1877 has only been recast time and again to serve immediate interests. For Richard Chase in the 1950s, the "Manichaean sensibility" of the Puritan mind laid the groundwork for a "culture of contradictions" meant to distinguish America from its European counterparts subject to class struggles and the dialectic of history.[13] Yet Marxists themselves can find in Puritanism, via Max Weber, a nation of Protestant capitalists. Those opposed to patriarchy can locate in Puritan authority the roots of the Vietnam War. Or Puritan patriarchy can be reconstructed to stand for all of our contemporary fiscal, social, and military ills. Moderns like Williams find an essential emptiness in our Puritan origins; conversely, fifty years later, in the aftermath of Vietnam, Sacvan Bercovitch rereads Cotton Mather's "Nehemias Americanus" to find an empty essentialism. By telescoping Puritan history into a historical totality, we chart the heavens in search of our own frustrations, vainly searching for answers in a new form of metaphysics we call "culture." We look through the glass; we cite ancestral delusions and bawl out "Eureka!", the image of our eyeball barely reflecting in the lens.

NOTES

Introduction

1. Charles Wentworth Upham, *Lectures on Witchcraft, Comprising a History of the Delusion in Salem, in 1692*, 2nd ed. (Boston: Carter & Hendee, 1832), 277–8.
2. Recent, excellent studies of Hawthorne that nevertheless dismiss his fellow practitioners of historical romance include: Michael Davitt Bell, *Hawthorne and the Historical Romance of New England* (Princeton: Princeton University Press, 1971); Michael J. Colacurcio, *The Province of Piety: Moral History in Hawthorne's Early Tales* (Cambridge, MA: Harvard University Press, 1984); John P. McWilliams, Jr., *Hawthorne, Melville, and the American Character: A Looking-glass Business* (Cambridge: Cambridge University Press, 1984); George Dekker, *The American Historical Romance* (Cambridge: Cambridge University Press, 1987). In *New England Literary Culture: From Revolution Through Renaissance* (Cambridge: Cambridge University Press, 1986), Lawrence Buell offers characteristically insightful discussion of the historical literature about Puritanism antedating Hawthorne's major work, but even his four-chapter sequence on "Reinventing Puritanism: The New England Historical Imagination" follows a critical teleology culminating in analysis of Hawthorne and Stowe. A good example of recent critical revisionism may be found in Lucy Maddox, *Removals: Nineteenth-Century American Literature and the Politics of Indian Affairs* (New York: Oxford University Press, 1991). See 128–30 for comparison of Hawthorne with Catharine Sedgwick and Lydia Child.
3. Jane Tompkins, *Sensational Designs: The Cultural Work of American Fiction, 1790–1860* (New York: Oxford University Press, 1986), 3–39, 25 for quotation.
4. Critical studies of the politics of canon formation are more than plentiful these days, too vast to survey here. Mathiessen's monumental *American Renaissance: Art and Expression in the Age of Emerson and Whitman* (New York: Oxford University Press, 1941) included

sections on Hawthorne, Melville, Emerson, Thoreau, and Whitman. For critique of the rubric of a white male "American Renaissance," see Nina Baym, "Melodramas of Beset Manhood: How Theories of American Fiction Exclude Women Authors," *American Quarterly* 33 (1981), 123–39. Judith Fetterley's introduction to *Provisions: A Reader from 19th-Century American Women* (Bloomington: Indiana University Press, 1985) similarly assails the exclusively masculine criteria of psychological romance by which nineteenth-century American fiction has been judged. See 26–31, 33–38.

5. See Thomas Hill Schaub, *American Fiction in the Cold War* (Madison: University of Wisconsin Press, 1991), vii–viii, 3–24, and passim, and Russell Reising, *The Unusable Past: Theory and the Study of American Literature* (New York and London: Methuen, 1986), 53–73, 93–128.

6. See Arthur Schlesinger, Jr., *The Vital Center: The Politics of Freedom* (Boston: Houghton Mifflin, 1949), esp. 35–50; Louis Hartz, *The Liberal Tradition in America: An Interpretation of American Political Thought Since the Revolution* (New York: Harcourt Brace Jovanovich, 1955), 14–20, 35, 67–86; Lionel Trilling, "The Meaning of a Literary Idea," in *The Liberal Imagination: Essays on Literature and Society* (Garden City, NY: Doubleday, 1953), 268–87. Trilling's paradigm is compatible with the view of romance as an expression of cultural contradictions that Richard Chase puts forth in *The American Novel and Its Tradition* (Garden City, NY: Doubleday, 1957). For specific discussion of these writers, see Schaub, *American Fiction*, 13–14, 16–17, 20–2, 31–7, and Reising, *Unusable Past*, 93–107.

7. Schaub, *American Fiction*, 21.

8. Richard Fogle, *Hawthorne's Fiction: The Light and the Dark* (Norman: University of Oklahoma Press, 1952), 4–5.

9. Schlesinger, *Vital Center*, 46.

10. Harry Levin, *The Power of Blackness: Hawthorne, Poe, Melville* (New York: Knopf, 1958), xii.

11. Frederick C. Crews, *The Sins of the Fathers* (New York: Oxford University Press, 1966), 6–7. As Crews here expresses a postlapsarian politics of new liberalism, he impugns as well older liberals' regard for social realism as a "sign of simplistic psychology that looks only at surfaces." He attacks specifically studies by Hubert Hoeltje, Randall Stewart, and Edward Wagenknecht.

12. Bell, *Hawthone and Historical Romance*, 14.

13. Dekker, *American Historical Romance*, 5.

14. Colacurcio, *Province of Piety*, 283–313, 221–38, 238 for quotations.

15. See John P. McWilliams, Jr., *Hawthorne, Melville and the American Character*, 41. See also Colacurcio, *Province of Piety*, 72–3: "[I]t should not be too surprising if someone actually learned to take seriously this [period's] project of historical literature." For recent work that rehistoricizes Hawthorne in context of contemporary politics in mid-nineteenth-century America, see Sacvan Bercovitch, *The Office of the Scarlet Letter* (Baltimore: Johns Hopkins University Press, 1991).

16. Carolyn L. Karcher, "Introduction" to *Hobomok and Other Writings on Indians* (New Brunswick, NJ: Rutgers University Press, 1986), xxi.

17. Mary Kelley, "Introduction" to *Hope Leslie; or Early Times in the Massachusetts* (New Brunswick, NJ: Rutgers University Press, 1987), esp. xx, xxvii, and xxxi.

18. Colacurcio, *Province of Piety,* 453–7 and passim.

19. Kelley, "Introduction," xiii, and Karcher, "Introduction," xx.

20. Nina Baym, *American Women Writers and the Work of History, 1790–1860* (New Brunswick, NJ: Rutgers University Press, 1995), 154–9.

21. A notable exception to this is Christopher D. Felker's *Reinventing Cotton Mather in the American Renaissance: Magnalia Christi Americana in Hawthorne, Stowe and Stoddard* (Boston: Northeastern University Press, 1993). However, Felker's examination of how Mather's *Magnalia,* republished by Thomas Robbins in 1820, became a "tutor text" for the historiographic and cultural experiments of nineteenth-century writers does concern texts that antedate those on which I focus in this book.

22. Buell, *New England Literary Culture,* and David S. Reynolds, *Faith in Fiction: The Emergence of Religious Literature in America* (Cambridge, MA: Harvard University Press, 1981).

23. Buell, *New England Literary Culture,* 240–1.

24. Maddox, *Removals,* 96.

25. I borrow this term "history-writers" from Nina Baym in order to distinguish the practice and methods of early-nineteenth-century antiquarians and other genteel amateurs from those of present-day professional historians. See Baym, "Women and the Republic: Emma Willard's Rhetoric of History," *American Quarterly* 43 (March 1991), n. 1, 19. See her *American Women Writers and the Work of History* as well.

26. The literature of and about the new historicism is too vast to catalogue here. In relation to my discussion here, see Stephen Greenblatt's *Renaissance Self-Fashioning: From More to Shakespeare* (Chicago: University of Chicago Press, 1980); Louis Montrose, "Renaissance Literary Studies and the Subject of History," *English Literary Renaissance* 16 (Winter 1986), 5–12; Michael Warner, "Literary Studies and the History of the Book," *The Book: Newsletter of the Program of the History of the Book in American Culture* 12 (July 1987), 3–9.

27. George Forgie, *Patricide in the House Divided: A Psychological Interpretation of Lincoln and His Age* (New York: Norton, 1979), 14.

28. One should bear in mind that historiographic and epistemological issues did not begin with the work of Hayden White – whom I discuss in Chapter 2. For background on this kind of philosophical inquiry, see Kenneth Burke, *Attitudes Towards History* rev. ed. (Berkeley: University of California Press, 1984), and R. G. Collingwood, *The Idea of History,* rev. ed., ed. Jan van der Dussen (Oxford: Clarendon Press, 1993). The work of Paul Ricoeur is also significant in the context of modern historiography, although Ricoeur, unlike

White, understands the narrativity of history as a potentially re-demptive phenomenon upon which human understanding of tem-porality may occur. See *Time and Narrative,* trans. Kathleen McLaughlin and David Pellauer (Chicago: University of Chicago Press, 1984).

29. See Hayden White, *Metahistory: The Historical Imagination in Nineteenth-Century Europe* (Baltimore and London: Johns Hopkins University Press, 1973), esp. 1–42, and "The Historical Text as Liter-ary Artifact" in *The Writing of History: Literary Form and Historical Understanding,* ed. Robert H. Canary and Henry Kozicki (Madison: University of Wisconsin Press, 1978), 41–62, 42 for the citation.

30. The discussion that follows is guided by George H. Callcott, *History in the United States, 1800–1860* (Baltimore: Johns Hopkins University Press, 1970), esp. 32–4, 48–9, 55–9, 88–90; David D. Van Tassell, *Recording America's Past: An Interpretation of the Development of Histori-cal Studies in America, 1607–1884* (Chicago: University of Chicago Press, 1960), 31–141, and esp. 89–91 for the rise of history text-books for public schools; Wesley Frank Craven, *The Legend of the Founding Fathers* (New York: New York University Press, 1956), esp. 66–7, 86–7, and 98–9 for the advent of historical societies. For the secularization of Revolutionary-era historiography, see also Lester H. Cohen, *The Revolutionary Histories: Contemporary Narratives of the American Revolution* (Ithaca, NY: Cornell University Press, 1980).

31. Callcott, *History in the United States,* 33.

32. One should not overestimate, however, the rapidity with which this occurred. The development of state-funded systems of public educa-tion was a gradual, and often heavily politicized, process that oc-curred throughout much of the nineteenth century. See Lawrence A. Cremin, *American Education: The National Experience, 1783–1876* (New York: Harper & Row, 1980), 148–86.

33. Callcott, *History in the United States,* 58–9.

34. Van Tassell, *Recording America's Past,* 90–1.

35. Ibid., 88–9.

36. "The Philosophy of History," *North American Review* 39 (July 1834), 30, 41.

37. Emma Willard, *History of the United States of America* (New York: White, Gallaher & White, 1831), xvi–xvii.

38. *The Christian Spectator* 7 (January 1825), 80–90, 82 for citation.

39. Rufus Choate, "The Importance of Illustrating New-England His-tory by a Series of Romances like the Waverly Novels," in *The Works of Rufus Choate with a Memoir of his Life,* ed. Samuel G. Brown (Bos-ton: Little, Brown, 1862), I:339.

40. "American Genius," *Collections, Historical and Miscellaneous; and Monthly Literary Journal,* 3 vols., ed. J. Farmer and J. B. Moore (Concord, MA: J. B. Moore, 1823), II, 261.

41. Catharine Maria Sedgwick, *Hope Leslie; or Early Times in the Massachu-*

setts, ed. Mary Kelley (New Brunswick, NJ: Rutgers University Press, 1987), 5.

42. See Cathy N. Davidson, *Revolution and The Word: The Rise of the Novel in America* (New York: Oxford University Press, 1986).

43. Choate, "Importance of Illustrating," in Brown, ed., *Works,* 319, italics added. The history-writers to whom Choate refers are John Marshall, Timothy Pitkin, Abiel Holmes, and David Ramsay.

44. See the *American Journal of Education,* II (Boston: Wait, Greene & Co., 1826), 683–7, for a critique of Goodrich. The accusations against Ramsay are in the *North American Review* 6 (March 1818), 335–6. For this stylistic criterion for historiography, see also "Materials for American History," *North American Review* 23 (October 1826), 275–6.

45. "Recent American Novels," *North American Review* 21 (July 1825), 97.

46. For the presence of historical fiction in historical magazines during this era, see Callcott, *History in the United States,* 48–9.

47. On Child, see Ernest Leisy, *The American Historical Novel* (Norman: University of Oklahoma Press, 1950), 70; on Cooper, see the "Historical Introduction" to *Lionel Lincoln; or, The Leaguer of Boston,* ed. Donald A. and Lucy B. Ringe (Albany: SUNY Press, 1984), xxvii.

48. Willard, *History,* viii.

49. James Fenimore Cooper, *The Wept of Wish-ton-Wish* (Philadelphia: Carey, Lea, & Carey, 1829), I:54. See also ix–x for Cooper's wry commentary on the reliability of Trumbull. James McHenry, *The Spectre of the Forest, or, Annals of the Housatonic* (New York: Bliss & White, 1823), II:92.

50. Benedict Anderson, *Imagined Communities: Reflections on the Origin and Spread of Nationalism,* rev. ed. (London and New York: Verso, 1991), 194–5.

51. Thomas's sometimes cranky critique perhaps unfairly assails new historicists for not trying to create a usable past, as earlier progressive historians had attempted. But he does expose the inconsistencies in new historicists' challenge to the literary canon. Thomas argues convincingly that many modern critics consider the canon inevitably to be an ideological construct and yet go about trying to expand it by relying on traditional methods for defining literary "traditions." See *The New Historicism and Other Old-Fashioned Topics* (Princeton: Princeton University Press, 1992), 7–10 and passim.

52. The issue of the status of Puritanism in popular culture, including an oral culture of songs and sayings that may include illiterate (or barely literate) members of lower classes is really beyond the ambit of this study. The title of the satiric ballad "Jonathan's Account of the Pilgrim People, or the Natural Freemasons" (Boston: G. Graupner, 1826) does suggest – through the allusion to masonry – that class indeed played a role in cultural representations of Puri-

.   tanism. The song debunks the republican mythology of the Puritans as industrious citizens that New England elites tended to emphasize.

53. For the subject of New England's disproportionate weight, see Van Tassel, *Recording America's Past,* 90–2. See also Ruth Miller Elson, *Guardians of Tradition: American Schoolbooks of the Nineteenth Century* (Lincoln: University of Nebraska Press, 1964), 7, 167–73, 217, 264, 294.

54. See, for instance, Bell, *Hawthorne,* 149–50, 170–71.

55. Charles Sellers, *The Market Revolution: Jacksonian America, 1815–1846* (New York: Oxford University Press, 1991). Much of my discussion in the paragraphs that follow derives from Sellers. For social and economic changes during this era, see also Steven Watts, *The Republic Reborn: War and the Making of Liberal America, 1790–1820* (Baltimore: Johns Hopkins University Press, 1987), esp. 2–62.

56. See Sellers, *Market Revolution,* 47–50, and Morton J. Horwitz, *The Transformation of American Law, 1780–1860* (Cambridge, MA: Harvard University Press, 1977), 31–62.

57. See Forgie, *House Divided,* 8–9; Fred Somkin, *Unquiet Eagle: Memory and Desire in the Idea of American Freedom* (Ithaca, NY: Cornell University Press, 1967); Marcus Cunliffe, *The Nation Takes Shape, 1789–1837* (Chicago: University of Chicago Press, 1959); and Marvin Meyers, *The Jacksonian Persuasion: Politics and Belief* (Stanford, CA: Stanford University Press, 1957).

58. R. C. De Prospo, "Marginalizing Early American Literature," *New Literary History* 23 (1992), 250. De Prospo's concern is with colonial literature, but his major point about the inevitable debasement of early texts within the framework of romanticized narratives of national, historical development applies as well to early-nineteenth-century writers.

59. See Tompkins, *Sensational Designs,* 147–85, and *The American Renaissance Reconsidered,* ed. Walter Benn Michaels and Donald Pease (Baltimore: Johns Hopkins University Press, 1985). For the continuing influence of this critical trope, see, for example, the introduction to Gillian Brown, *Domestic Individualism* (Berkeley: University of California Press, 1991).

Chapter 1

1. Salma Hale, *History of the United States* (London: John Miller, 1826), 34. The letter was written by both John Robinson, minister of the Scrooby congregation, and William Brewster, to Edwin Sandys, a principal member of the Virginia Company, while the Leyden group was negotiating with that body in November 1617 to obtain a patent for land in North America. Bradford's text was taken to England during the Revolutionary War, and so Hale never worked with it as a primary source. But he likely knew Bradford from reading Thomas Prince's *Annals of New England* (1736, 1755), since Prince had the

Bradford manuscript in his possession during the period in which he composed the *Annals*. See *Of Plymouth Plantation*, ed. Samuel Eliot Morison (New York: Knopf, 1952), 33 for Robinson and Brewster's letter.

2. Hale, *History*, 34.
3. Ibid., 50, 51.
4. Ibid., 53.
5. Ibid., 27.
6. See David D. Van Tassel, *Recording America's Past: An Interpretation of the Development of Historical Studies in America, 1607–1884* (Chicago: University of Chicago Press, 1960), 90.
7. Hale, *History*, 45.
8. Ibid., 53.
9. See Louis Hartz, *The Liberal Tradition in America: An Interpretation of Political Thought Since the Revolution* (New York: Harcourt Brace Jovanovich, 1955). For discussion of Hartz's ambivalence to "mass Lockianism," see Thomas Hill Schaub, *American Fiction in the Cold War* (Madison: University of Wisconsin Press, 1991), 11, 13–14, 126. Schlesinger's historical work is voluminous, but his liberal politics are perhaps most salient in *The Vital Center: The Politics of Freedom* (Boston: Houghton Mifflin, 1949). I include Hofstadter with this milieu because his interpretation of the Constitution's Framers as conservative skeptics reflects, I think, a revisionist liberal rejection of political idealism associated with Marxist ideologues. See "The Founding Fathers: An Age of Realism" in *The American Political Tradition: And the Men Who Made It* (New York: Knopf, 1948), 3–21.
10. The amount of scholarly literature that republicanism has spawned is quite large. For the seminal texts, see Bernard Bailyn, *The Ideological Origins of the American Revolution* (Cambridge, MA: Belknap/Harvard University Press, 1967); Gordon Wood, *The Creation of the American Republic, 1775–1787* (Chapel Hill: University of North Carolina Press, 1969); and J. G. A. Pocock, *The Machiavellian Moment: Florentine Political Thought and the Atlantic Republican Tradition* (Princeton: Princeton University Press, 1975). For a recent study showing the enduring influence of their work, see Ann Fairfax Withington's *Toward a More Perfect Union: Virtue and the Formation of American Republics* (New York: Oxford University Press, 1991).
11. Carl Becker, *The History of Political Parties in the Province of New York, 1760–1776*. 1909 (Madison: University of Wisconsin Press, 1968), 22.
12. Robert E. Shalhope, "Toward a Republican Synthesis: The Emergence of an Understanding of Republicanism in American Historiography," *William and Mary Quarterly*, 3rd ser. 29 (1972), 49–80.
13. Appleby's influential essays are anthologized in *Liberalism and Republicanism in the Historical Imagination* (Cambridge, MA: Harvard University Press, 1992), 163 for above quotation.
14. For revisions of the republican synthesis, see the special edition of

the *American Quarterly* 37 (Fall 1985), which Appleby edited, entitled "Republicanism in the History and Historiography of the
United States." See also Isaac Kramnick, *Republicanism and Bourgeois
Radicalism: Political Ideology in Late Eighteenth-Century England and
America* (Ithaca, NY: Cornell University Press, 1990), and "Republican Revisionism Revisited," *American Historical Review* 87 (1982),
629–63. In *The Lost Soul of American Politics: Virtue, Self-Interest and
the Foundations of Liberalism* (New York: Basic Books, 1984), John
Patrick Diggins attempts to articulate "the interrelated tradition of
Lockeanism and Calvinism," 9. Perhaps more interesting than his
general thesis is his theoretical critique of republican historians, for
it reveals how these historiographic differences rest upon deeper
issues involving the nature of language, causation, and even historical "reality" itself. See 347–65.

15. For a thorough, sophisticated analysis of eighteenth-century Scottish
philosophy, and particularly its influence on Jefferson, see Garry
Wills, *Inventing America: Jefferson's Declaration of Independence* (New
York: Doubleday, 1978). I take up the feminization of virtue and its
philosophical backgrounds much more thoroughly in Chapters 2
and 3.

16. See Gordon Wood, *The Radicalism of the American Revolution* (New
York: Vintage, 1993), 189–225, 196 for quotation. His discussion
of the softening of patriarchal authority derives in part from Jay
Fliegelman's *Prodigals and Pilgrims: The American Revolution Against
Patriarchal Authority, 1750–1800* (Cambridge: Cambridge University
Press, 1982).

17. Steven Watts, *The Republic Reborn: War and the Making of Liberal
America, 1790–1820* (Baltimore: Johns Hopkins University Press,
1987), xviii.

18. An early example of this trend is Drew McCoy's *The Elusive Republic:
Political Economy in Jeffersonian America* (Chapel Hill: University of
North Carolina Press, 1980); it articulates Jefferson's "hybrid" republicanism, which assimilated free trade and commercial growth
to traditional classical republicanism. See esp. 46–8, 67, 74–5. Gary
B. Nash's *The Urban Crucible: The Northern Seaports and Origins of the
American Revolution* (Cambridge, MA: Harvard University Press,
1986) is a good example of a "neoprogressive" study that considers
the subjects of virtue and ideology in context of urban class interests. For a thorough, though now somewhat dated, summary of
these changes in republican historiography, see Robert E. Shalhope,
"Republicanism and Early American Historiography," *William and
Mary Quarterly*, 3rd. ser. 39 (1982), 334–56. For more recent work
in this regard, see my "Virtue, Ideology and the American Revolution: The Legacy of the Republican Synthesis," *ALH* 5 (Fall 1993),
564–77.

19. Stephen J. Ross, "The Transformation of Republican Ideology," *Journal of the Early Republic* 10 (Fall 1990), 324, italics his.

20. This is one of the major arguments of Wood's recent study, *The*

Radicalism of the American Revolution. The quotation comes from his Afterword to an anthology of essays reevaluating the republican historiography, *The Republican Synthesis Revisited: Essays in Honor of George Athan Billias,* ed. Milton M. Klein, Richard D. Brown, and John B. Hench (Worcester: American Antiquarian Society, 1992), 149 for quotation.

21. Peter S. Onuf and Cathy Matson, "Republicanism and Federalism in the Constitutional Decade," in *Republican Synthesis Revisited,* 120. See also their *A Union of Interests: Political and Economic Thought in Revolutionary America* (Lawrence: University of Kansas Press, 1990).

22. See Tamara Plakins Thornton, *Cultivating Gentlemen: The Meaning of Country Life Among the Boston Elite, 1785–1860* (New Haven: Yale University Press, 1989), 45–6.

23. Charles A. Goodrich, *A History of the United States of America* (New York: G. C. Smith, 1829), 5.

24. See the Introduction to this book for a discussion of modernization in early nineteenth-century America. John M. Murrin offers various statistics that show the period's accelerated growth. From 1790 to 1814, for example, the number of federal patents almost doubled every five years. American banks increased from four in 1791 to eighty-nine in 1811, and to more than three hundred by the panic of 1819. International commerce multiplied more than five times to about $100 million between 1774 and 1807. See "The Great Inversion, or Court Versus Country: A Comparison of the Revolution Settlements in England (1688–1721) and America (1776–1816)" in *Three British Revolutions: 1641, 1688, 1776,* ed. J. G. A. Pocock (Princeton: Princeton University Press, 1980), 368–453. See also Bray Hammond, *Banks and Politics in America from the Revolution to the Civil War* (Princeton: Princeton University Press, 1957); Stuart Bruchey, *The Roots of American Economic Growth, 1607–1861: An Essay in Social Causation* (New York: Harper & Row, 1965), and *American Economic Growth and Standards of Living Before the Civil War,* ed. Robert E. Gallman and John Joseph Wallis (Chicago: University of Chicago Press, 1992).

25. The currency of classical republican ideology among a New England elite is apparent, for example, in a pamphlet Hale himself wrote in 1826 defending the presidency of John Quincy Adams, under the pseudonym of Algernon Sidney, who was one of the great Whig martyrs of republicanism, executed by Charles II during the English civil wars. See *The Administration of the Opposition. Addressed to the Citizens of New-Hampshire* (Concord, MA: Jacob B. Moore, 1826).

26. *The Dialogic Imagination: Four Essays by M. M. Bakhtin,* ed. Michael Holquist, trans. Caryl Emerson and Michael Holquist (Austin: University of Texas Press, 1981), 324.

27. John Farmer and J. B. Moore, eds., *Collections, Historical and Miscellaneous; and Monthly Literary Journal,* 3 vols. (Concord: J. B. Moore, 1822–1824), II:260.

28. David Ramsay, *History of the United States of America,* 3 vols. (Philadel-

phia: Mathew Carey, 1818), 1:75, 88. For Ramsay's regard for contemporary New England as a model of republicanism, see Arthur H.
Shaffer, *To Be an American: David Ramsay and the Making of the American Consciousness* (Columbia: University of South Carolina Press,
1991), 96. Shaffer, however, neglects the relationship between liberalism and republicanism that informs this paradigm. Critics of Ramsay's work generally tend to simplify it as a product of the "Enlightenment." See Lester H. Cohen, *The Revolutionary Histories:
Contemporary Narratives of the American Revolution* (Ithaca, NY: Cornell University Press, 1980), and Karen O'Brien, "David Ramsay and
the Delayed Americanization of American History," *Early American
Literature* 29 (1994), 1–18.

29. Ramsay, *History of the United States,* I:82.

30. "A Discourse Delivered at Plymouth, 22 December 1806, at the
Anniversary Commemoration of the First Landing of the Fathers,
A.D. 1620" (Cambridge, MA: William Hilliard, 1806), 15, and *The
Annals of America from the Discovery of Columbus in the Year 1492 to the
Year 1826,* 2nd ed., 2 vols. (Cambridge, MA: Hilliard & Brown,
1829), I:161. The first edition of *American Annals* appeared in 1805.

31. For further discussion of the role of Puritanism among conservative
Whigs, see Jean Matthews, " 'Whig History': The New England
Whigs and a Usable Past," *New England Quarterly* 51 (1978), 193–
208.

32. Holmes, *American Annals,* I:165, 45, 47.

33. Ramsay, *History of the United States,* I:53.

34. Ibid., 72.

35. Ibid., 79.

36. Ibid., 82.

37. Lemuel Shaw, "An Oration Delivered at Boston, July 4, 1815, Before
the Supreme Executive of the Commonwealth, and the Municipal
Authority and Citizens of the Town in Commemoration of American
Independence" (Boston: John Eliot, 1815), 6–7.

38. William C. Dowling, *Poetry and Ideology in Revolutionary Connecticut*
(Athens: University of Georgia Press, 1990), 17.

39. For the republican politics of Rush's medical theories, see Melvin
Yazawa, *From Colonies to Commonwealth: Familial Ideology and the Begin-
nings of the American Republic* (Baltimore: Johns Hopkins University
Press, 1985), 141–65.

40. See Goodrich, *History of the United States,* 63; Holmes, *American
Annals,* I:218.

41. Holmes, *American Annals,* I:218.

42. Abiel Abbot, *History of Andover from its Settlement to 1829* (Andover,
MA: Flagg & Gould, 1829), 177.

43. For example, see Orrin Grant Libbey, "Ramsay as Plagiarist," *Ameri-
can Historical Review* 7 (1902), 697–703. See also Elmer Douglass
Johnson, "David Ramsay: Historian or Plagiarist?" *South Carolina
Historical Magazine* 57 (October 1956), 189–98.

44. "Biographical Memoir of David Ramsay, M.D.," in Ramsay, *History of the United States*, 8.

45. Ibid., 8–9.

46. Ramsay, *History of the United States*, I:245–6.

47. Lawrence Buell, *New England Literary Culture: From Revolution Through Renaissance* (Cambridge: Cambridge University Press, 1986), 230.

48. See Buell, *New England Literary Culture*, 216; Sidney Kaplan, "*The History of New Hampshire:* Jeremy Belknap as Literary Craftsman," *William and Mary Quarterly*, 3rd ser. 21 (1964), 21; George B. Kirsch, "Jeremy Belknap: Man of Letters in the Young Republic," *New England Quarterly* 54 (March 1981), 35, 48; and Louis Leonard Tucker, *Clio's Consort: Jeremy Belknap and the Founding of the Massachusetts Historical Society* (Boston: Northeastern University Press, 1990), 34, 38.

49. Belknap and his lifelong correspondent, Ebenezer Hazard, mocked Mather's credulity at length, citing long passages from *Wonders of the Invisible World*. Most of Belknap's correspondence has been collected as the *Belknap Papers* in the *Massachusetts Historical Society Collections*, vols. 2 and 3 (1877), and vol. 4 (1891). See vol. 3 (1871), 188, 198–9, 204–5, for these particular references to Mather. Many of Belknap's anecdotes come directly from the *Magnalia:* the woodpile thief, the charity to widows, Winthrop's use of private funds for public projects, the speech in front of the General Court over the Hingham controversy. Mather highlights Winthrop's frugality and austerity, lauds his concern for "the common good of the nation," and holds up "the self-denial of this patriot" as the right object of memory. As I mention below, Mather also emphasizes Winthrop's wariness of a government "too democratical." See the *Magnalia Christi Americana: Books I and II,* ed. Kenneth B. Murdock (Cambridge and London: Belknap/Harvard University Press, 1977), 213–28, for the life of Winthrop. See also Richard S. Dunn, "John Winthrop Writes His Journal," *William and Mary Quarterly*, 3rd ser. 41 (1984), 186, 208, for Belknap's familiarity with Winthrop's *Journal.*

50. Belknap, *American Biography; or, an Historical Account of Those Persons Who Have Been Distinguished in America as Adventurers, Statesmen, Philosophers, Divines, Warriors, Authors, and Other Remarkable Characters. Comprehending a Recital of the Events Connected with Their Lives and Actions*, vols. 1–II (Boston: Isaiah Thomas & Ebenezer T. Andrews, 1794–8), II:340. All further citations come from this edition.

51. Belknap, *American Biography*, II:337–8.

52. Ibid., 341.

53. "Luxury and effeminacy," Belknap had written privately during the Revolutionary crisis, "have always been found the surest means to corrupt and enslave a people, while frugality and hardiness have always been favorable to liberty." See Jane Belknap Marcou, *Life of*

Jeremy Belknap, D.D., the Historian of New Hampshire (New York: Harper & Bros., 1847), 86–7.

54. Belknap, *American Biography* I:87, 101.

55. Ibid., 240.

56. Ibid., 241.

57. Ibid., 272. The historically judicious Belknap took Smith at his (dubious) word for just these reasons. Even such an enthusiastic partisan for Smith as Philip Barbour admitted that Smith's *The True Travels, Adventures, and Observations of Captain John Smith* (1630) contained "twenty chapters of apparent bombast that celebrate Smith's various deeds." See *The Complete Works of Captain John Smith*, vols. I–III, ed. Philip L. Barbour (Chapel Hill: University of North Carolina Press, 1986), III:127. Toward the end of the life of Smith, Belknap acknowledges his use of the *True Travels* and other writings by Smith. See *American Biography*, I:316.

58. Belknap, *American Biography*, II:v.

59. Ibid., I:264.

60. Ibid., II:347.

61. Ibid., 345, 348.

62. Ibid., 348.

63. Ibid., 349. This parallels, one might add, the virtue of Plymouth's William Bradford, who can see that the itinerant ne'er-do-wells John Oldham and John Lyford come to Plymouth to "excite a faction" and stir up "factious and disorderly conduct" (II:248, 250). And in this context, then, the often cited distinction between "Puritan" and "Pilgrim" is far less strident than is often supposed. Although early nationals often found the Plymouth colony more tolerant, and thus a model preferable to the Bay colony, much of this chapter articulates those ways in which the two were equivalently (and metaphorically) virtuous. For this kind of distinction, see, for example, Peter J. Gomes, "Pilgrims and Puritans: 'Heroes' and 'Villains' in the Creation of the American Past," *Massachusetts Historical Society Proceedings* 95 (1983), 1–16.

64. Sacvan Bercovitch, *The Puritan Origins of the American Self* (New Haven: Yale University Press, 1976), 87.

65. Jay Fliegelman, *Prodigals and Pilgrims*, 197–226, 210 for quotation. Fliegelman does note, however, that for conservative Federalists, Washington helped to serve as "an argument for aristocracy" (224).

66. John Davis, "An Eulogy on General George Washington Pronounced at Boston on Wednesday, February 19, 1800, Before the American Academy of Arts and Sciences," 16, 9, 21, 23.

67. Ibid., 9–10, italics added.

68. Ibid., 24.

69. See Buell, *New England Literary Culture*, 214–38, and Michael Vella, "Theology, Genre, and Gender: The Precarious Place of Hannah Adams in American Literary History," *Early American Literature* 28 (1993), 22–41.

70. For discussion of the political conservativism of Unitarianism, see Daniel Walker Howe, *The Unitarian Conscience: Harvard Moral Philosophy, 1805–1861* (Cambridge, MA: Harvard University Press, 1970), esp. "Unitarian Whiggery," 205–35. Howe notes how the Unitarian respect for the "old Puritan sense of corporate moral responsibility" (211) helped to create Unitarian affinities for the Puritan commonwealth. See also Henry F. May, *The Enlightenment in America* (New York: Oxford University Press, 1976), 268–9, 350–7. K. P. Van Anglen takes up the legacy of Milton's *Paradise Lost*. Unitarians "were even more glad that at the end of the poem Milton had made it clear that God (and with Him, the forces of order and hierarchy) would eventually triumph." See *The New England Milton: Literary Reception and Cultural Authority in the Early Republic* (University Park: Pennsylvania State University Press, 1993), 41–79, esp. 43.

71. Belknap, *American Biography*, II:355.

72. Ibid., 350, 355.

73. David Tappan, "A Sermon Preached Before His Excellency John Hancock . . . Being the Day of General Election," 1792. In *Political Sermons of the American Founding Era, 1730–1805*, ed. Ellis Sandoz (Indianapolis: Liberty Press, 1991), 1124, 1105–6. Compare his rhetoric to a fast day sermon given in the Orthodox environs of Andover, where the minister, John Hubbard Church, used this political typology to make the same kind of argument: "We have had Moses and Aaron to lead us; we have had teachings and instructions; – we have had ordinances and gospel dispensations the choicest of them." See "The First Settlement of New England, Delivered in the South Parish in Andover, April 5, 1810; being the Annual Fast in Massachusetts" (Sutton, MA: Sewall Goodridge, 1810), 18–19.

74. Jeremy Belknap, *The History of New Hampshire* (Philadelphia: Robert Aitken, 1784), I:80.

75. Hannah Adams, *A Summary History of New England from the First Settlement at Plymouth to the Acceptance of the Federal Constitution* (Dedham, MA: H. Mann & J. H. Adams, 1799), 34–5.

76. Mercy Otis Warren, *History of the Rise, Progress and Termination of the American Revolution interspersed with Biographical, Political and Moral Observations* (1805), ed. Lester H. Cohen 2 vols. (Indianapolis: Liberty, 1988), I:9.

77. Morse and coauthor Elijah Parish were accused of plagiarizing Adams's abridged version of the *Summary History* as they were preparing their own *Compendious History of New England* (1804). For the dispute between them, see Morse's *Appeal to the Public, on the Controversy Respecting the Revolution in Harvard College, and the Events which have Followed it; Occasioned by the use which has been made of certain complaints and accusations of Miss Hannah Adams, against the author* (Charlestown, MA: Printed for the Author, 1814); and Hannah Adams, *A Narrative of the Controversy Between the Reverend Jedidiah Morse, D.D. and the Author* (Boston, 1814). For the controversy be-

tween the two, see Buell, *New England Literary Culture*, 224, and Vella, "Theology."

78. Jedidiah Morse and Elijah Parish, *A Compendious History of New England* (London: William Burton, 1808), 126–7.

79. Adams, *Summary History*, 22.

80. For discussion of "civil millennialism," which politicized New England typology so as to interpret the coming of the New Jerusalem as a fulfillment of the principles of the American Revolution, see Nathan O. Hatch, *The Sacred Cause of Liberty* (New Haven: Yale University Press, 1977). The abridged edition of the *Summary History*, designed for schoolchildren, emphasizes the same theme: "From the first settlement [of New England] no nation had ever experienced more extraordinary interpositions of Providence than America; and at no period were those interpositions more singularly visible than during the controversy with Britain." See *An Abridgement of the History of New England for the Use of Young Persons* (Boston: B. and J. Homans, & John West, 1805), 162.

81. Adams, *Summary History*, 22.

82. Ibid., 94, 35, 102.

83. Morse and Parish, *Compendious History*, 59.

84. Adams, *Summary History*, 78.

85. Morse and Parish, *Compendious History*, 59. Adams, however, like so many of the Revolutionary generation, began to shift the balance between social order and civil liberty in the years after independence. See *The Works of John Adams*, vol. III, ed. Charles Francis Adams (Boston: Charles C. Little & James Brown, 1851), 452.

86. Michael Warner, *The Letters of the Republic: Publication and the Public Sphere in Eighteenth-Century America* (Cambridge, MA: Harvard University Press, 1990), 2.

87. Adams, ed., *Works*, III:452.

88. See Miller's famous essay, "From Edwards to Emerson," in *Errand into the Wilderness* (Cambridge: Belknap/Harvard University Press, 1956), 184–203. Mathiessen's comments at the outset of *American Renaissance* suggest the same historical role for Unitarianism: "One way of understanding the concentrated abundance of our mid-nineteenth century would be through its intellectual history, particularly through a study of the breakdown of Puritan orthodoxy into Unitarianism, and of the quickening of the cool Unitarian strain into the spiritual and emotional fervor of transcendentalism." See *American Renaissance: Art and Experience in the Age of Emerson and Whitman* (London: Oxford University Press, 1941), viii.

89. See the *Monthly Anthology and Boston Review* 2 (1805), 538–49, 543–4 for quotations.

90. William Emerson, "Oration Pronounced July 5, 1802, at the Request of the Inhabitants of the Town of Boston, in Commemoration of the Anniversary of American Independence," 1802. In *Political Sermons*, ed. Sandoz, 1559.

91. Sandoz, ed., *Political Sermons*, 1561.
92. Ibid., 1567.
93. Ibid., 1567.
94. Henry Ware, Sr., "A Sermon Delivered Before the Convention of Congregational Ministers of Massachusetts at their Annual Meeting in Boston" (Boston: Wells & Lilly, 1818), 9.
95. Henry Ware, Sr., "A Sermon Delivered Before His Excellency John Brooks, Governor, His Honor William Phillips, Lt. Governor, the Honorable Council, and the Two Houses Composing the Legislature of Massachusetts, on the Anniversary Election" (Boston: Russell & Gardner, 1821), 10.
96. Sandoz, ed., *Political Sermons*, 1560.
97. Ware, "John Brooks," 10–11, italics added.
98. Ibid., 14–15.
99. Ibid., 16, 22.
100. Ibid., 22.
101. "A Sermon Delivered in King's Chapel, Boston, 9 July 1826" (Cambridge, MA: Hilliard & Metcalf, 1826), 12, 18.
102. See, for example, "A Sermon Delivered October 12, 1820, at the Ordination of the Reverend William B. O. Peabody to the Pastoral Charge of the Third Congregational Church in Springfield" (Springfield, MA: A. G. Tannatt, 1820).
103. Holmes, "Oration," 18–19.
104. Ibid., 17.
105. For the relationship between Webster's political conservatism and lexical practice, see Richard Rollins, "Words as Social Control: Noah Webster and the Creation of the *American Dictionary*," *American Quarterly* 28 (1976), 415–30, and *The Long Journey of Noah Webster* (Philadelphia: University of Pennsylvania Press, 1980).
106. "Introduction: The Democratic Principle," *The United States Magazine and Democratic Review* 1 (1837), 1–2.
107. *The Dialogic Imagination*, ed. Holquist, 315.
108. See Thomas Gustafson, *Representative Words: Politics, Literature and the American Language, 1776–1865* (Cambridge: Cambridge University Press, 1992), esp. 37–65; Cynthia S. Jordan, *Second Stories: The Politics of Language, Form and Gender in Early American Fictions* (Chapel Hill: University of North Carolina Press, 1989), 1–26; Cathy Davidson, *Revolution and the Word* (New York: Oxford University Press, 1986), 152–63. The motif of the ambiguity of language in America runs throughout Michael P. Kramer's *Imagining Language in America: From the Revolution to the Civil War* (Princeton: Princeton University Press, 1992).
109. Gustafson, *Representative Words*, 53.
110. Rowland Berthoff, "Independence and Attachment, Virtue and Interest: From Republican Citizen to Free Enterprise, 1787–1837," in *Uprooted Americans: Essays to Honor Oscar Handlin*, ed. Richard L. Bushman (Boston: Little Brown, 1979), 106.

111. Samuel Knapp, *Lectures on American Literature* (New York: Elam Bliss, 1829), 43.
112. Ramsay, *History of the United States*, I:162.
113. Holmes, *American Annals*, I:161.
114. Goodrich, *History*, 36.
115. Holmes, *American Annals*, I 219–20.
116. Charles Sellers, *The Market Revolution: Jacksonian America, 1815–1846*. (New York: Oxford University Press, 1991), 152.
117. Timothy Dwight, *Travels in New-England and New-York*, 4 vols. (New Haven: T. Dwight, 1821–2), I:169–73.
118. Belknap, *The History of New Hampshire*, I:68–9.
119. Morse and Parish, *Compendious History*, 58.
120. Belknap, *History of New Hampshire*, I:68.
121. Morse and Parish, *Compendious History*, 9.
122. Adams, *Summary History of New England* (1805), 12.
123. See *Cotton Mather and Benjamin Franklin: The Price of Representative Personality* (Cambridge: Cambridge University Press, 1984), 153–70 for a discussion of the "Life of William Phips" in the context of the entire structure of the *Magnalia*.
124. Goodrich, *History*, 83.
125. Ibid., 86.
126. Ibid., 87.
127. Morse and Parish, *Compendious History*, 1–2.
128. Dwight, *Travels*, I:170.
129. See McCoy, *Elusive Republic*, 99.
130. Cathy Matson and Peter Onuf, "Toward a Republican Empire: Interest and Ideology in Revolutionary America," *American Quarterly* 37 (1985), 496–531.
131. Sellers, *Market Revolution*, 155–7.
132. Goodrich, *History*, 72–3.
133. Samuel Knapp, "Address," in *The New England Society Orations: Addresses, Sermons and Poems Delivered Before the New England Society in the City of New York, 1820–1885*, ed. Cephas Brainerd and Eveline Warner Brainerd (New York: The Century Co., 1901), 153–4.
134. Ibid., 154.
135. For a recent revision of the ideology of Puritan millennialism, see Theodore Dwight Bozeman, *To Live Ancient Lives: The Primitivist Dimension in Puritanism* (Chapel Hill: University of North Carolina Press, 1988).
136. John Lathrop, "A Discourse Delivered in Boston, April 13, 1815, the Day of Thanksgiving Appointed by the President of the United States in Consequence of the Peace" (Boston: J. W. Burditt, 1815), 13.
137. Ibid., 23.
138. Cohen, ed., *History of the Rise*, II:647.
139. Ibid., 688–9 (italics added).
140. Ibid., 698.
141. Ibid.

142. Dorothy Ross, "Historical Consciousness in Nineteenth-Century America," *American Historical Review* 89 (October 1984), 912.

143. For example, Salma Hale ends by reviewing "the rapid progress of the United States" and its "augmentation of wealth and power," which should give its citizenry "the loftiest anticipation for the future." Hale catalogues population growth, the rise in export trade, urban growth, internal improvements, new roads and canals. On America rests the patented fragility of the democratic experiment and thus "the destiny of mankind." See *History of the United States,* 465–7. Holmes similarly ends by taking stock of American modernity: the 10,000 boats passing through the Erie Canal each year, the plans for national roads, the Quincy railroad, and woolen factories in Paterson, New Jersey. See *American Annals,* 500–18).

144. Breitwieser, *Cotton Mather and Benjamin Franklin,* 94.

145. The trope of text as monument pervades the period's historical discourse. Joseph Felt, for example, admitted that his efforts constituted "no monument of brass. . . . But it speaks to us in clearer tones and with greater instruction and effect." Historical memory "covers us with the shield of its protection." See *Annals of Salem* (Salem, MA: W and S. B. Ives, 1827), 3, and ibid. (1845), iv, for the above citations.

146. For discussion of "Whig sentimentalism" during the Revolution, see Kenneth Silverman, *A Cultural History of the American Revolution* (New York: Columbia University Press, 1987), 82–7. Julie Ellison traces the legacy of sentiment into nineteenth-century conduct literature for men, noting particularly how it creates in Emerson's writings complex psychological tensions involving "homosocial affection." See "The Gender of Transparency: Emerson and the Conduct of Life," *ALH* 4 (1992), 584–606.

147. *North American Review* 26 (April 1828), 317–18.

148. Lyman Beecher, "Sermon Delivered at Plymouth, on the Twenty-Second of December, 1827" (Boston: T. R. Marvin, 1828), 24–5.

Chapter 2

1. This unpublished letter comes from the Emma Embury Collection, which is in the inventory of the 19th-Century Shop in Baltimore, Maryland. I would like to thank Stephen Loewentheil for his cooperation in allowing me to consult and use this material.

2. Letter to Charles Sedgwick, October 27, 1826, in *Life and Letters of Catharine M. Sedgwick,* ed. Mary Dewey (New York: Harper & Bros., 1872), 179–80.

3. Francis Jennings, *The Invasion of America: Indians, Colonialism, and the Cant of Conquest* (New York: Norton, 1976), 181. Other important revisionist studies include Richard Drinnon, *Facing West: The Metaphysics of Indian-Hating and Empire-Building* (Minneapolis: University of Minnesota Press, 1980), 35–45; and Neal Salisbury,

Manitou and Providence: Indians, Europeans, and the Making of New England, 1500–1643 (New York: Oxford University Press, 1982), 203–35. These historians address traditional accounts of the war, which place greater faith in the reliability of Puritan sources, such as found in Alden T. Vaughan's *New England Frontier: Puritans and Indians, 1620–1675* (Boston: Little, Brown, 1965). For an even earlier tradition of revisionist historians, see Vaughan, 134.

4. Stephen T. Katz, "The Pequot War Reconsidered," *New England Quarterly* 64 (June 1991), 207.

5. See, for example, Alfred A. Cave's "Who Killed John Stone: A Note on the Origins of the Pequot War," *William and Mary Quarterly*, 3rd ser. 49 (July 1992), 509–21. For an even more recent interpretation of whether or not the expedition qualifies as an act of genocide, see Michael Freeman, "Puritans and Pequots: The Question of Genocide," *New England Quarterly* 68 (June 1995), 278–93.

6. See Edwin Halsey Foster, *Catharine Maria Sedgwick* (New York: Twayne, 1974), 73–80.

7. Mary Kelley, "Introduction" to *Hope Leslie; or Early Times in the Massachusetts* (New Brunswick, NJ: Rutgers University Press, 1987), xxix, xxxi.

8. Sandra Zagarell, "Expanding 'America': Lydia Sigourney's *Sketch of Connecticut,* Catharine Sedgwick's *Hope Leslie,*" *Tulsa Studies in Women's Literature* 6 (Fall 1987), 235. For commentary that is less specific on Sedgwick's relationship to Puritan historiography but that still notes the novel's "subversion of male myth/history," see Christopher Castiglia, "In Praise of Extra-vagant Women: *Hope Leslie* and the Captivity Romance," *Legacy* 6 (1989), 12, and Lucy Maddox, *Removals: Nineteenth-Century American Literature and the Politics of Indian Affairs* (New York: Oxford University Press, 1991), 105 and n. 14, 191.

9. Dana Nelson, *The Word in Black and White: Reading "Race" in American Literature, 1638–1867* (New York: Oxford University Press, 1992), 72.

10. Ruth H. Bloch, "The Gendered Meanings of Virtue in Revolutionary America," *Signs: Journal of Women in Culture and Society* 13 (1987), 37–58. Bloch argues that through the affective epistemology of Edwardsian religion, Scottish Common Sense thinkers such as Francis Hutcheson who posited an emotional moral sense, and the rise of literary sentimentalism, virtue became increasingly associated with the workings of the heart and hence with women themselves. See also Jay Fliegelman, *Prodigals and Pilgrims: The American Revolution against Partiarchal Authority, 1750–1800* (Cambridge: Cambridge University Press, 1982).

11. Bloch, "Gendered Meanings," 56.

12. Gordon Wood, *The Radicalism of the American Revolution* (New York: Vintage, 1993), 216. See the entire section on "Benevolence," 213–25, for this change.

13. Nancy Cott, *The Bonds of Womanhood: "Woman's Sphere" in New England, 1780–1835* (New Haven: Yale University Press, 1977), 96.

14. Linda Kerber, *Women of the Republic: Intellect and Ideology in Revolutionary America* (Chapel Hill: University of North Carolina Press, 1980; New York: Norton, 1986). See also Mary Beth Norton's *Liberty's Daughters: The Revolutionary Experience of American Women* (New York, 1980). Rosemarie Zagarri recently has traced the intellectual roots of republican womanhood to the "civil jurisprudential school" of the Scottish Enlightenment. See "Morals, Manners, and the Republican Mother," *American Quarterly* 44 (June 1992), 192–215. For the importance of liberalism to women's political status, see Kerber's "The Republican Ideology of the Revolutionary Generation," *American Quarterly* 37 (Fall 1985), 474–95, esp. 485.

15. Kerber, *Women of the Republic,* 288.

16. The very notion of "separate spheres" has come under increasing scrutiny by historians of American women. In this chapter and the next, I treat this issue as an ideological construct rather than as an accurate description of social and political reality. For recent challenges to the concept of "woman's sphere," see Linda Kerber, "Separate Spheres, Female Worlds, Woman's Place: The Rhetoric of Woman's History," *Journal of American History* 75 (1988), 9–39, "Politics and Culture in Women's History: A Symposium," *Feminist Studies* 6 (Spring 1980), 26–64; Kathy Peiss, "Going Public: Women in Nineteenth-Century Cultural History," *ALH* (December 1991), 817–28; Lori D. Ginzberg, *Women and the Work of Benevolence: Morality, Politics, and Class in the Nineteenth-Century United States* (New Haven: Yale University Press, 1990); and Mary Ryan, *Women in Public: Between Banners and Ballots, 1825–1880* (Baltimore: Johns Hopkins University Press, 1990).

17. As Cott has shown, a number of factors made the home the "natural" place for the formation of virtuous citizens. See *Bonds,* 19–62, for changes that gradually devalued the home as a site of economic production. In this regard, see also Gerda Lerner, "The Lady and the Mill Girl: Changes in the Status of Women in the Age of Jackson," in *The Majority Finds its Place: Placing Women in History* (New York: Oxford University Press, 1979), 15–30, esp. 17–18, 25, 29. For the ideological legacy of Lockean and Rousseauist educational theories emphasizing the importance of nurturance, see Fliegelman, *Prodigals and Pilgrims,* 9–36.

18. Benjamin Rush, "A Plan for the Establishment of Public Schools and the Diffusion of Knowledge in Pennsylvania; to which are added Thoughts upon the Mode of Education Proper in a Republic. Addressed to the Legislature and Citizens of the State," 1786. In *Essays, Literary, Moral and Philosophical* (Philadelphia: Thomas and Samuel Bradford, 1798).

19. Rush, "Thoughts Upon Female Education Accommodated to the

Present State of Society, Manners, and Government in the United States of America," in *Essays*, 89.

20. *Life and Letters*, ed. Dewey, 91.

21. Ibid., 91, italics added.

22. *North American Review* 26 (April 1828), 403–20, 403 for citation.

23. Ibid., 408.

24. Ibid., 406.

25. George H. Callcott, *History in United States, 1800–1860: Its Practice and Purpose* (Baltimore: Johns Hopkins University Press, 1970), 104.

26. William Bradford gives some account of the machinations of John Lyford and John Oldham. See *Of Plymouth Plantation*, rev. ed., ed. Samuel Eliot Morison (New York: Knopf, 1991), 147–69, esp. n. 8, 149–50. See also Jennings, 188–90, and Vaughan, 123–4.

27. John Mason's "A Brief History of the Pequot War" was edited by Thomas Prince, who brought it to publication in Boston in 1736. It was reprinted in the *Collections of the Massachusetts Historical Society*, 2nd ser. 8 (1826), 120–53, 126 for citation. All future citations refer to this edition. As others have shown, *Hope Leslie* reveals Sedgwick's familiarity with Winthrop, Hubbard, and Bradford. I suspect that she likely was familiar with the *MHSC* reprinting of John Mason, but its virtual transmission in William Hubbard effectively skirts this problem. Let me say here, however, that my discussion in this chapter concerns the intertextual relations of these Puritan (and early national) histories. My references to the reprinted narratives of Gardiner, Underhill, and Vincent – all of which postdate the publication of *Hope Leslie* – are premised on those rhetorical and ideological features *common* to Puritan historians.

28. Mason, "Brief History," 129.

29. John Underhill, "Newes from America; or a New and Experimental Discoverie of New England," *Collections of the Massachusetts Historical Society*, 3rd ser. 6 (1837), 1–28. Lion Gardiner, "Leift Lion Gardiner his Relation of the Pequot Warres" in *Collections of the Massachusetts Historical Society* 3rd ser. 3 (1833), 131–60, and in *A History of the Pequot War* (Cincinnati: William Dodge, 1860), 5–32. All citations in the essay come from the 1860 edition; P[hilip] Vincent, "A True Relation of the Late Battell Fought in New-England, between the English and the Pequet Salvages: In which were Slaine and Taken Prisoners about 700 of the Salvages, and Those which Escaped Had Their Heads Cut Off by the Mohocks; with the Present State of Things There" (London: Thomas Harper, 1638), reprinted with Underhill's narrative in *Collections of the Massachusetts Historical Society*, 3rd ser. 6 (1837), 29–43.

30. Mason, "Brief History," 130.

31. Underhill, "Newes from America," 4.

32. See Gardiner, "Relation," 12–14, and Vincent, "True Relation," 35–7.

33. William Hubbard, *The Present State of New England. Being a Narrative of the Troubles with the Indians in New-England, from the First Planting Therof in the Year 1607 to this Present Year 1677: But Chiefly of the Late Troubles in the Last Two Years, 1675 and 1676; to which is added a Discourse about the Warre with the Pequods in the Year 1637* (London: Thomas Parkhurst, 1677), 116–17.
34. John Winthrop, *The History of New England from 1630 to 1649*, ed. James Savage (Boston: Phelps & Farnham, 1825), 190; Hubbard's account is virtually the same. See *A General History of New England from the Discovery to MDCLXXX* (Cambridge, MA: Hilliard & Metcalf, 1815), 249.
35. Mason, "Brief History," 129.
36. Benjamin Trumbull, *A Complete History of Connecticut, Civil and Ecclesiastical* (Hartford: Hudson & Goodwin, 1797), I:59–60.
37. Abiel Holmes, *American Annals* (Cambridge, MA: Hilliard & Brown, 1829), I:235; Jedidiah Morse and Elijah Parish, *A Compendious History of New England* (London: William Burton, 1808), 93; Epaphras Hoyt, *Antiquarian Researches: Comprising a History of the Indian Wars in the Country Bordering Connecticut River and Parts Adjacent* (Greenfield, MA: Ansel Phelps, 1824), 44. Even the famous antiquarian Samuel Drake, who initially argued that the English settlers "were too proud to court the favor of the natives," went on to recount the deaths of Norton, Stone, and Oldham. See the Appendix to his edition of Thomas Church's *The History of King Philip's War* (Exeter, NH: J&B Williams, 1829), 302–9.
38. Hannah Adams, *A Summary History of New England* (Dedham, MA: H. Mann & J. H. Adams, 1799), 68.
39. Catharine Maria Sedgwick, *Hope Leslie; or Early Times in the Massachusetts*, ed. Mary Kelley (New Brunswick, NJ: Rutgers University Press, 1987), 56. All quotations come from this edition and will be cited parenthetically in the text.
40. Hubbard, *Narrative of the Trouble with the Indians*, 116.
41. See Callcott, *History in the United States*, 139–47.
42. Ibid., 125.
43. Ibid., 136.
44. For a corrective to this commonly held misconception, see Salisbury, *Manitou and Providence*, 211.
45. Adams, *Summary History*, 68.
46. Trumbull, *Complete History of Connecticut*, 87.
47. *The Federalist Papers*, ed. Clinton Rossiter (New York: NAL Penguin, 1961), 353.
48. Timothy Dwight, *Travels in New-England and New-York* (New Haven: T. Dwight, 1821–2), III:19, italics added.
49. Trumbull, *Complete History of Connecticut*, 76.
50. Noah Porter, "A Discourse on the Settlement and Progress of New England" (Hartford: Peter Gleason, 1821), 10.
51. Epaphras Hoyt, *Antiquarian Researches*, 46.

52. Noah Webster, *An American Dictionary of the English Language* (New York: S. Converse, 1828), unpaginated.
53. See Merrill D. Peterson, *Thomas Jefferson and the New Nation* (New York: Oxford University Press, 1970), 57–61, and David P. Simpson, *The Politics of American English, 1776–1850* (New York: Oxford University Press, 1986), 81–90.
54. Salisbury, *Manitou and Providence*, 224.
55. See, for example, Adams, *Summary History*, 69; Trumbull, *Complete History of Connecticut*, 62; Dwight, *Travels*, III:12, and Morse and Parish, *Compendious History*, 95.
56. Gardiner, "Relation" (1860), 17. See Jennings, *Invasion of America*, 211–13, for European and Native American codes of warfare and the false stereotypes that have been pinned on the Pequot in this regard.
57. Morse and Parish, *Compendious History*, 95.
58. Ramsay, *History of the United States*, I:85.
59. Dwight, *Travels in New-England*, III:11.
60. Adams, *Summary History*, 70.
61. *American Annals*, I:241.
62. See, for example, Kelley, "Introduction," xxix, and Zagarell, "Expanding 'America,'" 233, 237.
63. See *The Power of Her Sympathy: The Autobiography and Journal of Catharine Maria Sedgwick*, ed. Mary Kelley (Boston: Northeastern University Press, 1993), 49.
64. Morse and Parish, *Compendious History*, 97.
65. See Kelley, ed., *Power of Her Sympathy*, 49.
66. See, for example, Isaac Goodwin's "An Oration Delivered at Lancaster," *Worcester Magazine and Historical Journal* 1 (Worcester: Rogers & Griffin, 1826), 327. Hawthorne's "Endicott and the Red Cross" investigates the ambiguities of Puritan rigor, as Endicott is described in this language. See *The Centenary Edition of the Works of Nathaniel Hawthorne*, vol. IX, ed. William Charvat, Roy Harvey Pearce, and Claude M. Simpson (Columbus: Ohio State University Press, 1974), 431, 444.
67. Ann Kibbey has argued for the "interchangeable" quality of Puritan and Pequot women as a way of showing the intimacy between Puritan racism and sexism. I would argue that despite the ostensible similarities, Sedgwick does not anticipate Kibbey's argument. Sedgwick issues much less of an indictment against "Puritan" sexism per se and more of one aimed at a political–cultural metaphor between Puritanism and republicanism that was popular during her own time. Sedgwick's feminization of Mystic Fort comments on the destructive capacity of male *virtu*, in which *both* Puritan and Native American men are implicated. Much of Kibbey's argument rests on the dubious conclusion that the diagram at the end of John Underhill's narrative symbolizes a vagina that "portrays both the Puritan men's genocidal violence and the sexual symbolism of their act" (110). Readers also might be warned that Kibbey gives an

idiosyncratic interpretation of Underhill's narrative to make it evidence of the "association between the violence of the war and [Puritan] men's attitudes toward women" (109). Underhill's reference to his wife mocks his *own* stubbornness. Kibbey also misreads Underhill's treatment of two captive, Puritan women, whom he mentions certainly not to serve misogynistic ends but only to show that the Lord chastens whom He loves. This fulfills the promotional dimension of the narrative: "You that intend to go to New England, fear not a little trouble" (22). One also wonders how Kibbey so easily associates Hutchinson with all Puritan women, and Puritan women with Pequot women in Underhill's narrative. See *The Interpretation of Material Shapes in Puritanism: A Study of Rhetoric, Prejudice, and Violence* (Cambridge: Cambridge University Press, 1986).

68. Ramsay, *History of the United States*, I:84.
69. Charles A. Goodrich, *A History of the United States of America* (New York: G. C. Smith, 1829), 15.
70. Morse and Parish, *Compendious History*, 96.
71. Salma Hale, *History of the United States* (London: John Miller, 1826), 43, 86.
72. Sedgwick likely read Philip Vincent's "A True Relation of the Late Batell Fought in New England," first published in 1638 and yet not reprinted in the *Massachusetts Historical Society Collections* until 1837. The description of Samoset's valor bears an uncanny resemblance to a passage in Vincent which is not present in any other of the firsthand Puritan accounts. Sedgwick reads as follows: "Samoset, the noble boy, defended the entrance with a prince-like courage, till they struck him down; prostrate and bleeding he again bent his bow, and had taken deadly aim at the English leader, when a sabreblow severed his bowstring" (49).
    And Vincent: "A stout Pequet encounters [an English soldier at the entrance], shoots his arrow, drawn to the head, into his right arm, where it stuck. He slashed the salvage betwixt the arm and the shoulder, who, pressing towards the door, was killed by the English" (37).
    Edward Johnson's *Wonder-Working Providence of Sions Saviour in New-England* (1654), with which, as Mary Kelley has demonstrated, Sedgwick was familiar, does specify that there were bowmen at the entrances to the fort who "wounded the foremost of the English in the shoulder" but gives nothing of the particular details found in both Vincent and Sedgwick. See *Wonder-Working Providence of Sions Savior in New England* (1653), ed. J. Franklin Jameson (New York: Charles Scribner's Sons, 1910), 167, and Kelley, n.5, 359, for Sedgwick and Edward Johnson.
73. Lydia Maria Child, *The First Settlers of New England: or, Conquest of the Pequods, Narragansetts and Pokanokets. As Related by a Mother to her Children. By a Lady of Massachusetts* (Boston: Munroe & Francis, 1829), 24.
74. The term comes, of course, from Hayden White, *Metahistory* (Balti-

more and London: Johns Hopkins University Press, 1973). White argues that "The same event [the attack upon Mystic Fort in this case] can serve as a different kind of element of many different historical stories, depending upon the role it is assigned in a specific motific characterization of the set to which it belongs" (7). See also "The Historical Text as Literary Artifact," in *The Writing of History: Literary Form and Historical Understanding*, ed. Robert H. Canary and Henry Kozicki (Madison: University of Wisconsin Press, 1978), 41–62. Selected essays have been compiled in *The Content of the Form: Narrative Discourse and Historical Representation* (Baltimore: Johns Hopkins University Press, 1987). While White has incurred the wrath of many historians, a more balanced theoretical dissent stressing the continuity between narrative and reality may be found in David Carr, *Time, Narrative and History* (Bloomington: Indiana University Press, 1986).

75. See Nelson, *The Word in Black and White*, n.13, 159.

76. Knapp, *Lectures*, unpaginated.

77. I have taken up this issue in part in my Introduction. See, for example, the review of David Ramsay's *History of the United States* in the *North American Review* 6 (1818), 335–7, and the review of Charles Goodrich's *History of the United States* in the *American Journal of Education* 2 (1827), 683–7.

78. *American Journal of Education*, 686.

79. Dewey, ed., *Life and Letters*, 192.

80. "History only becomes dramatic on two conditions: it must either have the passion of the politician or the imagination of the poet." Quoted from the *Edinburgh Review* 105 (January 1857), 23, in Callcott, *History in the United States*, 148–9. See 147–50 for the importance of emotion to the efficacy of historical narrative. David Levin also noted the "vital feeling of the past" with which the romantic historian was imbued: "One concentrated on responding emotionally to its [in this case, European ruins'] sound, on putting oneself or one's reader in proper imaginative relation with it." See *History as Romantic Art: Bancroft, Prescott, Motley and Parkman* (Stanford, CA: Stanford University Press, 1959), 7–8.

81. See Goodwin in *The Worcester Magazine and Historical Journal*, 327.

82. Ramsay, *History of the United States*, I:137.

83. *North American Review*, 340.

84. The entry for "recital" in the 1828 *American Dictionary* further suggests this lexical instability. Webster first distinguishes between an "enumeration" and a "narrative"; the latter he calls "a telling of the particulars of an adventure or of a series of events." But this distinction collapses because it fails to distinguish between an "enumeration" and a "telling." Another instance of this sense of "recital" may be found in one of the period's orations, where the speaker argues that war stories of the veterans of the War of 1812 actually swayed naive farmers and thus promoted a kind of dangerous militarism:

"The poor inhabitant of a remote retreat, who listens with enthusiasm to the *recital* of the exploits of his countrymen, and associates
himself in interest with those who never regarded him, discovers a
patriotism which we cannot but esteem. . . . Let them be better
informed, and know that the country which they love, demands
their zeal only for its rights . . . and that those who excite it in behalf
of their own personal renown, impose on their affections and betray
their interest." See Andrew Ritchie, "An Address Delivered to the
Massachusetts Peace Society at their Third Anniversary" (Boston:
Wells & Lilly, 1819), 14–15.

85. Ann Douglas, *The Feminization of American Culture* (New York: Knopf,
1977; Anchor, 1988), 165–99.

86. The extent of this rebuttal to Douglas is vast, but it originated
principally in Nina Baym's *Women's Fiction: A Guide to Novels by and
about Women in America, 1820–1870* (Ithaca, NY: Cornell University
Press, 1978) and Jane Tompkins's *Sensational Designs: The Cultural
Work of American Fiction, 1790–1860* (New York: Oxford University
Press, 1986). For a recent contribution to the politics of sentiment,
see Shirley Samuels, ed., *The Culture of Sentiment: Race, Gender and
Sentimentality in Nineteenth-Century America* (New York: Oxford Uni-
versity Press, 1992), esp. 10–15, for a reassessment of the Douglas-
Tompkins debate.

87. *North American Review* 26 (April 1828), 413.

88. Douglas, *Feminization*, 185.

89. Kelley, ed., *Power of Her Sympathy*, 69–70.

90. *The Linwoods: or "Sixty Years Since" in America* (New York: Harper &
Bros., 1835), 64.

Chapter 3

1. For these novels' critical acclaim, see, for example, Jared Sparks,
"Recent American Novels," in *North American Review* 21 (1825), 86–
95, and *North American Review* 26 (April 1828), 420. See Nina Baym,
American Women Writers and the Work of History, 1790–1860 (New
Brunswick, NJ: Rutgers University Press, 1995), 152–3, to keep such
popularity in a proper context. The objections to Child's treatment
of miscegenation voiced by contemporary readers I take up later in
this chapter.

2. John McWilliams's *Hawthorne, Melville, and the American Character: A
Looking-Glass Business* (Cambridge: Cambridge University Press,
1984), 40–43, 41 for quotation. McWilliams concludes that by the
1830s neither Massachusetts nor New York had produced historical
fiction that had convincingly challenged New England's commemorative tradition. In *The American Historical Romance* (Cambridge:
Cambridge University Press, 1987), George Dekker similarly claims,
"Fully to appreciate where a writer like Hawthorne came from and
how far he surpassed all rival historical romancers of colonial New

England, one must not only know his European literary antecedents but also follow Michael Davitt Bell's lead and sample many books like Lydia Maria Child's *Hobomok,* James Kirke Paulding's *The Puritan and His Daughter,* and Catharine Maria Sedgwick's more famous *Hope Leslie,*" 5. Lawrence Buell shows greater insight into cultural forces shaping historicity: "Another aspect of the Arminian [i.e., Unitarian] outlook more compatible than that of Orthodox Calvinism with historical fictionalizing was the greater extent to which Arminianism was committed to a present-minded value system that it more or less knowingly imposed on the past." See *New England Literary Culture: From Revolution Through Renaissance* (Cambridge: Cambridge University Press, 1986), 236. However, Buell's sense of *Hope Leslie's* "series of melodramatic adventures" and her "storybook marriage into the establishment" (234) overlooks the political messages encoded within literary conventions.

3. Michael Davitt Bell, *Hawthorne and the Historical Romance of New England* (Princeton: Princeton University Press, 1971), 170.

4. Ibid., 170.

5. See Mary Kelley, "Introduction" to *Hope Leslie; or Early Times in the Massachusetts* (New Brunswick, NJ: Rutgers University Press, 1987), xxxiv.

6. Sandra Zagarell, "Expanding 'America' ": Lydia Sigourney's *Sketch of Connecticut* and Catharine Sedgwick's *Hope Leslie,*" *Tulsa Studies in Women's Literature* 6 (Fall 1987), 237, 242.

7. Carolyn L. Karcher, "Introduction" to *Hobomok and Other Writings on Indians* (New Brunswick, NJ: Rutgers University Press, 1986), xxxi, xx, xxxviii. Much of her reading of the novel is republished in her recent study of Child, *The First Woman in the Republic: A Cultural Biography of Lydia Maria Child* (Durham, NC: Duke University Press, 1994), 22–34.

8. Dana Nelson, *The Word in Black and White: Reading "Race" in American Literature, 1637–1867* (New York: Oxford University Press, 1992), 69. This is also apparent in Lucy Maddox's conclusion that both novels constitute a "self-consciously feminist revision of male transmitted history." See Lucy Maddox, *Removals: Nineteenth-Century American Literature and the Politics of Indian Affairs* (New York: Oxford University Press, 1991), 103.

9. Baym, *American Women Writers,* 153.

10. See *American Women Writers,* 156–60, for Baym's treatment of the texts and issues discussed in this chapter. Many of the tensions I explore in these novels are actually embedded in much of Baym's powerful discussion of the didactic function of women's history-writing. For instance, she argues that history-writing served as "an example of women developing themselves as responsible civic beings" (11); history "helped form a good republican citizen" (18); history from the various regions "attempted to shape the developing United States by deriving a national ideology from the country's

beginnings" (103). I work from these same premises and yet maintain that the ambiguities of civic, national, and republican discourse during this transitional era allowed for a type of political revisionism, especially since the arena of Puritanism (as we have seen) was soaked in an outmoded, though resilient, masculine ideology.

11. Cathy Davidson, *Revolution and the Word: The Rise of the Novel in America* (New York: Oxford University Press, 1986), 134, and Cynthia S. Jordan, *Second Stories: The Politics of Language, Form and Gender in Early American Fictions* (Chapel Hill: University of North Carolina Press, 1989), 18.

12. Benjamin Rush, *Thoughts upon Female Education Accommodated to the Present State of Society, Manners, and Government in the United States of America* (Philadelphia: Prichard & Hall, 1787), 21.

13. Ibid., 12.

14. Ibid., 14, italics added.

15. Benjamin Rush, "A Plan for the Establishment of Public Schools and the Diffusion of Knowledge in Pennsylvania; to which are added Thoughts upon the Mode of Education Proper in a Republic" (1786), in *Essays, Literary, Moral and Philosophical* (Philadelphia: Thomas and Samuel Bradford, 1798), 19.

16. See Jay Fliegelman, *Prodigals and Pilgrims: The American Revolution Against Patriarchal Authority, 1750–1800* (Cambridge: Cambridge University Press, 1982), 227.

17. Ibid., 228.

18. Rush, "A Plan" in *Essays*, 9.

19. Ibid., 11.

20. See, for example, Nina Baym, "Reinventing Lydia Sigourney," *American Literature* 62 (September 1990), 393; or *American Women Writers*, 82, 103.

21. *American Journal of Education* (Boston: Wait, Greene, 1827), II:3.

22. The best recent discussion of this is Mary Kelley's " 'Vindicating the Equality of Female Intellect': Women and Authority in the Early Republic," *Prospects* 17 (1992), 1–27. See also, Jo Anne Preston, "Domestic Ideology, Reformers and Female Teachers: Schoolteaching Becomes Women's Work in Nineteenth-Century New England," *New England Quarterly* 66 (December 1993), 531–51, esp. 542–4.

23. Kelley, "Female Intellect," 20.

24. Rush, *Essays*, 19.

25. Rush, *Thoughts upon Female Education*, 25.

26. *American Journal of Education*, II:166–9, 676–82.

27. Jeremy Belknap, *American Biography; or, an Historical Account of Those Persons Who Have Been Distinguished in America as Adventurers, Statesmen, Philosophers, Divines, Warriors, Authors, and Other Remarkable Characters. Comprehending a Recital of the Events Connected with Their Lives and Actions* (Boston: Isaiah Thomas & Ebenezer T. Andrews, 1798), II:345.

28. This is important because so much has been said of late about the

importance of liberal, rather than republican, ideology to early American women's quest for autonomy. See, for example, Linda K. Kerber's recent reevaluations of republicanism and gender in "The Paradox of Women's Citizenship in the Early Republic: The Case of *Martin vs. Massachusetts,* 1805," *American Historical Review* 97 (1992), 349–78.

29. Judith Sargent Murray, "Desultory Thoughts upon the Utility of encouraging a degree of Self-Complascency, especially in FEMALE BOSOMS," *The Gentleman and Lady's Town and Country Magazine* (October 1784), 252. For the political context to seduction in the early republic, see Jan Lewis, "The Republican Wife: Virtue and Seduction in the early Republic" *William and Mary Quarterly,* 3rd ser. 44 (1987), 689–721, esp. 717–18, and Fliegelman, 230–67.

30. Murray, "Desultory Thoughts," 252.

31. See *The Massachusetts Magazine, or Monthly Museum of Knowledge and Rational Entertainment* (March 1790), 133.

32. *The Ladies Magazine* 1 (1828), 1, and 430.

33. Lydia Maria Child, *The Mother's Book* (Boston: Carter, Hendee & Babcock, 1831), 11.

34. Child, *Mother's Book,* 16, 18.

35. Ibid., 19.

36. Ibid., 86, 20.

37. Charles Sellers, *The Market Revolution: Jacksonian America, 1815–1846* (New York: Oxford University Press, 1991), 152–7.

38. For the strain of Enlightenment thinking directly opposed to Whiggish fears of luxury and corruption, which theorized that commerce enhanced the values of sociability and civilization, see Peter Onuf and Cathy Matson, *A Union of Interests: Political and Economic Thought in Revolutionary America* (Lawrence: University of Kansas Press, 1990), passim. During the nineteenth century this ideology evolved into the spiritualization of consumer goods, in which commodity culture invested things themselves with a quasi-religious significance that presumably enhanced one's spiritual refinement. See Lori Merish, " 'The Hand of Refined Taste' in Frontier Landscape: Caroline Kirkland's *A New Home, Who'll Follow?* and the Feminization of American Consumerism," *American Quarterly* 45 (1993), 485–523.

39. Murray, "Desultory Thoughts," 252.

40. Ibid., 252.

41. *Massachusetts Magazine* (April 1790), 223, italics added.

42. Child, *Mother's Book,* 26, 87.

43. Lydia Child, *The Frugal Housewife,* 2nd ed. (Boston: Carter & Hendee, 1830), 97.

44. Ibid., 126.

45. Ibid., 105.

46. Catharine Sedgwick, *Means and Ends, or Self-Training* (Boston: Marsh, Capen, Lyon & Webb, 1839), 244.

47. Noah Webster, *An American Dictionary of the English Language* (New York: S. Converse, 1828), unpaginated.
48. Lori D. Ginzberg, *Women and the Work of Benevolence: Morality, Politics, and Class in the Nineteenth-Century United States* (New Haven: Yale University Press, 1990), 19–35. Ginzberg states: "By describing women as victims in a lustful society – and men as the very personification of that lust – they sought to define respectability itself not by wealth, which they insisted was tenuous and under men's control, but by women's own virtues," 19. Ginzberg generally views the ideology of benevolence as ambiguous. While it made women of benevolent societies real political actors, it simultaneously set limits on political behavior that, for example, female abolitionists transgressed.
49. See "Works of Mrs. Barbauld," *North American Review* 23 (October 1826), 369.
50. See, for example, Michael Davitt Bell, *Hawthorne and Historical Romance*, 153, 155; Suzanne Gossett and Barbara Bardes, "Women and Political Power of the Republic: Two Early American Novels," *Legacy* 2 (1989), 15, and their *Declarations of Independence: Women and Political Power in Nineteenth-Century American Fiction* (New Brunswick, NJ: Rutgers University Press, 1990), ch. 2.
51. "Review of *Hope Leslie; or Early Times in the Massachusetts*, by the author of *Redwood*," *North American Review* 26 (April 1828), 409.
52. *Hope Leslie; or Early Times in the Massachusetts*, ed. Mary Kelley (New Brunswick, NJ: Rutgers University Press, 1987), 11. All further quotations come from this edition and will be cited parenthetically in the text.
53. On the power of Christian beneficence among women evangelicals, see Carroll Smith-Rosenberg, *Disorderly Conduct: Visions of Gender in Victorian America* (New York: Knopf, 1985), 131–2, 154.
54. Webster, *American Dictionary*, unpaginated and italics added.
55. This is a theme common to much criticism on Sedgwick's novel, though it is often decontextualized. See, for example, Erica Bauermeister, "*The Lamplighter, The Wide, Wide World*, and *Hope Leslie*: Reconsidering the Recipes for Nineteenth-Century American Women's Novels," *Legacy* 8 (Spring 1991), 17–28. See also Kelley's "Introduction," xxxv; Sandra Zagarell, 238; and Nelson, 69.
56. See *The Dialogic Imagination: Four Essays by M. M. Bakhtin*, ed. Michael Holquist (Austin: University of Texas Press, 1981), 270–4.
57. For a discussion of Rush in this regard, see Melvin Yazawa, *From Colonies to Commonwealth: Familial Ideology and the Beginnings of the American Republic* (Baltimore: Johns Hopkins University Press, 1985), 167–94, esp. 184, 193–4. For its potential for democratic "levelling," which some conservatives came to resist, see Linda K. Kerber, *Federalists in Dissent: Imagery and Ideology in Jeffersonian America* (Ithaca, NY: Cornell University Press, 1970), 108–9.

58. I can only speculate on the relationship between this ethos of republican behavior and later nineteenth-century satires of the "virtue" of New England industry as commentaries on this kind of dehumanization (e.g., Cooper's relentless antipathy for Yankee culture, Thoreau's metaphor of the train in *Walden*). A parallel objection to Sedgwick's may be found in Harriet Beecher Stowe, "Little Edward," published in 1843 and reprinted in *Regional Sketches*, ed. John R. Adams (New Haven, CT: College and University Press, 1972), 56–61.

59. Contemporary reviewers of the novel doubted the characterization of Magawisca in just these terms. Timothy Flint (quoting Byron) referred to Magawisca as " 'an incarnation of all the virtues.' " But he maintained that from "our knowledge of her race, we should have looked in any place for such a character rather than in an Indian wigwam." See *Western Monthly Review* 1 (1827), 294. "Some have questioned her verisimilitude as an Indian," the reviewer for the *North American Review* admitted, "They assert she is too noble, too delicate, too spiritual for an Indian" (418).

60. For a detailed description of these in the wake of the Panic of 1819, see Sellers, *Market Revolution*, 137–71.

61. Delia Bacon, *The Regicides*, in *Tales of the Puritans* (New Haven, CT: A. H. Maltby, 1831), 13–126, 68 for citation.

62. Ibid., 44.

63. *Hobomok and Other Writings on Indians*, ed. Carolyn Karcher (New Brunswick, NJ: Rutgers University Press, 1986), 13. All further quotations come from this edition and will be cited parenthetically in the text.

64. See *The Structural Transformation of the Public Sphere*, ed. Craig Calhoun, trans. Thomas Burger (Cambridge, MA: MIT Press, 1989). Michael Warner's *Letters of the Republic: Publication and the Public Sphere in Eighteenth-Century America* (Cambridge, MA: Harvard University Press, 1990) is a good example of the influence of Habermas in early American studies today. For recent reevaluations of Habermas, see *Habermas and the Public Sphere*, ed. Craig Calhoun (Cambridge, MA: MIT Press, 1992).

65. Mary Ryan, *Women in Public: Between Banners and Ballots, 1825–1880* (Baltimore: Johns Hopkins University Press, 1990), 10–14, 12 for quotation. See also her essay "Gender and Public Access: Women's Politics in Nineteenth-Century America," in *Habermas and the Public Sphere*, ed. Calhoun, 259–88, esp 261–2 for feminist appraisals of Habermas. Recently, Dena Goodman has taken feminist historians to task for misreading Habermas. Goodman argues that Habermas's conception of the public sphere accommodates the ways in which sociability – and specifically that enacted by women in the eighteenth-century salon – may be considered part of political culture. See "Public Sphere and Private Life: Toward a Synthesis of Current Historiographical Approaches to the Old Regime," *History and Theory* 3 (1992), 1–20.

66. See Fliegelman, *Prodigals and Pilgrims*, passim, and Gordon Wood, *The Radicalism of the American Revolution* (New York: Vintage, 1993), 189–225.
67. Wood, *Radicalism*, 204.
68. For the endurance of these values in later Romantic historiography, see David Levin, *History as Romantic Art: Bancroft, Prescott, Motley and Parkman* (Stanford, CA: Stanford University Press, 1959), 34–41; and Ann Douglas's discussion of the romantic historians' masculine values as an alternative to Victorian sentimentality in *The Feminization of American Culture* (New York: Knopf, 1977; Anchor, 1988), 169–80.
69. See Karcher, "Introduction," xxx–xxxi.
70. Lydia Maria Child, *The Rebels, or Boston Before the Revolution* (Boston: Cummings, Hilliard, 1825), 141.
71. Catharine Sedgwick, *The Linwoods, or "Sixty Years Since" in America* (New York: Harper & Bros., 1835), I:42.
72. Ibid., II:49.
73. Ibid., II:189.
74. Ibid., II:133.
75. Ibid., II:36.
76. David S. Reynolds, *Faith in Fiction: The Emergence of Religious Literature in America* (Cambridge, MA: Harvard University Press, 1981), 110.
77. Sedgwick, *Linwoods*, II:144.
78. Bacon, *Tales of the Puritans*, 278–9.
79. Ibid., 72.
80. Sedgwick, *Linwoods*, II:145, italics added.
81. Child, *Rebels*, 87.
82. For this phenomenon, see Norma Basch, "Equity and Equality: Emerging Concepts of Women's Political Status in the Age of Jackson," *Journal of the Early Republic* 3 (1983), 297–318, esp. 307.
83. Child, *Rebels*, 230, 251.
84. Sedgwick, *Linwoods*, I:192.
85. I do not mean to elide the many significant distinctions between traditional and revisionist views of the endings of these novels. Whereas the former see them as the final testament to these writers' shortcomings, the latter see them as evidence of an unwillingness to stick to the radical political logic that the novels themselves pursue until the end. For recent commentaries on the endings of these novels, see Karcher, "Introduction," xxxii–xxxiii, and Kelley, "Introduction," xxxvi. The value Kelley places on Esther's unmarried state suggests Esther is a progressive, even revolutionary, contrast of sorts to the wedded Hope Leslie. As Lucy Maddox has put it, "Both Sedgwick and Child . . . for all their efforts to dismantle the racist stereotypes imposed on the Indians by the colonial historians, manage only to tinker with them." See Maddox, *Removals*, 110.
86. Lewis, "Virtue and Seduction," 698. See also Carl N. Degler, *At Odds: Women and the Family in America from the Revolution to the Present* (New York: Oxford University Press, 1980), 8–25, for the importance of

volition and affection in the marriage union, and 38–42 for the ideal of the companionate marriage. See also Ruth H. Bloch, "The Gendered Meanings of Virtue in Revolutionary America," *Signs: Journal of Women in Culture and Society* 13 (1987): "American men were advised that good republican citizenship, as well as personal happiness, would follow ineluctably from true love and marriage" (47).

87. See n. 17 above. The case involved the son of a woman who during the Revolution had left Massachusetts with her husband (since both were Loyalists). The son was suing for restoration of his mother's property, which had been confiscated as a result of their departure. The case essentially hinged on the radical possibilities of a Massachusetts law of the time, which stated that if a wife or widow remained in the state, she was entitled to a third of the estate. This implied that she had the moral power as a citizen to stay in the state on her own accord. The court's ruling for the plaintiff in effect denied the radical implications of the law and of women's citizenship.

88. See 373–4 for Kerber's direct critique of Lewis. Lewis, however, does admit that for all its egalitarian rhetoric, this model of marital relations effectively subordinated women in the name of social stability. See Lewis, 711.

89. Kerber, "Paradox," 368.

90. Ibid., 375.

91. Some important qualifications must be made here. Lewis believes that as separate spheres evolved in nineteenth-century America, marital and political behavior could no longer be considered on a continuum. In the discussion that follows, however, I show that the political importance of the companionate marriage – especially its symbolic importance in literature – persisted into the early antebellum era. See Lewis, 721. Similarly, much of Kerber's argument about the ambiguities of republicanism would seem to separate marital and political relations: "The Federalist judges wanted it both ways – to abandon patriarchy in politics but maintain it . . . in their private lives" (375). Yet one cannot help but think that the ethos of female dependence, which the bench espoused in siding with the plaintiff, implied a pattern of order and stability in the state that conservative Federalists tended to idealize. Men like Sedgwick, as Kerber herself suggests, tried to substitute "republican" forms of hierarchical authority for previously rejected monarchical ones. See Kerber, 351–2.

92. *North American Review* (1828), 26, 404.

93. Introduction to *Ladies Magazine* (1828), 1–2.

94. Samuel Knapp, *Female Biography* (New York: J. Carpenter, 1834), iii.

95. Richard Slotkin, *Regeneration Through Violence: The Mythology of the American Frontier, 1600–1860* (Middletown, CT: Wesleyan University Press, 1973), 453. See also Kelley, "Introduction," xxix. For a dissenting view, see Baym, *American Women Writers*, 158–9.

96. For an analysis of Sedgwick's uneasiness with miscegenation, see

Alide Cagidemetrio, "A Plea for Fictional Histories and Old-Time 'Jewesses'," in *The Invention of Ethnicity*, ed. Werner Sollors (New York: Oxford University Press, 1989), 14–43, esp. 33–4.

97. I am aware that Child later sanctioned miscegenation in *An Appeal in Favor of That Class of Americans Called Africans* (1833), but I do not see any reason for reading her politics backward in time. Only after writing *Hobomok* during the late 1820s, as she supported her husband's opposition to the U.S. government's Indian removal policy, did Child's racial politics become relatively radical in her own society. Both Carolyn Karcher and Patricia Holland note the commercial and critical success Child was enjoying when she published the inflammatory *An Appeal*, with its denunciation of anti-miscegenation laws, and both see its appearance as a turning point in her personal and professional life. See Karcher, "Censorship American Style: The Case of Lydia Maria Child," *Studies in the American Renaissance*, ed. Joel Myerson (Boston: Twayne, 1986), 283–303, and Patricia G. Holland, "Lydia Maria Child as a Nineteenth-Century Professional Author," *Studies in the American Renaissance* (1981), ed. Joel Myerson, 157–67. See also Karcher, *The First Woman in the Republic*, 173–213.

98. See, for example, Annette Kolodny, *The Land Before Her: Fantasy and Experience of the American Frontier, 1630–1860* (Chapel Hill: University of North Carolina Press), 70–1, and Leland S. Person, Jr., "The American Eve: Miscegenation and a Feminist Frontier Fiction," *American Quarterly* 37 (1985), 679, 682, and Karcher, "Introduction," xxxii.

99. *North American Review* 19 (July 1824), 262–3.

100. "Recent American Novels," *North American Review* 21 (July 1825), 78–104, 87, 94 for citations.

101. See the Introduction to *The Culture of Sentiment: Race, Gender and Sentimentality in Nineteenth-Century America*, ed. Shirley Samuels (New York: Oxford University Press, 1992), 4.

102. For the relationship between Calvinist postlapsarian theology and a politics of hierarchy, see such works as Linda K. Kerber, *Federalists in Dissent;* James M. Banner, Jr., *To the Hartford Convention: The Federalists and the Origins of Party Politics in Massachusetts, 1789–1815* (New York: Knopf, 1970); and Nathan Hatch, *The Sacred Cause of Liberty* (New Haven: Yale University Press, 1977). See also Henry F. May, *The Enlightenment in America* (Oxford: Oxford University Press, 1976), for Puritan theological roots of republican theory's conception of cyclical history, 228, 253, 258–9.

103. Dewey, ed., *Life and Letters*, 90.

Chapter 4

1. See Warren S. Walker, *James Fenimore Cooper: An Introduction and Interpretation* (New York: Barnes & Noble, 1962), 102–15; Kay Seymour House, *Cooper's Americans* (Columbus: Ohio State University

Press, 1965), 117–45; Allan Axelrad, *History and Utopia: A Study of the World View of James Fenimore Cooper* (Norwood, PA.: Norwood Editions, 1978), 142–5; James W. Tuttleton, "The New England Characters in Cooper's Social Novels," *New York Public Library Bulletin* 70 (May 1966), 305–17; Donald A. Ringe, "New York and New England: Irving's Criticism of American Society," *American Literature* 38 (January 1967), 457–9; James D. Wallace, *Early Cooper and His Audience* (New York: Columbia University Press, 1986), 103; and George Dekker, *The American Historical Romance* (Cambridge: Cambridge University Press, 1987), 63, 112.

2. Warren Motley, *The American Abraham: James Fenimore Cooper and the Frontier Patriarch* (Cambridge: Cambridge University Press, 1987), 11.

3. Cooper sent *Notions of the Americans* to his American publisher, Matthew Carey, in the late spring of 1828 and began serious work on *The Wept* during that summer while living in Switzerland. On August 16 he wrote Luther Bradish that he was halfway done with the novel. He unsuccessfully tried to finish it in Marseilles and finally completed it in Florence, Italy. In an oft-quoted letter to Horatio Greenough, dated November 5, 1829, Cooper suggested its erratic composition when he claimed, "There are detached parts of it that are not bad, and nearly all the last volume, with a few chapters of the second will hold up their hands, but the book was written too much on the highway for the interest." See *The Letters and Journals of James Fenimore Cooper*, ed. James F. Beard (Cambridge, MA: Belknap/ Harvard University Press, 1960), I:269, 286, 364, 396.

4. Robert Spiller, *Fenimore Cooper: Critic of His Times* (New York: Minton, Balch, 1931), 64, 313.

5. House, *Cooper's Americans*, 120.

6. Axelrad, *History and Utopia*, 143.

7. Axelrad, *History and Utopia*, 143.

8. Jane Tompkins, *Sensational Designs: The Cultural Work of American Fiction, 1790–1860* (New York: Oxford University Press, 1986), 94–121.

9. Ibid., 103.

10. Ibid., 117.

11. Georg Lukacs, *The Historical Novel* (1924), trans. Hannah and Stanley Mitchell (London: Merlin, 1962), 34.

12. Dekker, *American Historical Romance*, 67–8.

13. James Franklin, *The New World of James Fenimore Cooper* (Chicago: University of Chicago Press, 1982), 123; Axelrad, *History and Utopia*, 85; Stephen Railton, *Fenimore Cooper: A Study of his Life and Imagination* (Princeton: Princeton University Press, 1978), 124. Spiller cites examples such as Fitzgerald De Roos's *Personal Narrative of Travels in the United States and Canada in 1826* (London, 1827) and Adam Hodgson's *Letters from North America* (London, 1824) as contexts for Cooper. See also Marvin Meyers, *The Jacksonian Persuasion: Politics*

and Belief (Stanford, CA: Stanford University Press, 1957), 67–8, which notes that New England is a force of social control in the text.

14. See Beard's Introduction to *The Letters and Journals of James Fenimore Cooper*, I, 1800–30 (Cambridge, MA: Harvard University Press, 1960), xxiii; Robert Spiller's Introduction to *Notions of the Americans Picked up by a Travelling Bachelor* (New York: Frederick Ungar, 1963), v.

15. See James D. Wallace, "Leatherstocking and his Author," *ALH* 5 (1993), 705–8, and Steven Watts, " 'Through a Glass Eye, Darkly': James Fenimore Cooper as Social Critic," *Journal of the Early Republic* 13 (1993), 60–3.

16. *Notions of the Americans: Picked up by a Travelling Bachelor*, ed. Gary Williams (Albany: State University Press of New York, 1991), 23–4.

17. Ibid., 45.

18. Ibid., 61.

19. Ibid., 62.

20. For example, Jedidiah Morse lauded "the excellent establishment of schools in every town," which contributed to "the consequent diffusion of learning." See *The Compendious History of New England* (London: William Burton, 1808), 199. See also Abiel Holmes, *The Annals of America* (Cambridge, MA: Hilliard & Brown, 1829), I:247, and Jeremy Belknap, *The History of New Hampshire* (Philadelphia: Robert Aitken, 1784), I:72–3.

21. Cooper, *Notions of the Americans*, 85.

22. Ibid., 100.

23. The generally negative English reviews of *Notions*, which unnerved Cooper to no end, often mocked the text's theme of American progress. The review in *Colbourn's New Monthly Magazine* was kinder in this regard than those in the *Literary Gazette* and the *Edinburgh Review*. See *Fenimore Cooper: The Critical Heritage*, ed. George Dekker and John P. McWilliams (London and Boston: Routledge & Kegan Paul, 1973), 148–54.

24. Cooper, *Notions of the Americans*, 108.

25. Ibid., 110.

26. Ibid., 117.

27. Ibid., 92.

28. *Letters and Journals*, ed. Beard, I:258.

29. A letter to Charles Wilkes, the president of the Bank of New York, suggests this sense of doubt about New England. Cooper was discussing *Notions*, then began castigating European vice, and turned next to the subject of the financial ruin of a large New York mercantile firm. He then commented on the Puritans: "The Pilgrims were certainly a praiseworthy and useful set, it must be allowed, but we could wish they had studied St. Paul a little less, and given more of their time to the simple, practical rules of the Levitical law, or at least to some law that might have elevated the standard of honesty

above the quibbles of a modern practice." See *Letters and Journals,* ed. Beard, I:245.

30. See Douglas Edward Leach, *Flintlock and Tomahawk: New England in King Philip's War* (New York: Macmillan, 1958); Francis Jennings, *The Invasion of America: Indians, Colonialism, and the Cant of Conquest* (New York: Norton, 1976), 254–326; and Russell Bourne, *The Red King's Rebellion: Racial Politics in New England, 1675–1678* (New York: Oxford University Press, 1990).

31. For Sassamon's role in precipitating events, as well as his status as a cross-cultural figure, see Jill Lepore, "Dead Men Tell No Tales: John Sassamon and the Fatal Consequences of Literacy," *American Quarterly* 46 (December 1994), 479–512.

32. See *The Worcester Magazine and Historical Journal* (Worcester: Rogers & Griffin, 1826), I:133.

33. See Emma Willard, *History of the United States of America* (New York: White, Gallaher & White, 1831), 67–8. "Had the resources of this hero been equal to those of his enemies," Samuel Drake proclaimed, "what would have been their fate? This exterminating war had not been known to millions!" See *History of King Philip's War* (Bowie, MD: Heritage, 1989), 123.

34. Salma Hale, *History of the United States of America* (London: John Miller, 1826), 53.

35. For nineteenth-century beliefs in the inevitability of Native American decline, see Brian Dippie, *The Vanishing American: White Attitudes and U.S. Indian Policy* (Middletown, CT: Wesleyan University Press, 1982); Ronald Takaki takes up the exclusionary work of republicanism vis-à-vis other races in *Iron Cages: Race and Culture in Nineteenth-Century America* (New York: Knopf, 1979), esp. 3–15.

36. Hale, *History of the United States,* 53.

37. *History of King Philip's War,* 123.

38. Morse and Parish, *Compendious History of New England,* 141, and *Worcester Magazine,* 161.

39. Belknap, *History of New Hampshire,* I:133, 123.

40. Ibid., I:124.

41. Willard, *History of the United States,* 67.

42. *Worcester Magazine,* I:161.

43. Benjamin Trumbull, *A Complete History of Connecticut, Civil and Ecclesiastical* (Hartford: Hudson & Goodwin, 1797), 367.

44. Rufus Choate, "The Importance of Illustrating New-England History by a Series of Romances like the Waverly Novels," in *The Works of Rufus Choate with a Memoir of his Life,* ed. Samuel G. Brown (Boston: Little, Brown, 1862), I:328.

45. Ibid., 329.

46. Ibid., 330, 332. For Choate's embrace of traditional premodern values, see Robert A. Ferguson, *Law and Letters in American Culture* (Cambridge, MA: Harvard University Press, 1984), 26–7. For his reconciliation of traditional values with America's economic devel-

opment, see Jean Matthews, *Rufus Choate: The Law and Civic Virtue* (Philadelphia: Temple University Press, 1980), 70–103.

47. See the prefatory material to Mather's history included in *So Dreadfull a Judgment: Puritan Responses to King Philip's War, 1676–1677*, ed. Richard Slotkin and James K. Folsom (Middletown, CT: Wesleyan University Press, 1978), 57–77. One should not read Puritan historiography as a monolith, however, and, as scholars have noted, both the theological and the narrative designs of Mather's history differed significantly from that of William Hubbard's *Narrative of the Troubles with the Indians* (1677). Hubbard saw the settlers as martyrs rather than sinners. Hubbard thus placed less emphasis on providential causation and was generally wary of theological extremism. See Anne Kusener Nelsen, "King Philip's War and the Hubbard–Mather Rivalry," *William and Mary Quarterly*, 3rd ser. 27 (1970), 615–29; Dennis R. Perry, " 'Novelties and Stile Which All Out-Do': William Hubbard's Historiography Reconsidered," *Early American Literature* 29 (1994), 166–82; and Stephen Carl Arch, *Authorizing the Past: The Rhetoric of History in Seventeenth-Century New England* (De Kalb: Northern Illinois University Press, 1994), 120–3.

48. Slotkin and Folsom, eds., *So Dreadfull a Judgment*, 101.

49. Ibid., 86.

50. Ibid., 99.

51. Church's son, Thomas, actually composed the narrative, which was later edited by Ezra Stiles and republished in 1772 under the name of *The Entertaining History of King Philip's War*. The antiquarian Samuel Drake issued another edition in 1825, entitled *The History of King Philip's War*, which was reprinted in 1827, 1829, and 1836. For the textual history of Church, see *Diary of King Philip's War, 1675–76*, Introduction by Alan and Mary Simpson (Chester, CT: Pequot Press, 1975), 53. All citations to the text come from *The History of King Philip's War* (Bowie, MD: Heritage, 1989), a facsimile reprint of the 1829 Drake edition.

52. Richard Slotkin has argued for the primitivist qualities of Church's narrative, concluding, "His chief aim is not to resign himself to the will of God," and "Divine providence is mentioned, but seems to figure anecdotally in the history, rather than as an organic causative principle." See *Regeneration Through Violence: The Mythology of the American Frontier, 1600–1860* (Middletown, CT: Wesleyan University Press, 1973), 158–9.

53. Drake, ed., *The History of King Philip's War*, ix.

54. Ibid., 71.

55. For a brief biography of Church, see Alan and Mary Simpson's Introduction to *Diary of King Philip's War*, 36–43.

56. See Wesley Frank Craven, *The Legend of the Founding Fathers* (New York: New York University Press, 1956), 79–82. For an instance of the regional competition over historical memory, see James Kent, "An Anniversary Discourse Delivered Before the New-York Historical

Society," in *Collections of the New York Historical Society*, 2nd ser. 1 (New York: H. Ludwig, 1841), 9–36, esp. 33.

57. *North American Review* 12 (1821), 488.

58. *The Wept of Wish-ton-Wish* (Philadelphia: Carey, Lea & Carey, 1829), I:v.

59. Ibid., x.

60. Ibid., x.

61. The best discussion of this is in Motley, *The American Abraham*, who argues, "In *The Wept* Cooper explores those qualities of the Puritan mind that led men west. . . . [and simultaneously] found in the patriarchal authority wielded by the founders of New England an antidote to social fragmentation," 11. See also 20, 22, 28–30, 38. This line of argument derives somewhat from John McWilliams's *Political Justice in a Republic: James Fenimore Cooper's America* (Berkeley: University of California Press, 1972): "A firm believer in individual liberty, distrustful of Divine Right and all Stuarts, Mark is an intriguing combination of deep submission to God's decrees and a very active practicality" (249). See also House, *Cooper's Americans*, 120–1, and Dekker, *American Historical Romance*, 112–13.

62. Perry Miller, "Declension in a Bible Commonwealth," in *Nature's Nation* (Cambridge, MA: Belknap/Harvard University Press, 1967), 14–49.

63. McWilliams, *Political Justice in a Republic*, 246–58. See also Motley, *The American Abraham*, 34–55; Harry Henderson, *Versions of the Past* (Oxford: Oxford University Press, 1974), 71; Michael Davitt Bell, *Hawthorne and Historical Romance of New England* (Princeton: Princeton University Press, 1971), 24–7, and Dekker, *American Historical Romance*, 68.

64. Joseph Felt, *Annals of Salem*, 2nd. ed. (Salem, MA: W. & S. B. Ives, 1845), 44. The first edition was published in 1827.

65. *The Borderers; or The Wept of Wish-ton-Wish* (London: Richard Bentley, 1833), 1. All further quotations come from this edition and are cited parenthetically in the text.

66. William Cronon, *Changes in the Land: Indians, Colonists, and the Ecology of New England* (New York: Hill & Wang, 1983), 126.

67. Wayne Franklin maintains that the forces of order and metaphysical evil/epistemological uncertainty are symbolized by the images of cultivation and wilderness. See *The New World of James Fenimore Cooper*, 119–49, esp. 123–4, 127–34, 141.

68. Dekker, *American Historical Romance*, 78–98.

69. Morton J. Horwitz, *The Transformation of American Law, 1780–1860* (Cambridge, MA: Harvard University Press, 1977), 43.

70. Ibid., 54.

71. See Charles Hansford Adams, *'The Guardian of the Law': Authority and Identity in James Fenimore Cooper* (University Park: Pennsylvania

State University Press, 1990), 67–8. Allan Axelrad similarly has argued, in the larger context of the importance of organic metaphors in Cooper's fiction, that the felling and girdling of trees "marks the wastefulness and destructiveness of white civilization, and portends the time when it, too, will be destroyed due to the wanton violation of nature." See *History and Utopia*, 58.

72. Francis Jennings takes issue with the view that either side launched a war of extermination, and argues instead that conspiratorial theories about Native American plans for exterminating the colonists were imposed upon the events immediately after the war's conclusion. See *The Invasion of America*, 282–326, esp. 298–300.

73. A relatively benign view of the sincerity propelling the first phases of colonial military efforts may be found in Charles Royster's *A Revolutionary People at War: The Continental Army and American Character, 1775–1783* (New York: Norton, 1979), esp. 25–53. For an example of skeptical revision of the "myth" of the disinterested citizen-army, see James Kirby Martin and Mark Edward Lender, "Toward an American Standing Army, 1776–1777," in *A Respectable Army: Military Origins of the Republic, 1763–1789* (Arlington Heights, IL: Harlan Davidson, 1982), 65–98.

74. Epaphras Hoyt, *Antiquarian Researches: Comprising a History of the Indian Wars* (Greenfield, MA: Ansel Phelps, 1824), 87.

75. *History of King Philip's War*, 128.

76. Hale, *History of the United States*, 56.

77. Hoyt, *Antiquarian Researches*, 117–18.

78. David Ramsay emphasized the cohesiveness of New England's effort against Metacom. "The confederation of the New England colonies was now found of great service . . ." Ramsay concluded. "They severally furnished their quotas, and proceeded, with combined forces and counsels, to attack their common foe." See *History of the United States* (Philadelphia: Matthew Carey, 1818), I:281. See also Trumbull, *Complete History of Connecticut*, 334.

79. See *The Wept*, 160, 164, 174, 217, 275–6, 280, 284, 287, 321, 350, for instances of this rhetoric and characterization.

80. Trumbull, *Complete History of Connecticut*, 352.

81. Cooper, *Wept* (1829), ix.

82. *Worcester Magazine*, I:213.

83. Ramsay, *History of the United States*, I:280.

84. See, for example, Adams, *Guardian of the Law*, 45–53, and Henderson, *Versions of the Past*, 56, 59.

85. Geoffrey Rans, *Cooper's Leatherstocking Novels: A Secular Reading* (Chapel Hill: University of North Carolina Press, 1991).

86. Nina Baym, "How Men and Women Wrote Indian Stories," in *New Essays on 'The Last of the Mohicans,'* ed. H. Daniel Peck (Cambridge: Cambridge University Press, 1992), 68.

87. *Southern Review*, 219.

88. William Hubbard, *The Present State of New-England. Being a Narrative of the Trouble with the Indians in New-England* (London: Thomas Parkurst, 1677). The page from which the passage is taken has no number.

89. The poem is included in *So Dreadfull a Judgment*, ed. Slotkin and Folsom. See 218, 220 for citations. For discussion of the contexts surrounding its composition and publication, along with those of "New England's Tears," see Jane Donahue Eberwein, " 'Harvardine quil': Benjamin Tompson's Poems on King Philip's War," *Early American Literature* 28 (1993), 1–21.

90. Samuel Knapp, *Lectures on American Literature* (New York: Elam Bliss, 1929), 229.

91. Jedidiah Morse and Elijah Parish, *Compendious History of New England*, 39–40.

92. See, for example, Trumbull, *A Complete History of Connecticut*, 342; David Ramsay, *History of the United States*, I:286; Abiel Holmes, *Annals of America*, 383; Epaphras Hoyt, *Antiquarian Researches*, 140–1.

93. Washington Irving, *The Sketch Book of Geoffrey Crayon, Gent.*, ed. William L. Hedges (New York: Penguin, 1988), 246–7.

94. Ibid., 246.

95. See Eugene Page's prefatory background to the play in *Metamora and Other Plays* (Princeton: Princeton University Press, 1941), 3–6. All citations that follow come from this edition, except those taken from the formerly missing fourth act, which was reprinted in Richard Moody, "Lost and Now Found: The Fourth Act of Metamora," *American Literature* 33 (1962), 353–64.

96. Roy Harvey Pearce, *Savagism and Civilization: A Study of the Indian and the American Mind* (Berkeley: University of California Press, 1988), 176. This is the revised edition of *The Savages of America* that appeared in 1953.

97. Bruce A. McConachie, *Melodramatic Formations: American Theatre and Society, 1820–1870* (Iowa City: University of Iowa Press, 1992), 68. McConachie's language here, as he elsewhere explains, derives from Raymond Williams's understanding of the relations between "emergent" and "residual" cultures. See Williams, *Marxism and Literature* (Oxford: Oxford University Press, 1977), 121–7.

98. Page, ed., *Metamora*, 37.

99. Ibid., 21, 36–7.

100. Ibid., 37.

101. See Bourne, *Red King's Rebellion*, 186.

102. For Cooper's familiarity with Irving's *The Sketch Book*, see Dekker, *American Historical Romance*, 64–65.

103. For the disagreement between the two, see Leslie Fiedler, *Love and Death in the American Novel*, rev. ed. (New York: Stein & Day, 1966), 184–5, 203–4, and George Dekker, *James Fenimore Cooper: The Novelist* (London: Routledge & Kegan Paul, 1967), 75–85.

104. James D. Wallace, "Race and Captivity in Cooper's *The Wept of Wishton-Wish*," *ALH* 7 (Summer 1995), 189–209. Readers will see that my argument differs significantly from that of Wallace, who sees the novel as about "the glories of amalgamation" (207) with Ruth as "a perfect medium, a natural bridge between the two cultures" (205). If one considers Conanchet's captivity, however, Wallace's contention that "historical events are seen as events within a family" (203) can be inverted to show how domestic events have historical and political consequences, specifically in the fate of Conanchet.

105. Ibid., 199.

106. See, for example, House, *Cooper's Americans*, 249–50, McWilliams, *Political Justice*, 255, and Franklin, *New World*, 133.

107. First published in America in 1923, Lawrence's landmark *Studies in Classic American Literature* at times bitterly mocked Cooper's psychological and symbolic treatment of the American wilderness. Fiedler followed Lawrence in his argument in *Love and Death in the American Novel* that American romance in general is shaped by a repressed sense of homoeroticism. See Russell Reising, *The Unusable Past: Theory and the Study of American Literature* (New York and London: Methuen, 1986), 130–2. A more indulgent view of Cooper's treatment of women may be found in Kay S. House and Genevieve Belfiglio, "Fenimore Cooper's Heroines," in *American Novelists Revisited: Essays in Feminist Criticism*, ed. Fritz Fleischman (Boston: G. K. Hall, 1982), 42–57.

108. See Dekker, *Fenimore Cooper*, 77–8.

109. See *Southern Review*, 207, 223. Recently, Lora Romero in "Vanishing Americans: Gender, Empire, and New Historicism," *American Literature* 63 (September 1991), 385–404, has argued that the domestication of Uncas by Cora leads to his downfall. Romero historicizes Cooper's treatment of Uncas's tragic feminization by looking particularly to the influence of Rousseau's misogynistic pedagogical theories on Cooper.

110. Hubbard, *Narrative*, unpaginated.

111. For the influence of Hubbard on early nationals in this regard, See James Eastburn and Robert Sands *Yamoyden, a Tale of the Wars of King Philip* (New York: Clayton & Kingsland, 1820), 282–3, which mentions Hubbard as the most interesting source for Conanchet's capture. Washington Irving's "Philip of Pokanoket" also includes this anecdote about Conanchet's death. Haskell Springer's notes to the text show that Irving borrowed extensively from Hubbard's history. See *The Sketch Book*, 243–4.

112. *The American Democrat*, Introduction by H. L. Mencken (Indianapolis: Liberty, 1993), 146. This is reprinted from the 1931 edition.

113. For an alternative reading of Cooper, language, and patriarchalism, see Cynthia S. Jordan, *Second Stories: The Politics of Lan-*

guage, Form and Gender in Early American Fictions (Chapel Hill: University of North Carolina Press, 1989), 102.

Chapter 5

1. James Fenimore Cooper, *The Borderers; or The Wept of Wish-ton-Wish* (London: Richard Bentley, 1833), 271, 273.
2. Ibid., 90.
3. Ibid., 57.
4. Ibid., 108–14.
5. G. Harrison Orians, "New England Witchcraft in Fiction," *American Literature* 2 (1930), 54–71, esp. 54–5. W. H. Gardiner's review was published in the *North American Review* 15 (July 1822), 250–82.
6. Lawrence Buell, *New England Literary Culture: From Revolution Through Renaissance* (Cambridge: Cambridge University Press, 1986), 360. Buell also notes in this section that witchcraft served as leverage for religious liberals against their orthodox counterparts. For the critical focus on witchcraft and literary nationalism, see also, for example, Lewis Leary, *John Greenleaf Whittier* (New York: Twayne, 1961), 34–5.
7. See Michael Davitt Bell, *Hawthorne and the Historical Romance of New England* (Princeton: Princeton University Press, 1971), 99–104, for discussion of witchcraft fiction; Michael P. Colacurcio, *The Province of Piety: Moral History in Hawthorne's Early Tales* (Cambridge, MA: Harvard University Press, 1984), 78–93, and 283–313; and George Dekker, *The American Historical Romance* (Cambridge: Cambridge University Press, 1987), 129–85.
8. See Bell, *Hawthorne*, 99–100.
9. See Colacurcio, *Province of Piety*, 78–93.
10. Buell's discussion of witchcraft fiction amply covers writers whose work postdates the 1820s, such as Longfellow, Josiah Gilbert Holland, Elizabeth Stoddard, and Hawthorne. See *New England Literary Culture*, 224–8 and 360–4.
11. I use this term specifically with regard to premodern fears about the gradual democratization of politics. Such fears characterized Federalists during the 1790s, and conservative National Republicans and Whigs later on. As I have shown in earlier chapters, however, "conservative" discourse could still embrace a decidedly "modern" (or "liberal") view of American economic development.
12. My argument here is distinct from Bernard Rosenthal's in *Salem Story: Reading the Witch Trials of 1692* (Cambridge: Cambridge University Press, 1993). After meticulously dissecting the historical evidence of Salem, Rosenthal argues that the episode has served as a metaphor for the persecution of the state, and as an instance of barbaric mistreatment that Americans have used to distance themselves from the past, thereby confirming their own relative, progressive enlightenment. My historical focus is narrower than Rosenthal's; I argue that the metaphoric meaning of Salem during the era be-

tween the 1790s and the 1830s signified fears of popular politics and representative democracy in the early republic. I clarify "persecution," in other words, within a specific historical moment.

13. Quoted in Bernard Bailyn, *The Ideological Origins of the American Revolution* (Cambridge, MA: Belknap/Harvard University Press, 1967), n.12, 151. See also Bailyn, *The Origins of American Politics* (New York: Vintage, 1967), esp. 45–9, 55, 140–9.

14. Gordon Wood, *The Creation of the American Republic, 1776–1787* (New York: Norton, 1972), 59.

15. William Stuart, "An Oration on Faction Delivered before the Uranian Society in the City of New York at a Quarterly Meeting" (New York: T. and J. Swords, 1794), 12, italics his.

16. Daniel Walker Howe, *The Political Culture of the American Whigs* (Chicago: University of Chicago Press, 1979), 29 for citation, 52–3. Jay Fliegelman also notes the anxieties about the need for reason in an uncertain political environment. See *Prodigals and Pilgrims: The American Revolution against Patriarchal Authority, 1750–1800* (Cambridge: Cambridge University Press, 1982), 227–67, esp. 230–5. See also Henry F. May, *The Enlightenment in America* (New York: Oxford University Press, 1976), 347–9.

17. Recently, Gordon Wood has argued persuasively that it was actually the Antifederalists during the Constitutional debates of the 1780s who argued that interests were inevitably sewn into politics. The Federalists (and, of course, Madison) only wanted to displace the interest group rivalries of the states to the newly empowered federal government, which in large part would still act as an arbiter of the public good. See *The Radicalism of the American Revolution* (New York: Vintage, 1993), 243–70, esp. 253.

18. John Murrin and Rowland Berthoff, "Feudalism, Communalism, and the Yeoman Freeholder: The American Revolution Considered as a Social Accident," in *Essays on the American Revolution*, ed. Stephen J. Kurtz and James H. Hutson (Chapel Hill: University of North Carolina Press, 1973), 275.

19. Ronald P. Formisano, *The Transformation of Political Culture: Massachusetts Parties, 1790s–1840s* (New York: Oxford University Press, 1983), 10. For a discussion differentiating between the first and second American party systems, see his "Federalists and Republicans: Parties, Yes – System, No," in *The Evolution of American Electoral Systems*, ed. Paul Kleppner (Westport, CT: Greenwood, 1981), 33–76.

20. See Major Wilson, "Republicanism and the Idea of Party in the Jacksonian Period," *Journal of the Early Republic* 8 (Winter 1988), 423.

21. See Formisano, *Transformation*, 15–16; Richard P. McCormick, *The Second American Party System: Party Formation in the Jacksonian Era* (New York: Norton, 1966), 12; and Wilson, "Idea of Party," 431. For the most recent – and most incisive – analysis of the self-serving

nature of this endurance of republican discourse about factions, see Marc W. Kruman, "The Second American Party System and the Transformation of Revolutionary Republicanism," *Journal of the Early Republic* 12 (Winter 1992), 509–37, esp. 516, 519, 529.

22. Benjamin Rush, *Essays, Literary, Moral and Philosophical* (Philadelphia: Thomas and Samuel Bradford, 1798), 137.

23. Ibid., 79–80.

24. Mercy Otis Warren, *History of the Rise, Progress and Termination of the American Revolution* (1805), ed. Lester Cohen, 2 vols. (Indianapolis: Liberty Press, 1988) I:3.

25. *The Speeches, Addresses and Messages of the Several Presidents of the United States* (Philadelphia: Robert Desilver, 1825), 109–10, italics added.

26. John Adams, *Discourses on Davila. A Series of Papers on Political History Written in the year 1790, and then Published in the Gazette of the United States* (1805), 56, 58. These writings first appeared in John Fenno's anti-Jeffersonian *Gazette of the United States*.

27. Stephen Peabody, "A Sermon Delivered at Concord Before the Honourable General Court of the State of New Hampshire at the Annual Election" (1797), and John Smalley, "On the Evils of a Weak Government" (1800), in *Political Sermons of the American Founding Era, 1730–1805*, ed. Ellis Sandoz (Indianapolis: Liberty Press, 1991), 1332 and 1444.

28. Timothy Dwight, "The Duty of Americans, at the Present Crisis" (1798) in Sandoz, ed., *Political Sermons*, 1382; Noah Webster, "The Revolution in France" (1794), in Sandoz, ed., *Political Sermons*, 1298.

29. Webster, "Revolution," in Sandoz, ed., *Political Sermons*, 1254.

30. Ibid., 1264.

31. Ibid., 1271.

32. Nathan O. Hatch, *The Democratization of American Christianity* (New Haven: Yale University Press, 1989), 10.

33. Ibid., 16.

34. See May, *The Enlightenment in America*, 337–8.

35. See Emma Willard, *History of the United States of America* (New York: White, Gallaher & White, 1831), xlii. The first edition, published in 1828, contained the same materials.

36. Francis Wayland, *The Duties of an American Citizen* (Boston: James Loring, 1825), 3.

37. Ibid., 37.

38. Pauline Maier, "Popular Uprisings and Civil Authority in Eighteenth-Century America," *William and Mary Quarterly*, 3rd. ser. 27 (January 1970), 3–35; the essay is collected in *In Search of Early America: The William and Mary Quarterly, 1943–1993*, ed. Michael McGiffert (Williamsburg, VA: Institute of Early American History and Culture, 1993).

39. J. G. A. Pocock, *The Machiavellian Moment: Florentine Political Thought and the Atlantic Republican Tradition* (Princeton: Princeton University Press, 1975), 471.

40. Adams, *Davila*, 49.

41. Jeremy Belknap, *A Discourse Intended to Commemorate the Discovery of America by Christopher Columbus* (Boston: Belknap & Hall/Apollo Press, 1792), 42–3. The oration was delivered before the Massachusetts Historical Society on October 23, 1792.

42. *The Federalist Papers*, ed. Clinton Rossiter (New York: NAL, 1961), 225.

43. Noah Webster, *An American Dictionary of the English Language* (New York: S. Converse, 1828). All citations are unpaginated.

44. Jedidiah Morse and Elijah Parish, *A Compendious History of New England* (London: William Burton, 1808), 165; Hannah Adams, *A Summary History of New England* (Dedham: H. Mann and J. H. Adams, 1799), 163; Epaphras Hoyt, *Antiquarian Researches: Comprising a History of Indian Wars* (Greenfield, MA: Ansel Phelps, 1824), 175; David Ramsay, *History of the United States of America*, 3 vols. (Philadelphia: Mathew Carey, 1818), I:90.

45. Cotton Mather, *The Wonders of the Invisible World*, 2nd ed. (London: John Dutton, 1693), 23; Robert Calef, *More Wonders of the Invisible World* (London, 1700; Bainbridge, NY: York Mail-Print, 1972), esp. 152–3.

46. Charles A. Goodrich, *A History of the United States of America* (New York: G. C. Smith, 1829), 6.

47. Abiel Abbot, *History of Andover from its Settlement to 1829* (Andover, MA: Flagg & Gould, 1829), 173, 172.

48. Charles Wentworth Upham, *Lectures on Witchcraft, Comprising a History of the Delusion in Salem, in 1692*, 2nd ed. (Boston: Carter & Hendee, 1832), 277–8.

49. See, for example, Adams, *Summary History*, 160; Salma Hale, *History of the United States* (London: John Miller, 1826), 62; Alden Bradford, *History of Massachusetts, for Two Hundred Years: From the Year 1620 to 1820* (Boston: Hilliard, Gray, 1835), 91; Abbot, *Andover*, 172; Emma Willard, *History*, 86; Morse and Parish, *Compendious History*, 165; Ramsay, *History*, I:90.

50. Adams, *Summary History*, 163.

51. Alden Bradford, *History of Massachusetts*, 91. Bradford, a descendant of Governor William Bradford of Plymouth, was an original member of the Massachusetts Historical Society. The first edition of this history appeared in 1829.

52. Hoyt, *Antiquarian Researches*, 183.

53. Morse and Parish, *Compendious History*, 165; Adams, *Summary History*, 160.

54. Morse and Parish, *Compendious History*, 170, 165; Adams, *Summary History*, 160, 162, 164–5.

55. See, for example, Abbott, *History of Andover*, 154; Hoyt, *Antiquarian Researches*, 175.

56. Noting the work of David Konig, Hall concludes "that anyone who threatened established authority – that is, who threatened social order – could be perceived as engaged in witchcraft. Witch-hunting

can thus be understood as a process of reaction against disruptively 'extralegal' outsiders." See his Introduction to *Witch-Hunting in Seventeenth-Century New England: A Documentary History, 1638–1692* (Boston: Northeastern University Press, 1991), 6, and David Konig, *Law and Society in Puritan Massachusetts: Essex County, 1629–1692* (Chapel Hill: University of North Carolina Press, 1979).

57. Morse and Parish, *Compendious History*, 168.

58. Goodrich, *History of the United States*, 80. See also Morse and Parish, *Compendious History*, 168.

59. See, for example, Morse and Parish, *Compendious History*, 168.

60. For a recent example of the scholarly challenge to traditional assumptions about deference in late-eighteenth-century America, see Richard R. Beeman, "Deference, Republicanism, and the Emergence of Popular Politics in Eighteenth-Century America," *William and Mary Quarterly*, 3rd ser. xlix (July 1992), 401–30.

61. Abbot, *History of Andover*, 173.

62. Goodrich, *History of the United States*, 114.

63. Formisano, *Transformation of Political Culture*, 10.

64. See McCormick, *Second American Party System*, 13–17.

65. See Buell, *New England Literary Culture*, 218–24.

66. Albert B. Cook, "Damaging the Mathers: London Receives the News from Salem," *New England Quarterly* 65 (June 1992), 307. Cook comments here on the status of Mather's reputation among historians today as a context for demonstrating how the London bookseller John Dutton promoted *Wonders of the Invisible World* and other writings on Salem in a way that sensationalized the event at the expense of Mather's reputation.

67. For a general discussion of Mather's modern reputation, see David Levin, *In Defense of Historical Criticism* (New York: Hill & Wang, 1967), 35–6. For a synopsis of "schools" of historians defending or (like Bancroft) excoriating Mather's role at Salem, see Richard H. Werking, " 'Reformation Is Our Only Preservation' ": Cotton Mather and Salem Witchcraft," *William and Mary Quarterly*, 3rd ser. 29 (1972), 281–90, esp. 281–2. Werking's view that witchcraft for Mather posed the possibilities of communal confession and hence the reaffirmation of the federal covenant derives (more than he acknowledges) from Perry Miller's famous essay "The Judgment of the Witches," in *The New England Mind: From Colony to Province* (Cambridge, MA: Belknap/Harvard University Press, 1953), 191–208, esp. 204, 207.

68. Ramsay, *History of the United States*, I:92.

69. Hale was a famous English jurist and one of the most prolific scholars on the English common law. Joseph Glanvill, Charles II's chaplain, defended the reality of ghosts as a defense against atheism, arguing that the belief in witchcraft was an English cultural legacy. See Morse and Parish, *Compendious History*, 170. For similar instances of how this argument inspired contemporary Anglo-

American rivalries, see Goodrich, *History*, 79; Salma Hale, *History*, 62; Willard, *History*, 86; Hoyt, *Antiquarian Researches*, 179; Abbot, *History of Andover*, 153–4.

70. Perry Miller, *The New England Mind*, 204. The metaphor actually comes from Samuel Eliot Morison, yet Miller appropriates it to argue instead for Mather's partial guilt.

71. Upham, *Lectures on Witchcraft*, 103–4.

72. Ibid., 111.

73. Ibid., iv–v.

74. The subject of witch-hunting echoed (and amplified) the same themes that emerged in accounts of Puritan treatment of Quakers during the 1650s. Except for the most stalwart of Orthodox apologists, such as Jedidiah Morse, historians associated Puritan persecution of Quakers with the behavior of factions. Mercy Otis Warren, for example, allowed that Puritan New England was not solely guilty of religious persecution, but warned that all intolerance derived from the desires of "the stronger party" in search of "superiority or power." Warren juxtaposed "the cultivation of reason" and "the cool moments of reflection" with "a strange propensity in human nature to reduce every thing within the vortex of [the party's] own ideas." See *History of the Rise, Progress and Termination*, ed. Cohen, I:10–11.

75. Rufus Choate, "The Colonial Age of New England," in *The Works of Rufus Choate with a Memoir of His Life*, ed. Samuel G. Brown (Boston: Little, Brown, 1862), 361, italics added.

76. Terence Martin, *The Instructed Vision: Scottish Common Sense Philosophy and the Origins of American Fiction* (Bloomington: Indiana University Press, 1961), esp. 4–5, 11–12, for the legacy of Common Sense philosophy in which fiction ideally promoted social cohesion and stability through the cultivation of reason; for specific dangers of the imagination, see 73–7, 83, 85–6, 92–5, 107. William Charvat, *The Origins of American Critical Thought, 1810–1835* (Philadelphia: University of Pennsylvania Press, 1936). For the theoretical configuration of the moral sense as function of reason, see, for example, Asa Burton, *Essays on Some of the First Principles of Metaphysics, Ethicks, and Theology* (Portland, ME: Mirror Office, 1824), esp. 5, 7, 35–45.

77. This short piece was published in three, separate sections in *The New York Literary Journal and Belles-Lettres Repository*. See 3 (September 1820), 329–35; 3 (October 1820), 417–20; and 4 (November 1820), 17–27.

78. Ibid., November 1820, 21.

79. Ibid., 21–2.

80. Ibid., 333.

81. *The Witch of New England; a Romance* (Philadelphia: Carey & Lea, 1824), 36, 33.

82. Ibid., 98.

83. Ibid., 168.

84. Ibid., 168.

85. Whittier edited the pro-Henry Clay *American Manufacturer* in 1828 and was later elected as a Whig to the Massachusetts legislature in 1835. Jackson's support from the slaveholding South undoubtedly exacerbated his partisanship. See Leary, *Whittier,* 27; Edward Wagenknecht, *John Greenleaf Whittier: A Portrait in Paradox* (New York: Oxford University Press, 1967), 51–3. For Whittier's Whiggish reference to Jacksonians as Tories, see John B. Pickard, ed., *The Letters of John Greenleaf Whittier,* 3 vols. (Cambridge, MA: Harvard University Press, 1975), I:159.

86. John Greenleaf Whittier, *Legends of New England* (Gainesville, FL: Scholars Facsimiles & Reprints, 1965), 57–8.

87. Ibid., 64, 66.

88. Ibid., 74.

89. Ibid., 74.

90. William Dunlap, *A History of the American Theatre* (New York: Jared J. Harper, 1832), 375.

91. See Paul H. Musser, *James Nelson Barker* (New York: AMS, 1969; reprint of 1929 edition), 2, 12–13, 103, 122.

92. See ibid., 87–96; and Arthur Hobson Quinn, *A History of the American Drama: From the Beginning to the Civil War* (New York: F. S. Crofts, 1946), 136–62.

93. *The Tragedy of Superstition; or the Fanatic Father,* in *Representative American Plays from 1767 to the Present Day,* ed. Arthur Hobson Quinn, 7th ed. (New York: Appleton-Century-Crofts, 1953), 127, 117, 137. All further quotations come from this edition and are cited parenthetically in the text.

94. "American Drama," *American Quarterly Review* I (1827), 355 for citation.

95. See Mark L. Sargent, "Thomas Hutchinson, Ezra Stiles, and the Legend of the Regicides," *William and Mary Quarterly,* 3rd ser. xlix (July 1992), 431–48. Sargent argues that "the roots of American ambivalence about the legend of Goffe and Whalley" (433) are found in the contrasting portrayals of them in Hutchinson's and Ezra Stiles's histories. In the discussion that follows, I offer reasons for this "ambivalence" that situate the respective "influence" of these histories within the context of the period's changing political culture.

96. Quinn, *American Drama,* 150.

97. Catharine Sedgwick, *Hope Leslie; or Early Times in the Massachusetts,* ed. Mary Kelley (New Brunswick, NJ: Rutgers University Press, 1987), 104–5.

98. Michael Warner, *The Letters of the Republic: Publication and the Public Sphere in Eighteenth-Century America* (Cambridge, MA: Harvard University Press, 1990).

99. *Whittier on Writers and Writing,* ed. Edwin Cady and Harry Hayden Clark (Syracuse, NY: Syracuse University Press, 1950), 93, 106, 115.

100. Whittier, *Legends,* 3.

101. Ibid., 63–4.
102. Ibid., 64.
103. *The Witch of New England*, 33.
104. Ibid., 33.
105. Ibid., 35, italics added.
106. Ibid., 35.
107. *North American Review* (July 1825), 97.
108. *The Witch of New England*, 69.
109. *Letters*, ed. Pickard, I:436.
110. David S. Reynolds, *Beneath the American Renaissance: The Subversive Imagination in the Age of Emerson and Melville* (Cambridge, MA: Harvard University Press, 1989), 198.
111. See Benjamin Lease, *That Wild Fellow John Neal and the American Literary Revolution* (Chicago: University of Chicago Press, 1972), 137–45; Donald A. Sears, *John Neal* (Boston: Twayne, 1978), 79–87; Bell, *Hawthorne and Historical Romance*, 99–104; Harold C. Martin, "The Colloquial Tradition in the Novel: John Neal," *New England Quarterly* 32 (December 1959), 455–75, esp. 458; William J. Scheick, "Power, Authority, and Revolutionary Impulse in John Neal's *Rachel Dyer,*" *Studies in American Fiction* 4 (1976), 143–55. Scheick sees, however, a tension between Burroughs's "antinomian impulse" and his ties to social order.
112. John Neal, *Rachel Dyer*, Introduction by John Seelye (Gainesville, FL: Scholars' Facsimiles and Reprints, 1964), 22. All further citations come from this edition and are cited parenthetically in the text.
113. See Cynthia S. Jordan, *Second Stories. The Politics of Language, Form and Gender in Early American Fictions* (Chapel Hill: University of North Carolina Press, 1989), 70.
114. For Neal's thoughts on Poe, see *The Genius of John Neal*, ed. Benjamin Lease and Hans-Joachim Lang (Frankfurt: Peter Lang, 1978), 201–11, 207 for citation; on Franklin, see Neal's *American Writers: A Series of Papers Contributed to Blackwood's Magazine, 1824–5*, ed. F. L. Patee (Durham, NC: Duke University Press, 1937), 101–10. For Neal on *Rachel Dyer*, see Lease and Lang, *Genius*, 283.
115. Webster, "Revolution," 1242.
116. Cooper, *Wept*, 13.
117. *The Works of Rufus Choate*, ed. Brown, I:366.
118. See McCormick, *Second American Party System*, 16, 27–9, 95.
119. See Benjamin Rush, "Influence of the American Revolution," in *Selected Writings of Benjamin Rush*, ed. Dagobert D. Runes (New York: Philosophical Society, 1947), 333. On Rush in this regard, see Melvin Yazawa, *From Colonies to Commonwealth: Familial Ideology and the Beginnings of the American Republic* (Baltimore: Johns Hopkins University Press, 1985), 152, and Kenneth Silverman, *A Cultural History of the American Revolution* (New York: Columbia University Press, 1987), 512.

Afterword

1. Review of *Merry-Mount, a Romance of the Massachusetts Colony, North American Review* 68 (1849), 205.
2. C. H. Weber and W. S. Nevins, *Old Naumkeag: An Historical Sketch of the City of Salem* (Salem: A. A. Smith, 1877), 1.
3. F. M. Hubbard, ed., *American Biography, by Jeremy Belknap,* 3 vols. (New York: Harper & Bros., 1877), III:33.
4. Ibid., 166.
5. V. L. Parrington, *Main Currents in American Thought: The Colonial Mind, 1620–1800* (New York: Harcourt Brace, 1954), 7, 5.
6. Ibid., 18.
7. Ibid.
8. William Carlos Williams, *In the American Grain* (New York: Albert and Charles Boni, 1925), 63–5.
9. Ibid., 65.
10. Ibid., 68.
11. Ibid., 63, 66.
12. Tully Atkinson, Letter, *Time* magazine, July 3, 1995, 8.
13. Richard Chase, *The American Novel and Its Tradition* (New York: Anchor; Baltimore: Johns Hopkins University Press, 1980), 11.

INDEX